POLITICS · IN · CONTEMPORARY
PORTUGAL

POLITICS · IN · CONTEMPORARY
PORTUGAL
PARTIES AND THE CONSOLIDATION OF DEMOCRACY

THOMAS C. BRUNEAU · ALEX MACLEOD

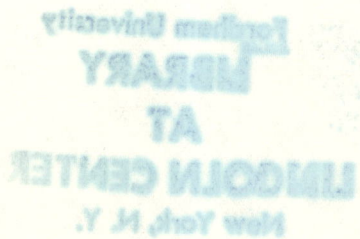

LYNNE RIENNER PUBLISHERS · BOULDER, COLORADO

Published in the United States of America in 1986 by
Lynne Rienner Publishers, Inc.
948 North Street, Boulder, Colorado 80302

©1986 by Lynne Rienner Publishers, Inc. All rights reserved

Library of Congress Cataloging-in-Publication Data

Bruneau, Thomas C.
  Politics in contemporary Portugal.

  Bibliography: p.
  1. Political parties—Portugal. 2. Portugal—
Politics and government—1974-   . 3. Political
participation—Portugal. I. Macleod, Alexandre,
1940-   . II. Title.
JN8651.A2B78 1986   324.2469'009047   85-30152
ISBN 0-931477-68-9

Distributed outside of North and South America and Japan by
Frances Pinter (Publishers) Ltd, 25 Floral Street,
London WC2E 9DS England. UK ISBN 0-86187-632-6

Printed and bound in the United States of America

For Celia and Elisabeth

Contents

List of Tables and Figures		ix
List of Abbreviations		xiii
Preface		xvii
Introduction		1
1	The Military: Goodbye to Politics?	12
2	The Party System and Political Participation	26
3	The Divided Left	45
4	The Parties of the Right and Center: CDS and PSD	77
5	The Political Role of Groups and Associations	98
6	The Constitution of 1976 and Its Revision in 1982	118
7	The Quest for Stable and Efficient Government	127
8	The Parliament Without Prestige	146
9	The Parties and the Media	165
10	The Politicized Role of the State in the Economy	181
Conclusion		198
Epilogue		203
Appendix 1	The Sample Survey: Questionnaire and Sample	214
Appendix 2	General Data on Industry and Economy	216
Bibliography		222
Index		229

Tables and Figures

Tables

0.1	What Should the Portuguese Be Most Proud Of?	9
2.1	Potential for Coalitions, 1976-1983	28
2.2	How Many Parties Should the Country Have?	33
2.3	What are the Goals or Objectives That Are Most Important for Political Parties?	33
2.4	Which Institution Is Most Necessary for Portugal to Be Democratic?	34
2.5	Do You Follow News and Information Concerning Politics and Government?	35
2.6	Results of Elections for the Assembly of the Republic, 1976-1985	36
2.7	Involvement or Participation in Party Activities	37
2.8	National and Regional Evolution of Party Vote and Abstention in Assembly Elections, 1975-1983	38
2.9	Voting in 1983 Assembly Election by Party Voted for in 1976	40
2.10	Voting in 1983 Assembly Election by Party Voted for in 1980	41
2.11	Ideological Tendency Identified Within Relationship to Party Voted for in 1983 Assembly Elections.	43
3.1	How APU and PS Voters Perceive the PCP	50
3.2	How APU and PS Voters Perceive the PS	50
4.1	Profession or Occupation of Members of the PSD and CDS in 1983	83

4.2	Distribution of Members of the PSD and CDS by Socio-Professional Strata	84
4.3	Profession or Occupation of Leaders of the PSD and CDS in 1983	85
4.4	Distribution of Leaders of the PSD and CDS by Socio-Professional Strata	86
4.5	Left-Right Positions of the Four Main Parties	88
4.6	Which Governments or Regimes Governed, or Govern, the Country Best, 1978	93
4.7	Which Governments or Regimes Governed, or Govern, the Country Best, 1984	94
4.8	Political Tendency Identified With?	95
4.9	How PSD and CDS Voters Perceive the PSD	96
4.10	How PSD and CDS Voters Perceive the CDS	96
5.1	What Type of Group or Association Are You Involved With?	100
5.2	Do You Consider Yourself Religious?	113
5.3	Which of These Do You Practice With a Certain Frequency?	114
7.1	Who or What Institution Really Governs the Country?	129
7.2	In Comparison to the Government: Should the President Have More, Less, or Equal Power?	130
7.3	Which of These Institutions Have Contributed Most to Defend Liberty and Democracy in Portugal?	131
8.1	Why Do You Consider the Assembly Extremely or Very Necessary?	154
8.2	Why Do You Consider the Assembly Not Very Necessary or Unnecessary?	155
10.1	Portugal: Components of Gross Product, 1973-1983	183

10.2	Participation of the Public Sector in Portugal's Economy Before and After the Revolution, by Industry or Branch	184
10.3	Weight of Public Enterprises in the Economy	189
10.4	Sources of Financing for the Public-Enterprise Sector	190
10.5	Financial Predicament of the Public-Enterprise Sector	191
10.6	Value Added of Public-Enterprise Sector	192
E.1	First Ballot of the Presidential Elections, 26 January 1986	208
E.2	First Ballot of the Presidential Elections, 16 February 1986	210
E.3	Percentages of Vote Totals, Both Ballots, January, February, 1986	211
A2.1	Comparative Indicators (1980)	216
A2.2	Portugal Public Enterprises	217
Chart A2.1	Structural Development of Portuguese Industry	220

Figures

2.1	Evolution of the Vote, Assembly of the Republic, 1975–1983	39
2.2	Percentage of Voters Who Voted for Same Party in Prior Elections	42
3.1	PCP Leadership Structure	59
3.2	PS Leadership Structure	68
4.1	PSD Leadership Structure	81
4.2	CDS Leadership Structure	82

Abbreviations

AD	Aliança Democrática Democratic Alliance	
AIP	Associação Industrial Portuguesa Portuguese Industrial Association	
ANP	Acção Nacional Popular National Popular Action	
APU	Aliança Povo Unido United People's Alliance	
ASDI	Acção Social Democrata Independente Independent Social Democratic Action	
ASP	Acção Socialista Portuguesa Portuguese Socialist Action	
CAP	Confederação de Agricultores de Portugal Confederation of Portuguese Farmers	
CCP	Confederação do Comércio Português Portuguese Confederation of Commerce	
CDE	Comissão Democrática Eleitoral Democratic Electoral Committee	
CDS	Centro Democrático e Social Social Democratic Center Party	
CEM	Comissão Eleitoral Monárquico Monarchist Electoral Committee	
CEUD	Comissão Eleitoral de Unidade Democrática Electoral Committee for Democratic Unity	
CGTP-IN	Confederação Geral dos Trabalhadores Portugueses— Intersindical Nacional General Confederation of Portuguese Workers— National Intersindical	

CIP	Confederação da Indústria Portuguesa Confederation of Portuguese Industry
CNAE	Conselho Nacional das Associações Empresarias National Council of Entrepreneurial Associations
CNARPE	Comité Nacional de Apoio à Recandidatura do Presidente Eanes National Committee for the Reelection of President Eanes
CNEP	Conselho Nacional dos Empresários Portugueses National Council of Portuguese Entrepreneurs
CPCS	Conselho Permanente de Concertação Social Permanent Council for Social Coordination
CR	Conselho da Revolução Council of the Revolution
EC	European Community
FEPU	Frente Eleitoral Povo Unido United People's Electoral Front
FP-25	Forças Populares 25 de Abril Popular Forces of the 25 April
FRS	Frente Republicana Socialista Socialist Republican Front
GIS	Grupo de Intervenção Socialista Socialist Intervention Group
IED	Instituto de Estudos para o Desenvolvimento Institute for Development Studies
IMF	International Monetary Fund
JSD	Juventude Social Democrata Social Democrat Youth
JUC	Juventude Universitária Católica University Catholic Action
MAD	Movimento para o Aprofundamento de Democracia

	Movement for a Democratic Debate
MDP	Movimento Democrático Português Portuguese Democratic Movement
MES	Movimento da Esquerda Socialista Movement of the Socialist Left
MFA	Movimento das Forças Armadas Armed Forces Movement
PCF	Parti Communiste Français French Communist Party
PCP	Partido Comunista Português Portuguese Communist Party
PDC	Partido Democrático Cristão Christian Democratic Party
PPD	Partido Popular Democrático Popular Democratic Party
PPM	Partido Popular Monarquico Popular Monarchy Party
PRD	Partido Renovador Democrático Democratic Renewal Party
PS	Partido Socialista Socialist Party
PSD	Partido Social Democrata Social Democrat Party
SEDES	Sociedade para o Desenvolvimento Económico e Social Society for Economic and Social Development
SI	Socialist International
SPD	German Social Democratic Party
TESIRESD	Tendência Sindical Reformista Social Democrata Social Democratic Reformist Union Tendency

TSD	Tendência Social Democrata Social Democratic Tendency
UDP	União Democrática Popular Popular Democratic Union
UEDS	União da Esquerda Democrática e Socialista Union of the Democratic and Socialist Left
UGT	União Geral dos Trabalhadores General Union of Workers
UN	União Nacional National Union

Preface

This book results from a completely cooperative research and writing effort of the two authors. Thomas Bruneau first conducted research in Portugal in 1973 on the political role of the Catholic Church. On returning to Portugal in the spring of 1974 he was present during the revolution of 25 April and decided to follow political events there at least until the consolidation of a new political regime. The result of this decade of involvement has been a book and several articles. Alex Macleod became interested in Portugal through his work on the Communist parties of France and Italy and their reaction to the Portuguese revolution. He has since focused on the Portuguese Communist party (PCP) and has published one book and several articles on the subject.

The authors met a number of times while researching in Portugal, at conferences dealing with Portugal and at the Interuniversity Centre for European Studies in Montreal. After cooperating with Victor M. P. da Rosa in a conference and subsequent publication of *Portugal in Development,* we decided there was much to recommend a comprehensive study of politics in Portugal after the transition from authoritarianism to liberal democracy. The vast majority of publications in history and political science on Portugal since the revolution, including our own, have dealt with the revolution and its immediate aftermath. We are convinced that Portugal today can be analyzed according to concepts and categories utilized in the study of other, mainly European, democracies. Such is our purpose in this book.

While drawing on our background experience in Portugal, the specific research for this book was conducted in Portugal between the winter and summer of 1984, and a first draft was written by September. In order to research and write a book that provided a comprehensive analysis of the political system, we necessarily utilized a variety of methods. Probably most important are the more than fifty interviews conducted with government officials, politicians, academics, and journalists in order to learn how the system in fact operates. (A list of the interviewees is included in the Bibliography.) Normally the interviews lasted an hour and sometimes we returned to clarify specific points; in all cases, the interviews were made with the understanding that the information obtained would remain confidential. For this reason there are no attributions in the text to the persons interviewed, and information from the interviews has been integrated with the data from other sources.

We have relied as well on extensive documentation of a primary and secondary nature published in Portugal and elsewhere, and some of the more useful sources are listed in the Bibliography. In order to follow through on certain themes and to achieve a perspective prior to and following the field research, we have utilized the Portuguese newspapers, particularly the high quality daily *Diário de Notícias* and the weeklies *Expresso* and *O Jornal*. In certain instances we have drawn on the partisan press such as *Avante!* for the PCP and *Acção Socialista* for the Socialist party (PS).

In our attempt to be as comprehensive as possible, it seemed extremely important to analyze the relationship between the population and the political system, with particular attention to the degree and forms of participation and popular support for the regime. With this in mind, we subcontracted a survey through Sociedade de Estudos para o Desenvolvimento de Empresas (NORMA) in Lisbon, which was administered and supervised by our Portuguese colleague, Dr. Mário Bacalhau. Bruneau had followed the same procedure, again in cooperation with Dr. Bacalhau, in 1978. We are convinced that this 2,400-interview survey is the most complete and thorough yet done in Portugal on political themes. Some elements of the methodology are described in Appendix 1.

Considering the scope of the task, our time was limited even though both of us were free from teaching and administrative responsibilities between January and September 1984. We thus subcontracted to have documents collected and texts prepared on four topics. In all instances, we utilized the documents and texts in conjunction with other research and our interviews; so the final sections or chapters generally bear little resemblance to the original texts. Without these four studies, however, our own work would have taken much longer or the book would have been more limited; we therefore consider the research and collection involved in these studies invaluable. The four studies were subcontracted through the Instituto de Estudos para o Desenvolvimento (IED) in Lisbon and were prepared by Dr. Mário Mesquita for the media, Dr. José Medeiros Ferreira for the armed forces, Dr. António Guterres for the state and the economy, and Dr. Menezes Ferreira for groups and associations. We wish to thank these four for their serious research efforts and willingness to rework sections according to our priorities.

The IED also played a critical support role for many other facets of our research. It provided a center, with telephones, telex, photocopying, secretarial assistance, and a library for our work while we were in Lisbon. Through the staff and the library we were able to obtain quickly any document or book we required, and this invaluable assistance continued long after we had left Portugal. The secretarial and research staff set up the vast majority of our interviews; this was frequently a complex and time-consuming process. It is hard for us to imagine conducting this type of project in less than a year without the efficient and willing staff and associates of the IED. For this reason we wish to extend our thanks to the coordinators of our project at the IED, Dr. Guy Clausse and Pe. Luis de Franca, to the librarian Conceição Carvalho, to the secretaries Dortea Santos and Conceição Toste, and to Graça Vasconcelos. In addition, Dra. Maria José Stock of the University of Évora deserves special mention for her help in providing us with her data and papers on the political parties.

We also wish to thank Linda Anderson who was involved in this project with us from beginning to end in assisting with the preparation of the grant proposal, administering the files and accounts, and transcribing and typing two drafts of the manuscript. Her willingness and efficiency are much appreciated. The cooperation, then, extends beyond the two authors to members of the IED and NORMA in Lisbon, Dra. Stock in Évora, Linda Anderson in Montreal, and to the more than fifty individuals in a variety of capacities who agreed to be interviewed.

The research and writing were made possible with a grant from the Social Sciences and Humanities Research Council of Canada. We wish to thank the Council and the assessors who made a number of very useful comments on the project. Thomas Bruneau also benefited from a fellowship from the Gulbenkian Foundation in Lisbon, which provided funds for travel and subsistence. We also thank the Social Science Research Grants Subcommittee of McGill University and the Comité des Publications at the Université du Québec à Montréal for assistance in completing this book.

Introduction

During the past fifteen years the speed of political change in Portugal has been vertiginous. The pace and direction of this change are particularly significant if we recall that since the demise of the First Republic in 1926 the country was ruled first by a military government (1926-1928) which gradually gave way to the personalized, conservative authoritarian regime designed and directed by António de Oliveira Salazar between 1933 and his incapacitation due to a stroke in 1968. In this avowedly corporatist Estado Novo Salazar was supreme, but the regime assumed none of the trappings of the fascist states of the interwar period with their deification of leaders, cult of violence, high level of political mobilization, and predominant role of the party. Rather, Portugal was defined by the conservative orientation of the regime which attempted to preserve a traditional society threatened by modernization and the corrosive effects of democratization. In the Estado Novo, the regime was expressedly antidemocratic, interests were either structured or co-opted through the corporatist system, and the population was not integrated into the system as citizens but rather as passive observers. Despite the combination of the Corporative Chamber and the National Assembly, interests were not represented in a government dominated by Salazar in his position as president of the Council of Ministers, or premier.

The government's goal in this society was not modernization via the normal means of industrialization. On the contrary, it discouraged industrialization in order to decrease the potential for the emergence of a significant working class which might pose a threat to the status quo. The economy was dominated by a relatively small number of economic groups or trusts, normally associated with approximately forty families. The state played a central role in the economy through regulation, economic policy, and some investment.

The domestic political and economic situation in Portugal cannot be considered separate from its colonial empire, the *Ultramar* (overseas). Despite the loss of Brazil in South America and a number of enclaves and islands in south and southeast Asia, Portugal still retained a far-flung empire consisting of Macau and Timor in east and southeast Asia, Goa, and other small enclaves on the Indian subcontinent, and the important African territories of Angola and Mozambique as well as Guinea-Bissau, Cape Verde, and São Tome and Principe. In 1961 the *Ultramar* constituted an area some twenty-two times the size of metropolitan Portugal. The colonies, particularly Angola and Mozambique, not only were important economically, but also provided a certain rationale or justification for Portugal's uniqueness as a society and polity. It was argued that Portugal was different and had found a political system appropriate for its culture and history. This culture and history reserved a special place for the Discoveries, the particular religious dimension of this process, and saw Portugal as a country with an Atlantic vocation and a civilizing mission, both past and present. Even after other, more modern and more powerful, European countries had surrendered their colonies in Africa and Asia, Portugal retained hers. When guerrilla wars broke out in Angola in 1961, and later in Mozambique and Guinea-Bissau, Salazar vowed to fight to keep the colonies. For the next thirteen years this remained the overwhelming priority of Portugal's polity and the economy and would have serious ramifications for the whole country.

With Salazar's stroke, Marcello Caetano was selected to continue the work of the founder of the Estado Novo. Initially Caetano attempted to liberalize somewhat, at least in the political realm. However, with the importance of the *Ultramar* as an issue and symbol, these efforts had been defeated by intransigent elements within the regime by 1972. Despite the pressures on the society, with the commitment to waging wars on three major fronts in Africa and the reorientation of the economy with the need to open it up to obtain foreign investment, there were no innovations in the political system. The government remained inflexible and would not allow a broadening of representation through the vote or other, more indirect, means. By preventing innovation or reforms, the regime brought on a revolution. The stability, order, and reliance on authority of the Estado Novo was replaced by instability, disorder, and a general questioning and even denunciation of authority during the revolution which began on 25 April 1974. Portugal, however, is one more case where the revolution was not instigated by the lower classes—proletariat or peasantry—but rather by a sector of the elite, in this case middle ranking officers in the Armed Forces Movement (MFA).

The Revolution of 1974-1975

The economic difficulties, aggravated by the OPEC oil embargo of late 1973, played a role in the general atmosphere of discontent in Portugal in the early 1970s. However, there were no structured means whereby the people could convey this discontent to the political level. There were indeed illegal strikes, demonstrations, and even terrorism, but politically they had little direct impact on the conservative authoritarian regime in which Marcello Caetano seemed as much a prisoner as a premier. Without institutionalized processes for change, action by a key element within the regime was required to transform the whole system. This was carried out by some two hundred officers composing the Armed Forces Movement (MFA) who organized a coup against the Estado Novo on 25 April 1974. Within twenty-four hours, the regime of almost half a century had disintegrated. The MFA moved primarily to bring an end to the interminable colonial wars. The specific motivation for the formation of the movement was a professional issue involving recruitment and training of the officer corps. The fact that it won so quickly attests to the professional competence of its members. That the coup rapidly became a revolution confirms the pent-up grievances and the complete bankruptcy of the Estado Novo.

From 25 April 1974, the process unleashed by the MFA began to assume a revolutionary momentum as the old structures were dismantled and new political groups and movements emerged to compete for power and to promote a fantastic variety of global models of politics and modernization. The MFA, in justifying the coup, promised the three Ds of Democracy, Development, and Decolonization. Decolonization was not simple, particularly in Angola where three guerrilla movements competed for power. It resulted in the disruption of already tenuous economic links and the return to Portugal of some 600,000 *retornados* (returnees). The other two Ds, development and democracy, provoked disagreement and conflict. With the elimination of the old regime, the system was potentially open and enormous transformations were needed, given the low level of development of the country.

Three political options seemed most probable. The Portuguese Communist party (PCP) advocated an orthodox Communist model. The second option was an institutionalized progressive military regime, which would be a continuation of the MFA and resemble Third World cases like Algeria, Peru, or Egypt. The third choice was a liberal democratic regime with a variety of political parties. Most of the parties to the right of the PCP, which by mid-1974 included the Socialist party (PS), Popular Democratic party [PPD; later the Social Democrat party (PSD)], and the Social Democratic Center party (CDS), favored this latter option.

During 1974 and 1975 there may not have been much development as politics became so conflictual and polarized with such widely varying groups and movements, but there was sufficient change to receive the definition of revolutionary. The Estado Novo had guaranteed a society and economy more in common with the nineteenth than the twentieth century. Its demise, and the pressures of the population, would have changed much in any case. Further, with the differing conceptions of Portugal's future, there was a high level of competition for power which involved dismantling elements of the old regime and replacing them with new structures, such as unions, cooperatives, neighborhood associations, and workers' committees. Finally, at the height of radicalization, in March of 1975, banks and insurance companies were nationalized, followed by large sectors in industry, transport, and basic services. Throughout most of 1975 an agrarian reform was underway, supported by the PCP. By late 1975 most of the structures of the old society and economy had changed but there was little agreement on what should replace them.

Politics in Postrevolutionary Portugal

By mid-1976 Portugal had opted for the liberal democratic solution. Within the military a group of moderates had realized that continuing radicalization would at the least erode their power base and possibly result in civil war. Headed by Lieutenant Colonel Ramalho Eanes, they took precautionary measures and easily put down an attempted coup from the military far left on 25 November 1975. The political actors promoting pluralism, the PS, PPD, and CDS, had together taken 72 percent of the vote in the Constituent Assembly elections on 25 April 1975. They demanded a liberal democratic regime which they promoted through their work at the grassroots level, in the unions, the media, and the military. And finally, foreign actors, including such countries as the United States and the Federal Republic of Germany, institutions such as the European Community (EC) and the World Bank, and groups such as the German Social Democratic Party (SPD), the Socialist International, and the International Confederation of Free Trade Unions all became involved in Portugal in a variety of ways. Through their pressure, particularly on the economy, foreign actors promoted the formation of a liberal democracy in Portugal just as other democracies were emerging (or reemerging) in Spain and Greece.

With a new constitution, elections to the Assembly of the Republic were held on 25 April 1976, followed by presidential elections in which the now-General Ramalho Eanes supported by the PS, PPD, and CDS won 61 percent of the vote; by mid-1976, the institutions of the new democratic Portugal were in place. The challenge of promoting the last D, development, now faced the country's leaders. The task has been formidable, given the legacy of the Estado Novo, the nature of decolonization, and the revolutionary turbulence, all in the context of the world economic recession. The recession brought a drop in tourism and exports and reduced remittances from emigrants. With higher oil prices, some large industrial projects also proved to be uneconomic, and potential investors showed less interest in putting their money into Portugal than during the period of world economic expansion of the 1960s.

Government might have been more effective if it had been more stable. Between mid-1976 and late 1977, the PS attempted to govern with 107 deputies of 263 in the Assembly but this minority government finally collapsed over the issue of an International Monetary Fund (IMF) standby agreement to bail out the economy. The first half of 1978 saw the PS in a coalition with the CDS (42 deputies) which fell apart by the summer. Between the middle of 1978 and early 1980, the president himself initiated three governments of "presidential inspiration" which were ostensibly nonpartisan and governed without support of a coherent majority in the Assembly. The last one, headed by Maria de Lourdes Pintasilgo, was formed especially to prepare for early elections in December 1979.[1] These elections brought in a conservative coalition, the Democratic Alliance (AD), which took enough seats to govern with a majority (128 out of 250). In the regular elections, in October 1980, the AD increased its representation to 134 but its candidate, General António Soares Carneiro, lost the presidential election to President Eanes in

December. Just a few days before this election the leader of the AD, Prime Minister Francisco Sá Carneiro, died in an airplane crash. The AD survived another two years but was internally unstable and constantly in conflict with the reelected President Eanes.

Revision of the 1976 Constitution seemed to offer a solution to the tensions between a popularly elected and potentially powerful president and a government based on results of elections for the Assembly. However, the AD could not pass the amendments it had originally intended because it depended on the PS for the necessary two-thirds majority in the Assembly. Revision dominated politics during 1981 and 1982; this theme obsessed the AD, which collapsed as soon as it was achieved, and generally changed the balance of power among the country's political institutions. For these reasons, revision has been made a reference point in this book. The 1982 constitutional revision represents a major step in the long process of institutionalizing the new regime after the *immobilisme* of the Estado Novo, the revolutionary ferment of 1974 and 1975, and the uneasy consolidation which followed. The challenge of development remains, as Portugal is still the most underdeveloped country in Western Europe. The economy has been extremely weak, necessitating two agreements with the IMF (1978 and 1983); the country imports no less than one-half of the food it consumes; the foreign investment is still very low. The revolution, and subsequent governments, did not resolve Portugal's problems of underdevelopment. Rather, the revolution created the conditions for development. As Portugal joins the EC, the process of integration will likely have mixed results, particularly from the impact of more-developed Spain, if precautions are not taken and measures implemented before full accession in 1996. The state must assume this responsibility as the country's private economic institutions are unable to do so on their own.

The political parties have emerged as the main agents defining the regime and have invaded all sectors of public activity. This is the central argument of this book, which explores the process in great detail. Portugal can now be studied as other liberal democracies are studied. The previously relevant but somewhat exotic topics, such as corporatism, militarism, and "alternative models of development," have been replaced by those common to the analysis of politics in Western Europe. Portugal, which heretofore had not been included in the vast majority of textbooks and comparative analyses of liberal democracies, and for good reason, has now become amenable to the same types of analyses used for parallel groups and institutions.

All Power to the Parties

Since World War II many of the countries of Western Europe have gone through a period of constitutional upheaval and been obliged to consolidate new institutions. Rarely have they had to start from scratch. In Italy and France, not only did many of the prewar parties reemerge in 1944-1945, but also the alliances that constituted the backbone of the resistance movement had already laid down the principles of future constitutions and had agreed on repudiation of the old regimes. In Spain the transition from authoritarian government followed a gradual process in which the monarch and governments led by supporters of the Francoist regime guaranteed a degree of continuity. Innovation was provided by previously outlawed parties and political groups which had already coalesced or negotiated in preparation for the inevitable disappearance of the Caudillo. In Spain, the military played an essentially negative role in the transition. The attempted *golpe* of February 1981 indicated that for some sections of the military, the new regime had already gone too far and too fast. Portugal has had much less reason to fear the reactions of military leaders nostalgic for the "good old days."

In all of the political systems born after 1945, organized political parties have become the major actors, often appearing to take over the system altogether to the detriment of democratic practices and effective government. The French Fourth Republic and Republican Italy represent extreme cases of political systems completely appropriated by the parties. Under the Fourth Republic, the parties within the system appeared to divide the spoils of government among themselves with little reference to the electorate, and politics became a game that excluded the voters, whose feeling of alienation increased as the parties vied with one another in Parliament. One can hardly be surprised that in addition to the permanent opposition of the Communist party, supported by some 25 percent of the electorate, the regime gave rise to several antisystem parties on the right, leaving barely half of the country supporting it at one moment.[2]

In Italy, party control of politics and society has reached such proportions that observers have coined the term *sottogoverno* to describe a system where the ruling parties have raised patronage to the level of a system of government. At all levels of state employment, partisan considerations play a vital role, especially in the top jobs, where the members of the ruling coalition divide up these leading positions on a basis that reflects the current balance of partisan forces within the government.

The Fourth Republic and Italy provide examples of what Giovanni Sartori has called "polarized pluralism."[3] A polarized-pluralist party system comes into existence when five or six relevant parties are seen to have an impact, negative or positive, on the functioning of the system. It is characterized by the existence of antisystem parties, mutually exclusive or bilateral oppositions, and a centrally placed party or group of parties. It has a highly polarized spectrum of political opinion which defines itself by strong ideological patterning. Opposition tends to be irresponsible, and parties frequently indulge in the politics of outbidding. In polarized-pluralist societies, party competition has a centrifugal rather than a centripetal effect, in that parties compete for votes more on the extremes than for the votes of the center.

Few systems correspond to the pure polarized pluralism analyzed by Sartori, but the Portuguese system reflects so many of its traits that this concept offers a useful tool for understanding the nature of Portuguese party politics. The

Communist party, although it supported the 1976 Constitution, resolutely opposes the regime without offering a plausible alternative. It cannot join forces with other parties, except in a negative fashion. Political opinion may no longer mirror the high degree of ideological mobilization of the revolutionary period, but, as the two chapters on the political parties show, voters are very conscious of ideological distinctions between parties and identify with them. At the same time, the parties practice the politics of outbidding, as they try to attract votes on their left and right. The CDS and the PSD compete on the right, and the PSD also seeks to prevent its more centrist followers from decamping to the PS. The PCP has largely outflanked its rivals on the left and fights the Socialists for the floating vote of the moderate left, while the PS must ensure that its centrist voters do not go over to the PSD. In this situation, parties engage in the politics of conflict, not accommodation, as each attempts to preserve and expand its ideological space. This does not mean that the Portuguese electorate is immutably frozen in its support for the various parties. However, parties now function within well-defined electoral limits beyond which there exists very little hope of significant growth.

We agree wholeheartedly with Di Palma when he says that "parties are the best indicators of the political society . . . they are what shapes and sets the tone of political society; they are by and large what the political society is all about."[4] This is true in the Portuguese case. Parties have not quite reached the point of establishing a *sottogoverno*, but they have successfully infiltrated so many aspects of Portuguese society that one can imagine few public offices or social institutions not subject to their dictates. Given the importance of the role of the state in society and the economy, which even extends to the media and total partisan control of the country's labor movement, it can be said that the parties have monopolized public life in Portugal.

The PCP exercises a negative veto power, reinforced through its control over the largest union federation, but is otherwise excluded from a share of the spoils. The three other main parties constitute the system of government, with a predominance of the two largest parties, the PS and the PSD. The PS has become the pivotal party of the political system, a concept which Jean-Claude Colliard calls "the essential axis of political life; governments are made around it, which is the general case, or by a reflex of opposition to it, and that supposes that all the other parties coalesce to win."[5] On the other hand, since 1980 the PSD has acted as a swing party, one which can turn to the left or to the right to form a government. By the same token, every crisis in this party has produced a crisis within the government.

Building New Institutions

The parties quickly filled the political vacuum created by the overthrow of the Caetano regime; the MFA could only fill this gap imperfectly because of its own internal conflicts and the determination of many military leaders to hand power over to Portugal's civilian political forces. The rapid rise of the parties, all—with the exception of the PCP—newly formed, was one part of a three-pronged process which has dominated Portuguese politics and includes demilitarization and institution building.

Demilitarization was not simply the result of the desire on the part of tired and frustrated soldiers to divest themselves of power they could no longer effectively wield, as in Greece in 1974, Peru in 1980, Argentina in 1983, or Brazil in 1985. It came from a conscious effort by the most important sectors of the military to return to civilian rule. It did not happen without friction. The civilian politicians and their parties scrambled to eliminate all traces of the MFA, leaving many of its former members frustrated and embittered. Despite these difficulties, Portugal remains a rare example of a successful withdrawal of the military from political power. At the same time, the armed forces have left their mark on the country's institutions.

The military signed two agreements with the political parties, which laid down guidelines for the future constitution. These ensured that the "conquests of 25 April" would constitute the philosophical basis of the constitution, whatever institutions might be adopted. With the adoption of a constitution in 1976, the regime began the vital process of institutionalization, the process through which institutions attain legitimacy and stability and develop recognizable and accepted norms of behavior. The pacts between the MFA and the parties gave the institutions an initial revolutionary legitimacy which only one party, the CDS, contested. Legitimacy has also been established through elections which have constantly produced high voter turnout and where no party openly attacking the regime has sought to be represented. Portugal's political institutions attained a reasonable degree of stable existence which remained unchallenged by the constitutional revision of 1982. As the various political bodies have become entrenched, norms have evolved which all politicians recognize and follow.

Portugal has not only given rise to new parties and institutions; the revolution also engendered a new political class: that group of individuals who constitute the main actors of the political system. Few of its members played prominent roles in the Salazar-Caetano era, at least not in the government. The country's new politicians are young, averaging forty to forty-five years of age and overwhelmingly middle class, with a strong representation of lawyers in Parliament and engineers and economists in government.[6]

Support for the New Regime

This book is primarily concerned with the structures and processes of Portuguese politics. Results from our public opinion surveys are cited throughout which indicate popular attitudes and behavior regarding this new regime. Have the Portuguese come to accept, or even support, the new political system and how do they participate in it? These are questions which will be dealt with throughout the text, but it might be useful to set out here some elements of this general theme. Our

Table 0.1

What Should the Portuguese Be Most Proud Of?

	1978	1984
1. Contribution to civilization	10%	9%
2. Government	1	2
3. The discoveries	14	26
4. Revolution of 25 April	15	14
5. Literature	1	1
6. Qualities of people	5	13
7. Religious life	3	3
8. The Constitution	1	1
9. Artistic heritage	0.3	2
10. Decolonization	1	2
11. Armed forces	1	2
12. Nothing	12	8
13. No response	36	17

general conclusion is that the Portuguese, with certain reservations and restrictions, have come to accept the new regime.

Identical questions were asked in the 1978 and 1984 surveys about what the Portuguese were most proud of. The data for both years are found in Table 0.1. In both surveys the population stressed historical events (the Discoveries), followed by the qualities of the Portuguese and their contribution to civilization. Government and the Constitution did not receive high marks, while the revolution of 25 April did. Both surveys included questions as to whether life had changed since the revolution. In 1984, 89 percent responded affirmatively, 7 percent negatively, and 4 percent did not answer. In 1978 these figures were, respectively, 72, 11 and 16 percent. The overwhelming majority, then, thought that there had been change. The 1984 survey asked whether the change was for the better or worse and 47 percent indicated it was for the better, 32 percent for the worse, and 22 percent did not respond. Most important was the response to an open question as to what was better or worse. Of those listing change for the better, the highest percentage (67 percent) cited liberty, followed very distantly by the economic situation (20 percent). Of the responses indicating change for the worse, 68 percent cited economic factors.

These same general findings are reflected in the responses to questions on changes in the respondent's own personal life. In both 1984 and 1978, exactly 44 percent reported that there was change in their life with the 25 April coup. (In 1984 54 percent said there was no change and 2 percent did not respond; in 1978 the response was about the same, with 50 percent saying there was no change and 6 percent not responding). More important, however, was the fact that in 1984, 57 percent said the change was for the better, 38 percent for the worse, and 6 percent did not respond. Of those indicating change for the better 40 percent cited liberty as the reason. Of those indicating change for the worse, the single highest factor was the cost of living (42 percent) and to this should be added unemployment (14 percent). What comes through clearly is an emphasis on liberty in the changes that came with the 25 April coup, an event the Portuguese are proud of, and an awareness that the country is faced with serious economic problems.

Is it possible that discontent with the economic situation will be directed against the regime? According to our data, this seems unlikely. As indicated, there is a keen awareness of a difficult economic situation. We asked whether there was an economic crisis: 93 percent responded yes, only 1 percent said no, 5 percent did not know, and a mere 0.6 percent did not respond. We then asked the causes for the economic crisis and found that respondents saw little relationship between it and any particular government. None of the responses to the questions gave indications of a serious alienation from the present regime. However, the data show that the population is not convinced of the government's capacity to deal effectively with economic and social problems. What our data show, supported by extensive observations and general discussions, is a broad acceptance of the new democratic system. If this system fails, it will not be because the people do not support democracy or because they yearn for the old regime.

Book Outline

The book is divided into four parts. The first, a chapter in itself, looks at the military as it gradually withdraws from the central stage of politics after 1976, but not without becoming an object of controversy between institutions, especially the presidency and the government, and the parties. The latter constitute the main subject of the second part, which deals with the organized political forces at work in Portugal. After a discussion of political participation and the party system as a whole, two chapters focus on the parties themselves. On the left, insurmountable divisions are apparent between the PCP, supported by the small but influential MDP, and the PS, creating a paradox where the left dominates electorally, ideologically, and in its capacity to mobilize, but cannot govern. On the center and the right two rivals, the PSD and CDS, dispute much the same electorate. Few ideological barriers prevent them from working together, yet factionalism and personal rivalries have undermined their cooperation. This part closes with an analysis of groups and associations, which have not yet played their full role vis-à-vis the parties, and among which the unions, divided on the same political lines as the parties, have assumed a prominent—albeit not necessarily effective—position.

In the three chapters which make up the third part of the book, we see the parties in action as they have sought to establish control over the country's political institutions. The battle over constitutional revision in 1982, which shows the PS, the PSD, and the CDS combining their forces to limit the powers of a president who did not control a party, is the subject of one chapter. The following two examine the evolution of the executive and the Assembly of the Republic, their changing relationship, and the difficulties of framing a parliamentary system of government in which the president continues to play an important role. The party rivalries, which have seriously impaired governmental efficiency, are also examined. The power of the parties extends well beyond the political institutions per se to affect important sectors of economy and society, a theme which occupies the last part. In the two final chapters we explain the inextricable symbiosis between state, government, and the parties in the media, the banks, and industry, areas opened to a high level of state intervention by the revolution, but which quickly turned into part of the battle between the parties.

Notes

1. According to the Constitution, the first legislature had to last until October 1980. To break the deadlock of an ungovernable Assembly, interim elections were held on the understanding that elections for the country's second official legislative term would take place ten months later.

2. In the 1951 legislative elections in France, Communists and Gaullists took just over 48 percent of the vote. The proregime forces were only able to ensure a comfortable parliamentary majority through extensive manipulation of the electoral system.

3. For the most complete formulation of this concept, see Giovanni Sartori, *Parties and Party Systems,* vol. 1 (Cambridge: Cambridge University Press, 1976), pp. 131-145. For an application of this model to the Italian case, see Guiseppe Di Palma, *Surviving Without Governing: The Italian Parties in Parliament* (Berkeley: University of California Press, 1977), pp. 219-253.

4. Guiseppe Di Palma, *Surviving Without Governing,* 1977, p. 222.

5. Jean-Claude Colliard, *Les régimes parlementaires contemporains* (Paris: Presses de la Fondation Nationale des Sciences Politiques, 1978), p. 80.

6. Between 1976 and 1983, the average age of deputies at election varied between 40 and 44, and for members of the government at appointment, between 40 and 45. In the same period, it has been calculated that 86 percent of all deputies and all members of government have come from the middle classes. Vinício Alves da Costa e Sousa, "Caracterização da classe política portuguesa"(unpublished paper, Instituto Damião de Góis, n.d.), pp. 95-99.

1
The Military: Goodbye to Politics?

Adoption of the new Constitution in 1976 did not signal the end of military intervention in Portuguese politics. On the contrary, it institutionalized the role of the armed forces by maintaining a highly visible position for the Council of the Revolution, made up only of members of the military. This was hardly surprising; the Constitution itself was based on the pact (signed on 26 February 1976) between the MFA and all major political parties and replaced the one drawn up after the attempted right wing coup of 11 March 1975. It was generally agreed that the Council of the Revolution would eventually be abolished with the expected constitutional revision that would take place after the first legislature in 1980. In the meantime, the role of the military was to become a crucial political issue, dividing parties, institutions, and the military itself.

The Military in Politics 1976 to 1980

The 1976 Constitution maintained an official role for the military through the Council of the Revolution, but in actual fact the central link between politics and the armed forces throughout the period was the president of the Republic. In 1976 all parties favored a military man as the next president of the Republic. The PCP presented its own civilian candidate, but this was for purely tactical reasons; the party had no real desire or hope of electing one of its own to the presidency. It was obliged to present a candidate mainly because one of the main contenders, General Otelo Saraiva de Carvalho, represented a threat to its own electorate on the left.[1] However, the PCP was careful never to attack General Antonio Ramalho Eanes himself, thereby preserving the party's room to maneuver. Once elected, General Eanes emulated his predecessor, General Francisco Costa Gomes, and remained chief of the General Staff. In other words, the president was not only the actual head of the armed forces, but a head who also enjoyed a position given to him by universal suffrage. As General Eanes explained much later, maintaining himself as chief of the General Staff of the Armed Forces allowed him to keep his authority over the military.[2]

Thus the election of Ramalho Eanes apparently signaled that the military were now subordinate to civil authority. This subordination was, however, ambiguous. According to the 1976 Constitution, control of national defense was divided among different institutions: the presidency, the Assembly of the Republic, the government, and the Council of the Revolution. This division presaged both conflicts and possible paralysis within the country's governing institutions, events which soon happened.

To begin with, the president faced a divided military. Indeed, most of the officers closely associated with the far left or the PCP during the revolution had been eliminated in one way or another. However, a division still existed between left and right within the armed forces. More specifically, it centered around those who favored an active political role in defense of the 1976 Constitution, which embodied most of the principles of the revolution, and those more conservative officers who believed that the military should return to a more neutral role in society. For example, in April 1977 President Eanes appointed as vice-chief of the General Staff of the Armed Forces Lieutenant Colonel José Alberto Loureiro dos Santos who had to be promoted to four-star general to carry out his new post. The rapid promotion of Loureiro dos Santos, whose main task was to organize and modernize the country's armed forces, raised the hackles of some leading members of the armed forces and created such opposition that he was forced to resign.[3] Another example involved the resignation of General Vasco Lourenço from his post as commander of the Military Region of Lisbon in 1978 after becoming involved in a conflict with the head of the army, General Vasco Rocha Vieira. The then-General Lourenço, a well-known figure of the moderate left in the army and a member of the Council of the Revolution, was a prime target for the pressures of the more conservative members of the military hierarchy who were determined to remove him from his job. Despite support from General Eanes he was unable to retain his position.[4]

The president also had to contend with rivalry between the different branches of the military and in particular with the rising strength of the air force which appeared as an increasingly autonomous force. In 1976, the air force had already indicated its opposition to Eanes by encouraging Mário Soares to put forward his own presidential candidacy at a time when there seemed to be a wide consensus around General Eanes.[5] The growing importance of the air force was shown in 1979 when its chief, General Lemos Ferreira, publicly attacked Parliament for rejecting the budget and suspended air force participation in military exercises within NATO without previous notice to the General Staff to put pressure on the Assembly of the Republic.[6]

To most observers the most obvious instrument of military intervention in Portuguese politics was the Council of the Revolution. However, when the Council of the Revolution's activities were scrutinized, it became apparent that this was by no means the deus ex machina depicted by the right or the undying defender of the revolution so often imagined, at least publicly, by the Portuguese Communist party. Theoretically the Council disposed of sweeping powers. It acted as a political adviser to the president, who was also its chairman. It acted as a protector of the Constitution and as a constitutional tribunal. It was responsible for legislation dealing with the military. And finally it was the body that decided on promotions to top levels in the various branches of the military. When the Council's role as an adviser to the president is evaluated, it becomes clear that the president felt no obligation to heed its opinions. In one of the most important decisions made by the president during his first mandate, the Council of the Revolution opposed his position. This incident involved the decision to dismiss Mário Soares as prime minister in 1978 on the grounds that he no longer retained sufficient support within the Assembly to continue as an elected head of government. The majority of the Council, still wishing to maintain links with the Socialist party and with Mário Soares, advocated prudence and suggested that the president back away from his threat to dismiss the prime minister. This advice was not followed. On the contrary, the president preferred to rely on other advisers, in particular his own personal staff (led also by a member of the military) and his own military staff then headed by General Amadeu Garcia dos Santos who was later to figure prominently in another conflict between the military and the civil authorities. As for military legislation, the Council usually left it to the General Staff of the Armed Forces and the military hierarchy to prepare the necessary legislation; the Council rarely raised any fundamental objections. The same can be said for promotions. Despite its name, the Council of the Revolution made no attempt to challenge tradition and in fact played a prominent role in ensuring that the rules governing promotions in the armed forces before 1974 continued to be enforced. When it came to appreciating the constitutionality of various bills, the Council adopted an activist stance which upset many civilian politicians, rejecting no fewer than thirty-five of the seventy-four bills that were submitted to it.

Until January 1980, the military and civil authorities were also linked by the presence of military officers in the Cabinet and in the government. Following a tradition dating back to Salazar, the post of minister of defense was held by a military man. The two officers who assumed this portfolio, Colonel Mário Firmino Miguel and Lieutenant Colonel Loureiro dos Santos, could both be classed as strong-minded individuals with definite personal views on the organization of the country's armed forces and the role of the military in politics.[7] Both drafted important bills on the reorganization of national defense, and even though neither plan was adopted they served as a point of departure for the Law on National Defense finally passed in 1982. Except during the short-lived PS/CDS government headed by Mário Soares in 1978, the military also controlled the Ministry of the Interior.

However, real power over the military remained in the hands of the General Staff of the Armed Forces, which was still governed by decree-law 3/74 of 14 May 1974. This law established the General Staff's autonomy vis-à-vis the civil authorities and invested the chief of the General Staff with a position equivalent to that of a prime minister and the chiefs of the different services with the powers of ministers within the armed forces. The minister of defense acted as a link between the military and the government through the General Staff, which was headed until January 1981 by the president of the Republic, General Ramalho Eanes.

The Democratic Alliance and the Battle Over the Militiary

On 2 December 1979 a government of the right headed by Francisco Sá Carneiro was elected and a new period in military-civilian relations began. Sá Carneiro, the uncontested leader of the Democratic Alliance (AD), the coalition between the PSD and the CDS, was a purposeful individual with definite ideas regarding the future orientation of Portuguese politics. He was determined to rid the country of what he called "excesses of the revolution" and to exclude the military from any further political activity. By 1979 his former support for General Eanes was at an end and he made it clear that he would do everything to make sure that the president was not reelected. His methods, however, raised as many divisions within the armed forces as those of which he accused President Eanes and the Council of the Revolution. He launched the slogan "one government majority, one presidential majority" and suggested a radical change in the Constitution which would circumvent the problem of the necessary two-thirds majority for any constitutional revision by proposing that the new president simply change the Constitution by referendum. Sá Carneiro shortly realized that he could not simply avoid getting involved with the military and therefore selected and threw his support behind another military candidate, General Soares Carneiro. The ensuing campaign hardened partisan lines within the military and did little to ensure the political neutrality of the armed forces.

Before taking office in January 1980, Sá Carneiro sought to neutralize any military opposition by offering the post of minister of the interior to an army officer, who declined the invitation to join the government, even when the prime minister designate subsequently offered him the defense portfolio. For the first time since 1926, there would be no representative of the military in the Cabinet. This left the field open for a new civilian minister of defense, Adelino Amaro da Costa, second in the hierarchy of the CDS. Amaro da Costa and Sá Carneiro became the leading protagonists in the legislative elections of October 1980 and the battle for the presidency in December of the same year. Their untimely death in December and Eanes's subsequent defeat of Soares Carneiro forced a change in the Democratic Alliance's strategy but not in its aim to put the militiary completely under civilian control.

President Eanes's reelection in December 1980 presaged a new phase in the struggle for civilian control of the military. From then on until adoption of a new Law on National Defense in November 1982, which was an integral part of the whole attempt to revise the Constitution, a series of skirmishes occurred which involved not only the AD and the military but also the leadership of the Socialist party. These disputes took the form of declarations to the press and articles from the military denouncing various aspects of governmental incompetence.[8] The government answered in kind. For example, the Balsemão government, the successor to Sá Carneiro, suddenly decided to divulge a devastating report on East Timor showing the irresponsibility of a certain number of officers during decolonization. Needless to say, these were officers close to General Eanes himself.

During this time the military was preparing for the gradual return of all political powers to the civilian politicians. In January 1981 President Eanes took the first step when he renounced his position as chief of the General Staff, putting an end to a concentration of powers which he himself later acknowledged was "exhausting and negative" for the presidency.[9] This was followed by the dissolution of the Council of the Revolution in the autumn of 1982.

No one within the military had seriously questioned the dissolution of the Council with the adoption of a new, totally civilian constitution. It was thought, however, that the members of the Council deserved some recognition for their contribution to restoring democracy to the country from politicians who had played no direct role in the overthrow of the dictatorship. However, far from receiving any demonstration of gratitude, the Council of the Revolution was liquidated in an atmosphere of embarrassment on the part of Portugal's civilian politicians. The minister of defense, Diogo Freitas do Amaral, set the tone by declaring that 30 October 1982 (the last official day of the Council's existence) would be "Portugal's day of freedom," a comment that provoked the reply from the Council's official spokesman, Lieutenant Colonel Vítor Alves, that he had "offended the Portuguese people and their recent history."[10] After some difficult negotiations, the Council managed to have television cameras record its last meeting. Vítor Alves took advantage of this opportunity to attack all the political parties for being "incapable of finding adequate answers for the people's aspirations" and held them responsible for the "social climate of frustration, disenchantment and even discouragement" which had led to a "dangerous disbelief in the functioning of democratic institutions."[11] On the day the Council's powers were to be officially transferred to the civilian authorities, the Socialist and Communist parties only sent along second-level representatives, and the AD simply boycotted the ceremony. The government sent a junior minister, the minister for parliamentary affairs, whose late arrival prompted the president to ask him if he had done it on purpose.[12]

It was in this very tense atmosphere that the AD government, supported by the Socialist party, debated the major piece of legislation establishing full civil control over politics, the Law on National Defense.

The Final Step toward Civil Control

Until the new Law on National Defense was adopted in November 1982, the armed forces still functioned largely on their own. The only political official to whom they owed any subservience was the president. The constitutional revision of 1982 indicated that the role of the armed forces in Portuguese politics would change; in effect, the military would become subordinate to civilian authorities. The new Law on National Defense precisely specified what that relationship would be. When the first version of the law was presented to Parliament in September 1982 the minister of defense, Freitas do Amaral, also introduced a document explaining what the government was doing and delineating its basic philosophy toward the armed forces.[13] Basically, the government wanted to redefine the whole concept of national defense in a much more restrictive way; the new view would be limited to national security seen solely as a problem of *external* security. The so-called *internal* enemy, which could necessitate armed forces intervention to control the limits of politics within the country, ceased to exist. As the document took great pains to show, the government intended to make the Portuguese conception of national defense completely compatible with that of other NATO countries. In other words, the government claimed it was only emulating other democratic countries with which Portugal wished to identify. To achieve this end the new law would clearly subordinate armed forces to civilian authority. Secondly, it would establish co-responsibility for the armed forces between the country's three governing bodies. Since the Council of the Revolution had disappeared with constitutional revision, its role in military matters would be taken over by the other bodies. It was understood that none of these powers would revert to the president of the Republic, who, in accordance with the aims of constitutional revision, would lose many of his powers or at least the capacity to exercise these powers without any other form of control. In fact, this so-called co-responsibility was heavily weighted in favor of the government itself as the principal articles of the law were to show. The president would remain supreme commander of the armed forces, but as in most other West European countries this would be a purely titular role. The minister of defense would become the real master of the armed forces. Obviously such elemental changes met much opposition from within the military and from those who supported the president of the Republic. But the greatest bone of contention, or at least the issue which drew the attention of both General Eanes and the military hierarchy, was the question of who should appoint and dismiss the members of the General Staff of the Armed Forces.

From then on, the choice of the chief of the General Staff and the heads of the three services would be in the hands of the government. The Council of the chiefs of the General Staff would prepare a list of possible candidates for the vacancy, and the prime minister and the minister of defense would jointly select a candidate to be confirmed by the government. In such a process the president of the Republic could only accept or reject the government's appointment; should he reject it, then the whole process would begin again. He would not be able to impose his own choice. As for dismissals, the government itself would decide who should or should not be dismissed and the president again would only be able to confirm or reject their decision. For general questions of defense policy and for promotions to the position of general the government would use an advisory body called the Higher Council for National Defense, presided over by the president, but in which the government enjoyed a solid majority.

Freitas do Amaral conscientiously consulted all interested parties during the passage of the bill. Admittedly, he could not always count on their cooperation, but he balked at trying to push through a measure that would certainly provoke total opposition on the part of the military. However, Freitas do Amaral also had to contend with the realities of the political complexion of the Assembly. After presenting the original version of his bill in late September 1982, he was then forced to negotiate with the Socialist party to ensure that Parliament would support the law in its final form. The PS leadership took full advantage of this opportunity to tighten up certain aspects of the bill; by doing so they struck another blow in the ongoing battle between Mário Soares and President Ramalho Eanes. For example, the final version of the bill more stringently restricted the military's right to participate in any form of association with possible political connotations than did the original proposal. The PS also increased the powers of the minister of defense by putting the heads of the three services firmly under his control. The bill was finally approved by the Assembly of the Republic, supported by the AD and the Socialist party with over a two-thirds majority, on 29 October 1982.[14] Three weeks later President Eanes announced officially that he had vetoed the law.

In his message to the Assembly, the president commented that too much power had been given to the minister of defense to the detriment of the military chiefs in certain areas. He also complained that the president of the Republic's position as supreme head of the armed forces was now unclear. As to the Higher Council for National Defense, its real power as an autonomous body was questionable, not only because it was weighted too heavily in favor of the government but also because its position seemed highly ambiguous.[15] However, Eanes was not prepared to cast his veto on constitutional grounds, although he was certain that many of its articles were demonstrably unconstitutional. President Eanes was certainly expressing his own displeasure at a law which diminished his position as laid down in the constitutional revision, but he was above all responding to the discontent felt with the law by the military hierarchy and among the majority of members of the now-defunct Council of the Revolution. The military hierarchy were not only venting their anger at the loss of autonomy and power but also expressing a deeply felt fear that the new law, by giving the power of appointment and dismissal of the leading members of the military to the government, would finally introduce a form of party politics in the military from which it had until then been relatively free. However, the parties that had voted the law remained intransigent. They correctly realized that even an amended bill could fall under presidential veto. Since it was common knowledge that the government coalition was on its last legs, another presidential veto could effectively hold the bill up and perhaps even introduce it as an election issue. Thus on 26 November 1982 the majority of the Assembly reiterated its support for the Law on National Defense, and the president had no choice but to promulgate it the following day. The first application of the new law appeared to fully justify the fears of those generals who had thought that the questions of promotion, appointments, and dismissals would become a political issue.

The First Test: The Garcia dos Santos Affair

To assert the government's authority, Freitas do Amaral requested the dismissal of one of the members of the General Staff. He chose General Amadeu Garcia dos Santos who seemed to be the best target for the AD. As former head of the president's personal military staff, a member of the Council of the Revolution, and also one of the military organizers of President Eanes's reelection campaign in 1980, General Garcia dos Santos represented the most politically visible and vulnerable member of the military hierarchy from the government's point of view. His appointment to head the army in January 1981 had also raised a certain amount of opposition among those officers of the right associated with the Soares Carneiro's campaign for the presidency.

The decision to dismiss Garcia dos Santos as head of the army was not carried out at the time due to the disintegration of the AD government. The new PS/PSD government which took office after the elections of April 1983 acted cautiously on this issue; presumably it wished to avoid a head-on collision with the military, especially as the military hierarchy had already indicated that it would not accept a Socialist as minister of defense.[16] The government decided to force the dismissal of Garcia dos Santos at a Cabinet meeting on 21 July 1983. For the next four months President Eanes put off making any decision over the government's request. Things came to a head at the beginning of November that year at a meeting of the Higher Council for National Defense when the government-controlled majority rejected General Garcia dos Santos's proposal to appoint General Aurélio Trindade as commander over the eight military regions of the north. The minister of defense, supported by a majority of the Higher Council for National Defense, rejected this proposal despite its unanimous support in the High Council of the Army and by the military members of the Higher Council for National Defense. General Garcia dos Santos's resignation became inevitable, since now the normal functioning of the army was effectively blocked. Four days later the general offered his resignation to the president. It was announced publicly a few days later that the president had refused his resignation, but in fact, in the meantime, both the president and the prime minister, Mário Soares, had been working out a compromise solution to the situation. The basis for this compromise had already been laid by General Eanes in the Higher Council for National Defense when he suggested that from now on members of the General Staff should enjoy the confidence of both the government and the president and that if a member of the General Staff should lose the confidence of either he should resign with no explanation.

This suggestion was turned down. A few days later Prime Minister Soares wrote General Eanes and proposed a new interpretation of the Law on National Defense, suggesting that the president should only take fifteen days to follow the government's suggestion for dismissing a member of the General Staff. On the other hand, both the government and the president would have the right to propose the dismissal of a member of the General Staff who had lost their confidence without any reasons given. This compromise would only be valid for the presidency of

General Eanes and during the lifetime of the PS/PSD government. Of course, the compromise also included the dismissal once and for all of General Garcia dos Santos. Although General Eanes accepted a compromise solution similar to the one he had put forward himself, he made it clear that he considered the reasons given by the government for dismissing General Garcia dos Santos to be invalid and commented that his agreement was a purely political gesture aimed at maintaining institutional operations.[17]

On the face of it, the government had won an important victory. It had finally forced the president to get rid of one of his most trusted supporters. But on closer examination, it could also be said that the president really came out the winner since he clarified the Law on National Defense in his own favor by ensuring that he could also dismiss without question a member of the General Staff with whom he did not agree; by implication, the government should consult him on future appointments to the General Staff. Three months later the chief of General Staff, General Melo Egídio, reached the age of retirement and was replaced by the head of the air force, General Lemos Ferreira. The ease with which this change was made at the top of the armed forces showed clearly that the Garcia dos Santos affair had been completely political in nature, a test of strength between the government and the president. The fact than an air force general had assumed leadership of the General Staff, rather than the head of the army as was traditionally the case, also indicated the rising strength of the air force in the balance of forces between the branches of the military. However, the battle over the right to dismiss a member of the General Staff was by no means the end of the political struggle over the role of the armed forces in Portuguese society.

The 25th April Association

As the Law on National Defense was being finalized in the Assembly, twenty-seven members of the defunct MFA, including one of its leading protagonists, President Eanes himself, were founding a new association to defend the ideas of the revolution. They called it the 25th April Association. Major Vasco Lourenço was the driving force behind this group; he was elected to head its interim executive committee and ultimately became its president in February 1984. By that time the Association had attracted some 1,900 members, representing about one-quarter of the total active officer corps.[18] From the beginning, the Association was attacked by the right and by those parties that supported constitutional revision. There was even a demand that the Association should be outlawed with the promulgation of the Law on National Defense. As yet no government had dared to invoke Article 31 of this new law which expressly forbade the military to belong to a political association. The military hierarchy absolutely refused to comply with such a demand and have, on the contrary, constantly reaffirmed their demand for the continued existence of the Association.

There is little agreement on the exact nature of this association. Some see it as nothing more than a military front for more sinister purposes, that is, as some form of a Communist-dominated left-wing army coup. Others view it as a club for old soldiers who simply want to meet and relive old times. And others seem to consider it a sort of pressure group aimed at defending progressive causes, or, in the words of a *New York Times* correspondent, a sort of left-wing Lions Club.[19] It is, however, certain that the Association well expresses the continued distrust between Portugal's civil governments and those officers who made the coup d'état on 25 April 1974.

The Association gained rapid popularity among Portugal's military officers, except in the air force, and its membership far exceeded the 136 captains and lieutenants who constituted the original group that led the coup. Above all, it appeared to reflect the bitterness of those who had the foresight and audacity to overthrow the old regime and to create the conditions of democratic government in Portugal in 1974 and 1976 and who now felt unrecognized and excluded from the ensuing process. They also strongly resented the tendency within Portuguese civil politics to forget what they consider essential, and to resort too frequently to petty squabbling among personalities and politics. These feelings were expressed by a leading figure of the Captains' Movement, Vítor Alves, in a speech given to members of the Association in which he denounced the fact that Portugal had once again fallen into "the baseness of partisanship, patronage, decisions without transparency." He added that the 25th April did not happen so that "parties of notables could be formed to dedicate themselves to struggles of influence which had nothing to do with the interests of their electors nor with the country's situation."[20] At the same time, Alves warned that it was futile to depend on the military to intervene again. In other words, the 25th April Association refused to be considered some form of embryonic organization to carry out a military coup. On the other hand, as this speech made abundantly clear, the officers supporting the 25th April Association were by no means adverse to creating new parties. This, probably more than the hypothetical coup, is what the country's present party politicians would seem to fear most: a new political party with some military support.

The antagonism between the 25th April Association and the civil politicans supporting the PS/PSD government has been expressed symbolically. Both the government and the Association decided to organize separate celebrations for the tenth anniversary of the 25th of April. Some attempt at cooperation between the government and the Association was begun in July 1983, but as a letter from Vasco Lourenço to the Association pointed out, there was an unfortunate coincidence between the beginning of these negotiations and the government's decision to oust General Garcia dos Santos.[21] From then on a series of quasi-diplomatic negotiations took place between the two bodies without either side yielding an inch. In the end two separate ceremonies took place; the one organized by the Association enjoyed great popular success, while that run by the government attracted very few spectators indeed.

Goodbye to Politics?

Since 1976, Portugal's politicians—at least those who supported constitutional revision and the Law on National Defense—have been waging a battle to reduce the role of the military in politics. At times the battle has been so ferocious that outside observers cannot help feeling that the politicians want to eradicate the military in order to forget that they themselves had little or nothing to do with the overthrow of the former dictatorship. In their anxiety to rapidly "Europeanize" Portuguese politics, civilian politicians have frequently behaved callously towards the military, and their actions have taken on petty overtones, such as the atmosphere which surrounded the disintegration of the Council of the Revolution and made it appear as if the country's politicians wanted to sweep the military under the carpet as quickly as possible. At the same time, as the Eanes/Soares agreement over Garcia dos Santos showed, there is tacit admission that the military cannot be ignored, and that as yet there are limits to civilian handling of the military. The weight of the military presence could still be felt in the period leading up to the 1986 presidential elections. With the exception of the PS, the major parties all considered the possibility of supporting a military candidate. Carlos Mota Pinto's decision to promote the candidacy of General Firmínio Miguel was the immediate cause of his defeat in the PSD National Council in February 1985 and his subsequent loss of party leadership and resignation from the Cabinet, both as deputy prime minister and as minister of defense. During the inevitable shuffle that followed, the chief of the General Staff met with Mário Soares to inform the prime minister of his opposition to one prospective candidate for the defense portfolio and to point out that the armed forces expected the post to be held, as was the custom since 1982, by the deputy prime minister. The prime minister acquiesced. When Mota Pinto's successor, Rui Machete, fell in May 1985, the armed forces once again let it be known that they wanted this practice maintained. There are few grounds for fearing that the military might be tempted by another coup.

To be sure, many officers, especially among the members of the 25th April Association, have not hesitated to vigorously criticize the parties and government inefficiency in general, but they have also stressed that they do not wish to return to a full role in politics. After all, it should never be forgotten that the Portuguese military not only returned the country to civilian rule, but also actively made sure that the transition was relatively smooth. This does not mean that the military lack political interest or demands. At the least what they desire would seem to be recognition once and for all on the part of the civilian politicians for their role in bringing democracy to Portugal and, at the most, the possibility of exercising some form of political influence to make sure that the principles of the 25 of April for which so many of them worked are still maintained.

It is true that not all the military would go that far. One must distinguish between those who strongly hold to "the principles of the 25th April" and those of a more conservative orientation—many of whom supported Soares Carneiro in his bid for the presidency in 1980. Nonetheless, there is a general collective reaction to attacks on the military as an institution. This was demonstrated during the debate over the Law On National Defense, in particular over the question of how members of the General Staff should be promoted and dismissed. Many of the demands made by the military deal with straightforward corporatist matters, concerning such issues as status and pay. The politicians have not always recognized the importance of this, or in some cases seem to have gone out of their way to provoke the military on such matters. The sensitivity of these corporatist demands can be underscored by the fact that it was precisely these types of demands that sparked the creation of the MFA in 1973.[22] Thus in the month leading up to the 1980 presidential campaign, Prime Minister Sá Carneiro refused the increase in the armed forces' salaries (which had been proposed by the Council of the Revolution), while granting a 19 percent raise to the militarized Republican National Guard and Public Security Police, two institutions that have always been regarded with suspicion by the armed forces. In February 1984, a fourteen-page typewritten document attributed to Vasco Lourenco appeared in the barracks throughout the country. In this document the president of the 25th April Association denounced a law passed in December 1983 which gave equal pay and social privileges to the officers of the Republican National Guard and the regular armed forces. The deliberate exclusion of the military from the organizing committee for the celebrations of the tenth anniversary of the coup of 25 April 1974 by the government was just a further example of this type of pettiness.

The politicans also appear to underestimate the importance the military attach to any sign that they are being taken for granted. Like most armed forces, the Portuguese military are sensitive about the budget allotted them. As noted earlier, the head of the air force reacted strongly when Parliament refused to vote the budget in 1979 and five years later General Lemos Ferreira, now chief of the General Staff, complained in the presence of the prime minister, Mário Soares, that Parliament had failed to provide the armed forces with sufficient funds. Just in case the civilian government had forgotten about the political role of the military, he reminded them that the military had intervened on 25 November 1975 to maintain democratic freedoms.[23]

Politicians seem much more concerned that the military remains too popular and takes up too much room in public opinion. Our survey shows that 54 percent of the population agrees that either much or very much recognition should be given to the armed forces for their role in the revolution. Furthermore, 36 percent feel that the armed forces should play a role at least equal to the role that they have today in politics, and more than 28 percent thought that their role should be more important (only 10 percent thought it should be less important). On the other hand, when asked about which institutions they thought really governed the country less than one-tenth of 1 percent spontaneously named the armed forces. This response is all the more significant because the question immediately followed the two on the role of the military since 1974.

Despite the skirmishes between civil politicians and some of the military, a high degree of civilian control of the military has been attained in Portugal. The question remains as to what type of civilian control has been established. The distinction made by Samuel Huntington between so-called "subjective" and "objective" civilian control is of some help here. According to Huntington, in a situation of "subjective" control, a particular civilian group or groups will use the military, or more probably a section of the military, to further its/their own power aims. Where there is "objective" civilian control, the military are treated essentially as a professional body which is used by the civilian authorities and is responsible to them in spheres that belong to their professional competence. In the words of Huntington: "Subjective civilian control achieves its ends by civilianizing the military, making them the mirror of the state. Objective civilian control achieves its ends by militarizing the military, making them the tool of the state."[24]

Portuguese politics appears to have wavered between these two distinctions. In the 1980 presidential campaign Sá Carneiro was hoping to use Soares Carneiro as an instrument to put an end to the role of the military left and in so doing was aligning himself with the military right. The battle over General Garcia dos Santos also was a political battle; this incident set the government against the president, seen as the last important vestige of the military in politics. The subsequent ease with which both Garcia dos Santos was replaced as head of the army and a successor found for Melo Egídio as chief of the General Staff shows that the regime is approximating the desired model of objective civilian control. It remains to be seen whether civilian officials can exercise the same maturity toward the military that they expect from the military in their dealings with politicians.

Notes

1. Alvaro Cunhal, *A revolução portuguesa: O passado e o futuro* (Lisbon: Edições Avante!, 1976), pp. 204-210.
2. "Preponderância do parlamento não é a solução para o país," interview with president Eanes in "Dez anos de democracia," special supplement of the *Diário de Notícias,* 24 April 1984, p. 9.
3. Ibid.
4. Avelino Rodrigues, Cesário Borga, and Mário Cardoso, *Abril nos quartéis de novembro* (Lisbon: Livrária Bertrand, 1979) pp. 213-215.
5. "PR partidário não significa a partidarização do Estado," interview with Mário Soares in "Dez anos de democracia," *Diário de Notícias,* 24 April 1984, p. 13.
6. Alberto Santos, "La péninsule ibérique: enjeu stratégique," *Les cahiers de la fondation pour les études de défense nationale,* no. 18, 1980, pp. 139-40.
7. The views of Loureiro dos Santos on the political role of the military have been expressed in various articles and speeches which have been collected in José Alberto Loureiro dos Santos, *Forças armadas, defesa nacional e poder político* (Lisbon: Imprensa Nacional–Casa da Moeda, 1980).
8. See, for example, Major Vasco Lourenco's denunciation of corruption in high places, "Estranha democracia esta," *Diário de Notícias,* 3 November 1981.
9. "Dez anos de democracia," *Diário de Notícias,* 24 April 1984, p. 9.
10. Autunes Ferreira, "Sete anos e meio de vida atribulada," in "Dez anos de democracia," p. 95.

11. "Militares de abril perdem a última batalha no CR," *Expresso*, 30 October 1982.
12. Ibid.
13. For the full text of this document, see "Memória justificativa," in Diogo Freitas do Amaral, *A lei de defesa nacional e das forças armadas* (Coimbra: Coimbra Editora, 1983) pp. 100-157.
14. However, the military chiefs were hostile to many of the Socialist party's proposals, which nullified Freitas do Amaral's attempts to create a large consensus on a bill whose basic principles met general agreement from the military hierarchy. See Miguel Almeida Fernandes, "PS não negociará com a AD a proposta de governo?" *Expresso*, 25 September 1982.
15. For the complete text of the president's message, see, *Diário da assembleia da república*, 2nd series, no. 17, 23 November 1982, pp. 225-227.
16. For a full account of the Garcia dos Santos affair, see Augusto de Carvalho, "Garcia dos Santos: história da exoneração," *Expresso*, 26 November 1983.
17. "Proponderância do parlamento não é a solução para o Pais," in "Dez anos de democracia," p. 9.
18. John Darnton, "Lisbon Officers Club: Coup Makers or Breakers?" *New York Times*, 18 February 1984.
19. Ibid.
20. Vítor Alves, speech given before the 25th April Association, Cascais, 8 March 1984, mimeographed, p. 9.
21. Letter from Vasco Lourenco to all members of the Association, November 1983.
22. The best account of the founding of the MFA remains Avelino Rodrigues, Cesário Borga, and Mário Cardoso, *O movimento dos capitães e o 25 de Abril* (Lisbon: Moraes Editores, 1974).
23. *Diário de Notícias*, 26 November 1984.
24. Samuel P. Huntington, *The Soldier and the State* (Cambridge: Harvard University Press, 1957) p. 83.

2
The Party System and Political Participation

During the Estado Novo elections were regularly held for the National Assembly and the presidency (until 1959 when these were made indirect). Indeed, Philippe Schmitter has claimed that no country in Western Europe seems to have held as many national elections between the 1930s and 1970s as Portugal.[1] It must be emphasized, however, that Portugal during these years was a "unitary, corporative republic" in which the legitimation was explicitly antidemocratic and the authoritarian regime was well structured and tightly controlled. There was little real question that the locus of power was in the premier and Cabinet, and no lower level of government had power over a higher level.[2] Elections did not have the same function in prerevolutionary Portugal as they do in liberal democratic regimes (including that founded in Portugal by 1976). Schmitter has argued convincingly that the function of elections in the Estado Novo was to maintain the system by promoting unity among the elite and dividing the potential opposition.[3] Suggestive of the great differences in the function and meaning of elections during and after the Estado Novo are data pertaining to political parties and elections.

The Estado Novo did not allow any political parties. The official National Union (UN) was founded in 1930 as an "association without partisan character" and was never allowed to develop as a party during the following forty-four years, even when renamed National Popular Action (ANP) in 1969 by Marcello Caetano. The opposition was allowed to emerge and "contest" elections after World War II, but only for one month during which press censorship and restrictions on freedom of speech were decreased. The opposition was not constituted as political parties but rather as "formations." It must be stressed that these elections were for the largely symbolic and marginal National Assembly; they did not extend to the Corporative Chamber, which was advisory in any case.

Marcello Caetano, taking over from the incapacitated Salazar in 1968, was aware that the system was somewhat stagnant and attempted to rejuvenate it, not only by renaming the UN (to ANP) and the secret police, but also by including newer and more liberal elements on the ANP's list for the 1969 elections as well as allowing opposition formations to contest the elections. Of the three opposition formations one was monarchist, the Monarchy Electoral Committee (CEM), and two were on the left. The Democratic Electoral Committee (CDE) was dominated by the Communists, whereas the CEUD, or Electoral Committee for Democratic Unity, brought together Socialists and Social Democrats.[4] The initial reforms of Caetano encouraged the formation of many groups, but the promises quickly wore off. The opposition did not elect a single deputy to the National Assembly, nor did they contest the 1973 elections. The liberal elements elected on the ANP's slate all quit the Assembly before the 1973 election. Awareness that the elections could only serve to support the regime and did not offer any possibility whatsoever for change eliminated any interest in the 1973 elections.

Elections were not utilized by the regime for broad political mobilization, nor were they seen by the population as a viable instrument for change in the regime. The regime limited voting registration severely by restrictions on age (over 20), literacy (when over 30 percent of the population was illiterate), and sex (only men, or women who were heads of households or paid a certain amount of tax) as well as by bureaucratic complications. Consequently, the percentage of the total population that was registered to vote remained virtually stagnant from 1945 until 1965 at some 15 percent. In preparation for the 1969 election, Caetano allowed the opposition to review the electoral rolls but more importantly allowed women to register without restrictions and ordered an overhaul of the voter registration records. The percentage of registered voters thus rose to 19.5 percent, but in the elections themselves only 62 percent of this registered electorate actually voted. Schmitter has shown that Portugal placed eighty-eighth out of ninety-two countries in terms of voter turnout, the lower rates being found in four African countries.[5] Clearly, Portugal was not a liberal democracy during the Estado Novo. There were elections, but no legal political parties, and the regime was conservative and authoritarian.

As to the parties themselves, the PCP, founded in 1921, was outlawed during the Estado Novo and survived in a clandestine existence as an orthodox and tightly integrated "organizational weapon" which did not evolve in a Eurocommunist direction. The PS was founded only in 1973, and the other two main parties after the revolution—the PPD/PSD and the CDS—were founded only in mid-to-late 1974. There was, then, slight experience in politics during the almost half century of the Estado Novo.

Although the parties had not been founded entirely from scratch, as there was always some historical reference to draw upon, they were nonetheless without recent histories, lacking in cadres, and inclined to formulate instantaneous and frequently misleading programs. Because the revolution was made against the corporatist and conservative Estado Novo a strong initial tendency existed to define the political spectrum much to the left in order to contrast the new organizations and their programs with the old regime.

Following the initial explosion of group formation immediately after the revolution, which continued until the elections for the Constituent Assembly on 25

Table 2.1

Potential for Coalitions, 1976–1983

	1976	1979	1980	1983
PS	35.0	27.4	27.8	36.1
PSD	24.0			27.2
PCP	14.6	19.0	16.8	18.1
CDS	15.9			12.6
PS/PSD	59.0			63.3
PS/CDS	50.9			48.7
PSD/CDS	39.9	42.2	47.6	39.8
PS/PCP	49.6	46.4	44.6	54.2

April 1975, there has been substantial stability in the number, rank ordering, and support for a limited number of parties. During the first year after 25 April 1974 at least twenty-three organizations, which called themselves political parties, came into existence. In the elections of 25 April 1975 twelve parties ran and four (the PCP, PS/PPD, PSD, and CDS) emerged as predominant. In the 1983 elections, for example, these four received 94 percent of the vote. The four major party groupings have all 250 deputies from the 1983 elections in which thirteen parties put up candidates.[6] In the 6 October 1985 legislative election this pattern was shattered with the emergence of the pro-Eanes PRD (Democratic Renewal party) which took 18 percent of the vote and 45 seats. As is clear from the data in Table 2.1, Portugal is a multiparty system with no dominant party.

Not all the minor parties are to the left of the PCP, and not all were formed in the immediately postrevolution period. For example, the Union of the Democratic and Socialist Left (UEDS) was formed from a faction of the PS in 1979 and the Independent Social Democrat Action (ASDI) broke off from the PSD in the same year. The former ran in the elections of 1979 and received 0.7 percent of the vote, whereas the ASDI ran in the local elections of 1982 and received 0.1 percent. Both of these parties joined the PS in the Socialist Republican Front (FRS) for the Assembly elections in 1980, but, as will be discussed below, the PS broke up this coalition in 1982. Candidates from these two parties ran as independents on the PS slate in 1983. However, the PS endured these elements of the UEDS and ASDI primarily in order to compete with coalitions to its left, the United People's Alliance (APU) led by the PCP, and to its right, the AD. With the collapse of the AD in late 1982 and the creation of Central Bloc government with the PSD in June of 1983, there was much less need or justification in the PS for either the UEDS or the ASDI. Consequently, the ASDI voted itself out of existence in January of 1985. Without an arrangement with a major party these two minor parties would have no representation in the Assembly. The problem facing small parties can be illustrated by reference to the case of the Popular Monarchist Party (PPM). This minor party of the right received some 0.5 percent of the vote in both the 1976 and 1983 elections and elected no deputies. By joining the AD for the 1979 and 1980 elections it received, because of the list arrangement, five deputies in the former and six in the latter election. In sum, there seems to be negligible potential for minor parties to grow into major parties and the only means whereby they can survive is in a coalition with one of the four major parties.

Entrenching the Party System

A political party system is strongly determined by the legal context in which it is located. This applies both to the Constitution of 1976, as revised in 1982, and legislation following from it. The individuals who framed the Constitution had a number of concerns at hand as they elaborated this document in late 1975 and early 1976. They wanted to avoid the experience of the First Republic, 1910-1926, which was the most unstable of any European government during this period.[7] The instability was due at least in part to the fragmented party system. The Constitution of 1976 sought to integrate, rather than fragment, the political parties. With the case of the Estado Novo in mind, the individuals who wrote the Constitution sought to guarantee the presence of several political parties. Closer at hand was the experience of 1974-75 when the MFA was discussing the institutionalization of a progressive military regime in which the parties would play a small role. Indeed, a number of proposals came from the left in the summer of 1975 for just such an institutionalization which left little room for the political parties. The success of the Document of the Nine, written by officers of the moderate left and calling for democratic socialism, put an end to these suggestions. The Constitution sought to avoid this situation by including various stipulations which guaranteed the parties' presence. Presumably, as long as the Constitution survives so will the political parties.

The Constitution was written by an Assembly dominated by the four major parties. They drafted a document in line with their own political interests and ensured that it could be revised only with their cooperation. It could not be revised until 1980, and then only by a two-thirds majority on most items and not at all on certain "reserved" articles, including the electoral law.

The extent and detail of the articles in the Constitution of 1976, and of the legislation emanating from it, dealing with political parties is incredible; it has become the topic of an excellent and comprehensive thesis by Marcelo Rebelo de Sousa.[8] The author demonstrates most convincingly the extent and importance of the parties in the legal framework of democratic Portugal and indicates the exhaustiveness of this framework in comparison to other European countries.

The Constitution and the legislation springing from it define political parties in some detail; it is clear that political parties are *necessary* in Portuguese democracy—this democracy is interlinked with political parties. Item 290 of the Constitution specifically excludes the possibility of revising the proportional representation system of voting and also mentions political parties as an expression of pluralism. The constitutional revision of 1982 did nothing to change the overall situation regarding the prominent role of the political parties. If anything, as we shall see in Chapter 6, their roles and powers have been increased.

The Constitution also ensures that each party receives a subsidy determined by the number of votes it received in the last election; this is based on a formula in which the number of votes for each party is multiplied by 1/225 of the national minimum salary. In 1984 this meant that the PS and PSD, for example, received the equivalent of U.S. $90,000 and $67,000, respectively. These sums compared to membership dues for the PS of U.S. $52,000 and PSD of $19,000. It is almost impossible to determine all sources of party funds, but clearly the public funding is far more important than dues.[9]

The Electoral System

Critics claim that the electoral system has reinforced the hold of the parties over the whole political system. They assert that it has rendered the party system completely rigid and has estranged the electorate from the political system—in particular from the Assembly. Many of these criticisms are well founded. For example, it is almost impossible for the average voter to identify himself with his local deputy when Article 152/3 of the Constitution specifically stipulates that members "shall represent the whole country, not the districts for which they are elected." On the other hand, as Marcelo Rebelo de Sousa has noted, it was the parties (and particularly the PS and the PSD) which saw advantages in establishing a voting system which not only perpetuates the main political parties and reduces the possibilities of smaller parties achieving any parliamentary representation, but which also tends to favor larger parties and those able to form viable coalitions.[10] The basic principles for the present electoral system were established in 1975, and enshrined in the 1976 Constitution and the electoral law of 1979. The revised Constitution merely confirms these principles, which include not only proportional representation (Article 116/5), but also the use of the d'Hondt system of the highest average for distributing seats among the parties. Parties do not have to obtain a minimum percentage of votes either at the local or national level to ensure party representation in Parliament, and only political parties may present candidates for the Assembly.

The electoral system adopted in 1975 has directly affected the political parties. It has effectively reduced the number of parties represented in the Assembly; in addition, the parties have been obliged to adopt strategies that will maximize the benefits reaped by the larger parties from the d'Hondt system of proportional representation. In general, the electoral map has reinforced the effects of the d'Hondt system and given a slight advantage to the country's more populous, urban areas at the expense of the rural districts. At the same time, by reserving four seats for emigrants and residents outside Portugal (two for Europe and two for the rest of the world, including Macau) the electoral law has a built-in bias which favors the PS and the parties to its right at the expense of the PCP. Since 1976, the PSD has won two of these seats and the PS and the CDS one each. This is hardly surprising since most of these emigrants are natives of areas where these parties are relatively strong. In addition, in two countries with large Portuguese communities, Brazil and South Africa, the PCP has not been able to campaign legally; the situation is not very different in practice in the United States.

The results of Portugal's legislative elections have confirmed what most observers have known for a long time: the d'Hondt method "systematically favors parties which have obtained the most votes in the different constituencies, i.e., generally the big parties."[11] Since 1976 the PS and the PSD have systematically been overrepresented in the Assembly in relation to the percentage of votes received. On the other hand, the PCP and the CDS have neither suffered nor gained in terms of percentage of seats to percentage of votes. The smaller parties have been the losers and, with one exception, the Maoist People's Democratic Union (UDP), have never won a seat in the Assembly on their own, despite the fact that no minimum percentage is required.

Because of the obvious advantages the d'Hondt system holds for a big party, the major Portuguese parties have formed electoral coalitions at one time or another to further improve their standing in Parliament. The first party to take advantage of this strategy was the PCP which, after running on its own in the 1976 elections, formed a coalition with the small Portuguese Democratic Movement (MDP) and ran in the 1979 legislative elections under the banner of the United People's Alliance (APU). It increased its votes by 5 percentage points. However, the parties which benefited most from a coalition were the PSD and the CDS which joined forces with the small PPM to form the Democratic Alliance (AD) for the 1979 and 1980 elections. In 1979 with 46 percent of the vote the coalition took 52 percent of the seats, and in 1980 with just 47 percent of the vote their total share of the seats increased to 54 percent. In effect, the d'Hondt system allowed them to obtain a majority of the seats in the Assembly without winning an absolute majority of the electorate. The PS also formed a coalition when it saw its electoral support drop from 35 percent in 1976 to 28 percent in 1979. It thus joined forces with two smaller parties, the UEDS and the ASDI, to form the Socialist Republican Front (FRS). It was not successful; the FRS only gained 0.5 more percentage points in the legislative elections of 1980 than the PS had won on its own in 1979. However, it is doubtful whether any alliance could have upheld the PS against the popularity of Sá Carneiro and the AD among voters who remembered the poor performance of the Socialist government between 1976 and 1978.

The effect this electoral system has on the structure of the political parties is less clear. In theory, proportional representation naturally favors the centralization of political parties; no one will deny that the Portuguese political parties are highly centralized. However, it remains uncertain whether the electoral system has caused this centralization or merely amplified an underlying trend. Party discipline is certainly increased under such a system; if a deputy or a prospective candidate finds himself at odds with the party's central office he may find his name omitted from the party's local list of candidates, or at least put in a position with little hope of being elected. Yet, with the exception of the PCP, which definitely exercises central control over the choice of candidates and the order in which they are presented, the parties usually allow local branches substantial participation. However, this autonomy can have its limits when the authority of the leadership is at stake. Such an incident occurred within the PS during the 1983 elections, in the battle between majority and minority factions. The central party organization, controlled by Mário Soares, attempted to determine how the lists were made up. It suggested that one of the leading figures of the minority, António Guterres, a *bête noire* of the party hierachy, should switch his position as leader of the party list in his home district of Castelo Branco to that of third on the list of Socialist candidates in Braga; Guterres not unnaturally refused. No compromise could be reached and the minority group withdrew from the election altogether.

Despite proportional representation, Portugal has not been inundated with a multitude of parliamentary parties which could make governing even more difficult. Portuguese elections may not present the electorate with the clear option between two parties, as in Britain, or between two reasonably coherent blocks, as in France, but in every election since 1976 a choice has been offered. In 1976, the electorate was asked to support or reject the notion of a homogeneous Socialist government. In 1979 and 1980 it had the opportunity to vote for the conservative program of the AD and to pass judgment on the performance of the two governments led by Mário Soares. In 1983, the electorate realized that it was voting for or against a PS/PSD government even though the coalition had not yet been officially formed. The 1985 elections were somewhat confused by the coming presidential elections, but clearly the voters were being invited to comment on the behavior of the two government parties after the breakdown of the Central Bloc. Whatever its shortcomings, the electoral system cannot be held responsible for the poor functioning of Portugal's political system. It merely reflects the absolute control of the parties over the country's political life: it is not the cause of the problems.

Public Opinion and the Parties

Our survey included a number of generic questions related to the political party system. In some cases comparable questions are available from the 1978 survey. Table 2.2 reflects comparable data on how many parties the respondents thought the country should have. These data suggest a number of points: First, much continuity is apparent in the responses to these surveys carried out six years apart; this

Table 2.2

How Many Parties Should the Country Have?

	1978	1984
0	6%	7%
1	20	20
2	16	13
3 or more	26	40
Don't know	26	17
No response	7	3

is particularly obvious regarding the first three possibilities which together total 42 percent in 1978 and 40 percent in 1984. It should be noted, however, that the possibility of 0 and 1 in the 1984 survey varied tremendously by class and by whether the respondent was an opinion leader. For example, only 13 percent of the upper-middle class gave these responses, compared to 37 percent of the lower class. Also, those favoring three or more parties increased from 26 percent in 1978 to 40 percent in 1984, suggesting that the multiparty system is gaining greater acceptance.

Table 2.3 reflects roughly comparable data on what the respondent thought the primary goals of political parties should be. These data demonstrate a great

Table 2.3

What Are the Goals or Objectives That Are Most Important for Political Parties?

	1978	1984
Achieve power	5%	6%
Express popular will	15	18
Defend democracy	21	21
Link people and government	14	14
Promote political clarification	2	2
Have assemblies and meetings	1	1
Govern the country *	--	13
No response/Don't know	43	26 (of which 5% don't know)

* This question was included only in 1984

deal of continuity between responses in the two surveys. Most important is the decrease in "no response" from 43 percent in 1978 to 21 percent in 1984.

Roughly similar questions were asked concerning the institution necessary for Portugal to be a democratic country; the data are found in Table 2.4. What stands out in these data is the 5 percent increase for "parties with different ideologies," making it the highest cited institutional feature; the continuation and even increase in the "single party"; and the decrease in "don't know" from 41 percent to 29 percent. There is increasing attention to the parties (even including the single party) and more overall awareness of the party system.

Political Participation

To what degree has the population participated in this new regime dominated by the political parties and how is it involved? Central to participation and involvement is information and interest. The 1978 and 1984 surveys included similar questions on these two topics. In the 1978 survey slightly more than half the sample (51 percent) indicated that they followed news and information concerning politics and government. By 1984 this had increased slightly to 56 percent, but it should be noted that the figure varied from a low of 37 percent in the interior of the north to 58 percent in the Oporto area and 74 percent in the Lisbon area. The increase in frequency of following news and information as displayed in Table 2.5 is also suggestive.

Table 2.4

Which Institution Is Most Necessary for Portugal to Be Democratic?

	1978	1984
Presidency of the Republic	24%	19%
Parties with different ideologies	18	23
A single party	6	10
Organized armed forces	5	4
Assembly of the Republic *	--	14
Others	4	1
Don't know	41	29
No response	4	2

* This question was included only in 1984

Table 2.5
Do You Follow News and Information Concerning Politics and Government?

	1978	1984
Frequently	39%	40%
Sometimes each week	21	25
Once in a while	38	33
No response	1	3

Both surveys also included a question on whether the respondents discussed politics with others. In 1978 34 percent reported that they did, and by 1984 this has increased slightly to 37 percent. However, in the intervening six years the frequency had dropped with 37 percent in 1984 reporting they discussed politics sometimes each week or more in comparison to 50 percent in 1978. But political discussion does continue and again there are great variations by region (low of 18 percent discussing politics in the Algarve to 45 percent in the Lisbon area) and class (11 percent of the lower class and 60 percent of the upper class) as well as by other variables.

In a liberal democracy, elections represent the most important act of political participation for the vast majority of the population. As noted above, Portugal prior to 1974 was not a democracy, suffrage was extremely restricted, and the percentages registered and voting were low. This is certainly not the case since the revolution as indicated in Table 2.6.

In the electoral census of 1975, 72 percent of the *total* population was registered. Since then, the census was updated with an increase of 860,770 registered voters between 1976 and 1983; virtually all potential voters are now registered in Portugal where registration, but not voting, is obligatory. Thus in contrast to the less than 20 percent registered in 1969 at least 75 percent of the total population is now registered. And whereas only 62 percent of the 20 percent registered in 1969 actually voted, in 1975 the figure was 92 percent. Since then abstention rates have increased from the very low 8 percent to 21 percent in the 1983 elections. These latter abstention rates are lower than in Canada (29 percent in 1974) and the United States (50 percent in 1978), about the same as in Great Britain (21 percent in 1974) and Norway (17 percent in 1977), and higher than in Germany (9 percent in 1972 and 1976). In addition to the five elections for the Assembly since 1975, there have been two for the presidency (75 percent turnout in 1976 and 84 percent in 1980) as well as three elections for local offices (1976, 1979, 1982). The Portuguese have had abundant opportunities to vote since 1974 and have taken full advantage of them.

In order to better understand motives for voting, the 1984 survey included a question on why the respondent voted. This pertained to the 1983 Assembly election and included seven possible responses. The overwhelming majority (63 percent) gave patriotic or democratic duty as their response, followed by 21 percent

Table 2.6 Results of Elections for the Assembly of the Republic, 1976–1985[1]

	1976	Percentage of vote (number of deputies) 1979	1980	1983	1985
% of votes cast	85.6	87.2	83.9	78.6	75.4
Socialist Party (PS)	35.0 (107)	27.3 (74)	1.1 (3)	36.3 (101)	20.8 (56)
Republican and Socialist Front (FRS)			26.7 (71)		
Communist Party (PCP)	14.6 (4)				
United People's Alliance (APU)		18.8 (47)	16.8 (41)	18.2 (44)	15.6 (38)
Social Democratic Party (PSD)	24.4 (73)	2.4 (7)	2.5 (8)	27.0 (76)	29.8 (86)
Social Democratic Center Party (CDS)	16.0 (42)	0.4 (0)	0.2 (0)	12.4 (29)	9.7 (21)
Democratic Alliance (AD)		42.5 (121)	44.9 (126)		
(AD+PSD+CDS)[2]	40.9 (115)	45.3 (128)	46.7 (134)	39.9 (105)	
Democratic Renewal Party (PRD)					18.0 (45)
Total[3]	100.0 (263)	100.0 (250)	100.0 (250)	100.0 (250)	100.0 (246)

[1] Includes the noncontinental electoral districts.

[2] Totals include the Monarchist party (PPM) in all elections; figures for the 1976 and 1983 elections represent the totals for the parties of the AD (which did not then exist); the separate figures for the PSD and CDS in the 1979 and 1980 elections are for the islands where they campaigned separately.

[3] Totals include other small parties.

hoping for a better economic situtation and only 9 percent wanting to change the government. Other possible responses added up to 10 percent. It seems clear, then, from the data on voting and the responses to the questionnaire, that the Portuguese take voting seriously as a duty that should be carried out in a democratic country.

In both surveys questions were asked on whether the respondents were interested in political parties and how they were involved with them. In both, 26 percent responded that they were interested in the parties. The nature of this interest, or involvement, of the 26 percent can be seen in Table 2.7.

Except for exposure to the media, these figures on involvement with political parties are somewhat low compared to the data available on other countries.[12] What stands out is the continuity or consistency of popular involvement with the parties, as exactly 26 percent in both surveys, six years and seven governments apart, expressed interest in or involvement with the political parties. Probably the most important change is the increase from 5 percent to 9 percent (of the original 26 percent) of those who claim party membership. Thus from a low point, as there were virtually no party activities prior to 1974, there has been a generally increasing involvement in the postrevolutionary period even while there are fewer street demonstrations, popular outbursts, and other unstructured political activities. The parties have become *the* structures of power and the population has gradually increased its involvement with them. This is important, particularly as the population has little involvement with other groups or associations which might link it to the political system.

Both surveys included questions on membership in groups and associations. In 1978, 11 percent reported that they belonged to some kind of group or association and this had increased to 15 percent in 1984. Compared to elsewhere these figures are very low,[13] particularly when the types of groups are considered, as will be done in Chapter 5.

Table 2.7
Involvement or Participation in Party Activities

	1978	1984
Party functionary	3%	4%
Party member	5	9
Distribute party materials	4	5
Attend meetings or demonstrations	14	16
Read or hear about or see party activities in media	87	90
No response	5	5

Table 2.8 National and Regional Evolution of Party Vote and Abstention in Assembly Elections, 1975-1983

		North Coast	North Interior	Center Coast	Center Interior	Lisbon Santarem Setubal	Alentejo	Algarve	Country
Abstention %	75	7.0	10.1	9.6	9.7	7.8	6.6	9.4	8.3
	76	12.9	21.8	18.8	20.0	16.5	13.6	19.5	16.7
	79	9.9	15.7	13.6	13.7	12.4	11.2	15.4	12.5
	80	11.6	19.7	16.1	17.1	13.7	12.9	16.6	14.6
	83	18.7	29.0	23.0	25.6	19.5	16.7	23.0	21.4
PCP/APU %	75	5.6	2.8	1.9	3.4	22.0	32.2	12.3	12.5
	76	7.1	3.0	5.8	3.7	25.4	37.4	14.5	14.6
	79	12.8	6.0	9.7	7.5	29.7	44.0	20.2	19.0
	80	10.8	5.0	8.6	6.6	26.7	40.6	16.7	16.9
	83	11.9	5.0	8.8	6.6	28.7	42.7	18.7	18.2
PS/FRS %	75	36.7	26.0	35.8	28.9	44.0	41.1	45.5	37.9
	76	37.0	24.7	34.0	27.6	37.1	34.1	44.5	35.0
	79	33.2	24.5	29.6	24.9	26.0	23.0	35.0	27.1
	80	31.8	22.2	28.5	24.9	27.5	23.4	34.7	27.1
	83	41.0	31.5	38.1	33.3	35.0	29.5	43.0	36.3
PSD+CDS+PPM AD %	75	44.1	54.5	43.6	50.1	17.8	10.0	17.3	34.6
	76	47.0	59.1	49.9	55.9	26.7	17.4	26.0	40.4
	79	47.4	58.8	52.9	59.1	36.5	25.5	34.5	45.0
	80	50.0	63.3	55.2	60.1	38.1	28.0	37.2	47.1
	83	41.7	55.6	47.4	52.8	30.4	21.7	30.5	39.9
PSD %	75	32.3	44.8	35.8	35.5	13.7	7.1	13.9	26.4
	76	27.8	36.5	31.4	27.8	15.2	9.1	19.3	24.0
	83	27.1	39.5	32.9	33.6	20.3	16.4	23.1	27.0
CDS %	75	11.8	9.7	7.8	14.6	4.1	2.9	3.4	7.6
	76	19.0	22.5	18.5	28.1	11.5	8.3	6.7	15.9
	83	14.6	16.1	14.5	19.2	10.1	5.3	7.4	12.4

The surveys asked whether the respondents thought they could be involved in the resolution of local, regional, or national problems. In 1978 some 16 percent responded positively and by 1984 this had increased to 19 percent. The follow-up to the question was an open-ended question on how they could be more involved. The responses here, although more specific in 1984 than 1978, were very vague and conveyed little awareness on how to be involved. There are negligible indications in the responses to other questions that there exist other means of linkage and involvement through other structures than the political parties.

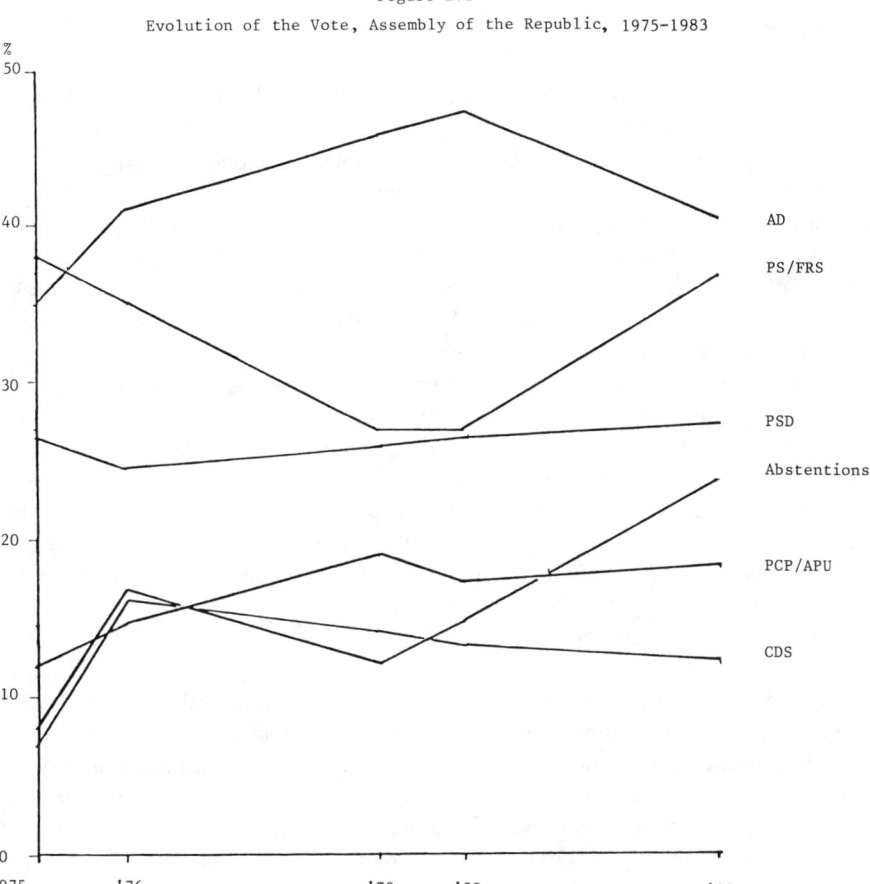

Figure 2.1
Evolution of the Vote, Assembly of the Republic, 1975–1983

Table 2.9 Voting in 1983 Assembly Election by Party Voted for in 1976

Party Voted for in 1976	PS	PSD	CDS	APU	OTHER	DIDN'T VOTE	DON'T KNOW/ NO RESPONSE
PS	88%	3%	0.5%	4%	0.5%	5%	0.1%
PSD	10	79	6	2	0.2	2	-
CDS	4	14	75	-	-	7	1
PCP	6	-	-	89	1	4	1

Voting Trends

If we review the data from Table 2.6 and regard Table 2.8, a number of points are obvious. Until 1985 the party system was characterized by the following features: First, no single party ever won a majority of the votes, let alone a majority of seats in the Assembly. Second, there was no tendency in the electorate for a splitting, fracturing, or restructuring of the party system. The minor parties' share of the vote decreased from 5.8 percent in 1976 to 3.3 percent in the 1983 election. Third, these tables show apparent stability of the vote until 1985. The order of the parties remained generally the same with the PS the single largest party, the PSD second, the PCP generally third, and the CDS fourth. For example, in 1976 the PS received 35 percent of the vote and in 1983 36 percent; the PSD received 24 percent in 1976 and 27 percent in 1983; the PCP received 14 percent in 1976 and 18 percent in 1983; and the CDS went from 16 percent to 13 percent. Figure 2.1 illustrates these observations on voting behavior.

Exhaustive studies in electoral geography have shown that the national trends are replicated at the regional level. While the support for the parties varies by region, the general patterns are identical between the national and regional levels.[14] Probably the most variable element is the increase in abstentions, to levels still comparable to other European countries.

The electoral stability at the aggregate level is supported by data from the 1984 and other surveys at the individual level. In the 1984 survey we asked questions on previous Assembly elections as well as future voting intentions. The data showing continuity between 1976 and 1983 and between 1980 and 1983 are found in Tables 2.9 and 2.10. These data, as well as results from another survey,[15] are described in Figure 2.2, in which those not voting have been removed.

While there are slight shifts among the parties, with the PCP (APU) voters being the most stable, and slight movement to other parties, not knowing, or not voting, overall tendencies are clear and very strong. Party loyalty was defined early, in 1975, and continued with very little movement of the voters from one party to another between 1976 and 1983. If we look at the data displayed in Table 2.11 on identification with ideological tendencies, we note the fairly high degree

Table 2.10   Voting in 1983 Assembly Election by Party Voted for in 1980

Party Voted for in 1980	PS	PSD	CDS	APU	OTHER	DIDN'T VOTE	DON'T KNOW/ NO RESPONSE
PS (FRS)	95%	0.7%	0.2%	2%	0.6%	3%	0.2%
AD	10	84	-	0.4	0.1	4	0.5
APU	5	-	-	94	-	1	-

to which one party has become identified with each tendency. This is particularly clear with the APU and PS, but remains significant for the other two major parties although there are ambiguities which will be clearer from the discussion of the parties in the two following chapters.

The 1985 legislative elections suggested a serious break with previous electoral behavior which was already obvious from our survey of 1984 and showed that certain sectors of the electorate were available to shift their support. This was confirmed by the impressive showing of the PRD as demonstrated in Table 2.6.

Notes

1. Philippe C. Schmitter, "The Impact and Meaning of 'Non-Competitive, Non-Free and Insignificant' Elections in Authoritarian Portugal: 1933–1974," in Guy Hermet, Richard Rose, and Alain Roquié (eds.), *Elections Without Choice* (London: The Macmillan Press, 1978), p. 146.

2. This has been extensively analyzed in many studies. See Bruneau's 1984 book as well as chapters by Lucena, Riegelhaupt, Schmitter, and Wiarda in Lawrence Graham and Harry Makler (eds.), *Contemporary Portugal: The Revolution and its Antecendents* (Austin: University of Texas Press, 1979).

3. Schmitter, "The Impact and Meaning," p. 167. It would seem that foreign experts did not consider these elections as proof of democratic experience. Portugal is included in neither of the following books on elections, although the second does include the Republic of South Africa. Stein Rokkan and Jean Meyriat, *International Guide to Electoral Statistics, Volume I* (The Hague: Mouton, 1969), and Thomas Mackie and Richard Rose, *The International Almanac of Electoral History* (London: Macmillan, 1974).

4. For a discussion of the opposition and its many problems see Mário Soares, *Portugal's Struggle for Liberty*, trans. Mary Gawsworth (London: George Allen & Unwin Ltd., 1975).

5. Schmitter, "The Impact and Meaning," p. 146.

6. These and other election results utilized in this book are taken from the volumes on the elections by the Secretariado Técnico dos Assuntos Políticos e Eleitorais, Ministério da Administração Interna.

7. For these data seen Juan J. Linz, *The Breakdown of Democratic Regimes: Crisis, Breakdown, and Requilibration* (Baltimore: Johns Hopkins University Press, 1978), pp. 111-12. On the republic see Douglas Wheeler, *Republican Portugal: A Political History* (Madison: University of Wisconsin Press, 1978).

8. Marcelo Rebelo de Sousa, *Os partidos políticos no direito constitucional por-*

42 Politics in Contemporary Portugal

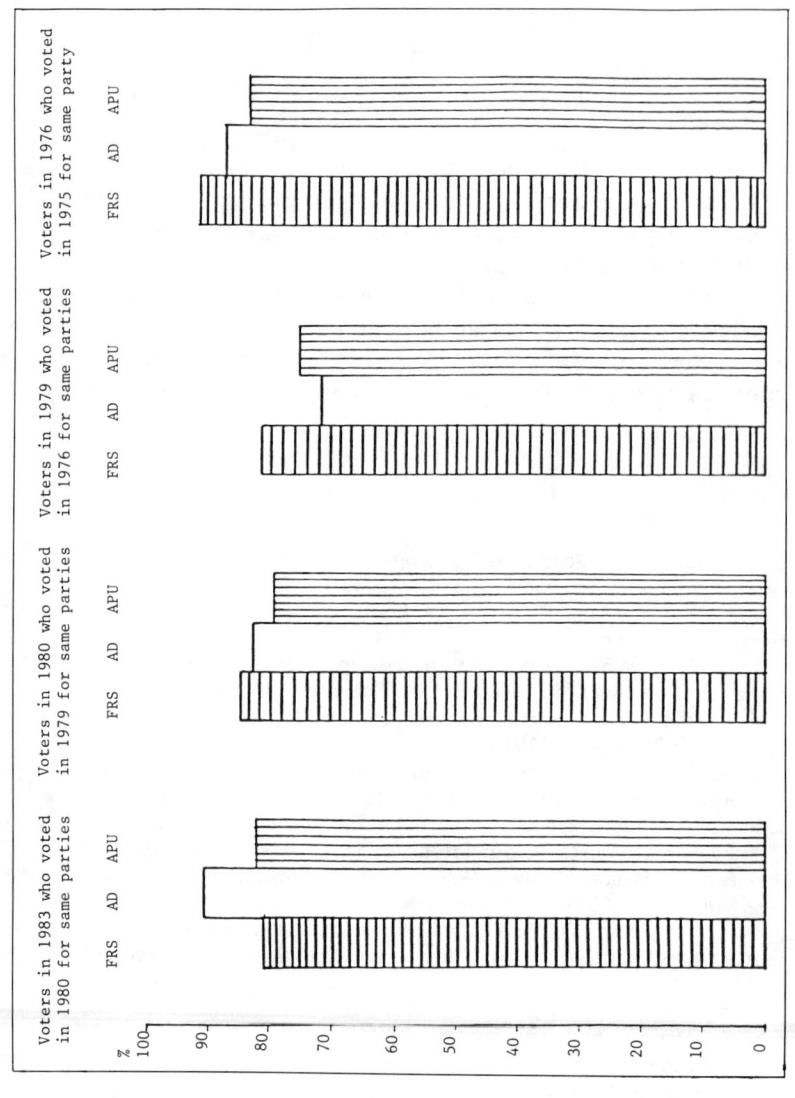

Figure 2.2
Percentage of Voters Who Voted for Same Party in Prior Elections

Table 2.11

Ideological Tendency Identified with in Relationship to Party Voted for in 1983 Assembly Elections*

Party Voted for in 1983	Christian Democratic	Social Democratic	Socialism	Tendency Identified With Communism	Revolutionary	None	Don't Know/ No Response
PS	18%	21%	88%	9%	27%	53%	41%
PSD	19	67	2	2	0	24	35
CDS	60	11	–	–	–	8	19
APU	2	1	9	89	36	15	5
MDP	–	–	–	–	–	6	–
UDP	–	–	–	–	36	–	–

*Those not voting or not responding excluded for calculation.

tuguês (Braga: Livraria Cruz, 1984).

9. Editorial Progresso Social e Democracia, *Atlas eleitoral* (Lisbon: EPSD, 1984), pp. 20-22.

10. Rebelo de Sousa, *Os partidos políticos,* 1984, p. 644.

11. Jean-Marie Cotteret and Claude Emeri, *Les systèmes électoraux* (Paris: Presses Universitaires de France, 1970), p. 91.

12. For comparative data and an analysis of political participation see Sidney Verba, Norman Nie, and Jae-On Kim, *Participation and Political Equality: A Seven Nation Comparison* (Cambridge: Cambridge University Press, 1978), pp. 58-59.

13. Ibid.

14. Isabel André, Jorge Gaspar, and Fernando Honório, *As eleições para o assembleia da república, 1979–1983: Estudos de geografia eleitoral* (Lisbon: Instituto Damião de Góis, 1984), figures 2-8. On electoral geography see as well Jorge Gaspar, "Portugal, Ten Years of Democracy: Changes in the Political Geography" (paper presented to the International Conference Group on Modern Portugal, May 1984), and Jorge Gaspar and Nuno Vitorino, *As eleições de 25 de abril: Geografia e imagem dos partidos* (Lisbon: Livros Horizonte, 1976). For short analyses, see J.R. Lewis and A.N. Williams, "Social Cleavages and Electoral Performance: The Social Basis of Portuguese Political Parties, 1976-83," in Geoffrey Pridham (ed.), *The New Mediterranean Democracies: Regime Transition in Spain, Greece and Portugal* (London: Frank Cass, 1984), pp. 119-137; David B. Goldey, "Elections and the Consolidation of Portuguese Democracy: 1974–1983," *Electoral Studies*, vol. 2, no. 3 (1983), pp. 229-240; and Eusébio Majal-Leon, "The Portuguese Elections of April 1983: The Portuguese Party System in Flux," in Howard Penniman (eds.), *The World Votes—1983* (Durham: Duke University Press, forthcoming).

15. The data for 1975–1980 were reported by our colleague, Dr. Mário Bacalhau, from a survey he supervised in October 1980.

3
The Divided Left

The Portuguese left emerged irremediably split after the revolution. The Socialists accused the Communists of trying to establish a "People's Democracy" with the help of their supporters in the MFA, while the Communists blamed the Socialists for siding with the right and sabotaging the revolutionary movement. As for the splintered far left, which had shown amazing strength during the revolutionary period, it attacked both Communists and Socialists, the former for their attempts to dominate the course of events in their own interests and the latter for their social-democratic opportunism. The revolution inevitably hardened the divisions within the left, but the ground had already been well prepared in the late 1960s and early 1970s.

The small underground left in Portugal was led by the Communist party during much of the Salazarist dictatorship. Though a small party,[1] it was well organized and had gained a reputation for resisting the constant repressive measures carried out against it by the regime.[2] It was the party which naturally attracted intellectuals opposed to Salazar, and many of Portugal's present politicians active on the left today joined it at one moment in their political life, including the Socialist leader, Mário Soares.

In the 1960s the Communist party's hegemony over the left no longer remained unquestioned. The party itself felt the impact of the Sino-Soviet split as pro-Maoist factions began to appear within its ranks. Both its dogmatic political style and wait-and-see attitude toward the regime were being attacked from within by those who saw little hope of overthrowing the dictatorship if the leadership continued its cautious policies. Outside the party, on its left and on its right, other small groups were being created such as the Portuguese Socialist Action (ASP), forerunner of the Socialist party, and the more violent League for Union and Revolutionary Action.

The Communists neither expected nor wanted closer ties with the various Maoist factions and small revolutionary groups which became more active in the early 1970s. Instead, they established links with the new in-exile Socialist party, founded in Bad Münstereifel in April 1973. Formally, the Socialist and Communist parties were committed to working together when the old regime disappeared. It soon became apparent after the coup, when both parties served in the government, that they had very different conceptions of what that commitment meant.

The Left and the Revolution

During the revolution, the PCP, well aware that it could not hope to win power simply by running for election, used all the means at its disposal to establish positions of influence throughout Portuguese society. It allied itself tactically with the more radical elements of the MFA, since the military wielded effective power for much of that period. It also occupied key positions in the media, in the state apparatus, in the municipalities and in the trade unions. For many, it seemed that Portugal was inexorably headed for a Communist-dominated government. Till this day the debate about the PCP's true intentions during the revolution continues among politicians and scholars,[3] but the consequences of its actions for the Portuguese left after the revolution are very clear. The party remains politically isolated, and there can be little hope for any long-term unity on the left.

While implementing a policy that caused many to compare the PCP's maneuvers with those used by Communist parties in Eastern Europe, the PCP had to face challenges on several fronts. Within its own ranks, it had to contend with the sudden influx of thousands of enthusiastic but inexperienced new members.[4] New pressures were created as the inadequately staffed party attempted to organize militants who often gloried in their sectarian attitude toward all other parties. In addition, the new membership was influenced by the revolutionary activities of the far left.

Throughout the revolution the various groups and parties of the Portuguese far left exercised an influence far beyond their support in votes.[5] In the unions, workers' committees, the media, and the armed forces, the far left, and especially the Maoists, often put the Communist party on the defensive. In its struggle to maintain control over the working class, the PCP was forced to resort to a series of apparently contradictory measures, ranging from strikebreaking to tacit acceptance of adventurist actions on the part of the far leftists, in order not to be outflanked. In the "hot summer" of 1975, the far left also challenged the PCP in an area where it had always demonstrated its superiority—that of mass mobilization. For a few days in August and September 1975, the PCP even entered a tactical alliance with certain non-Maoist far left groups, from which it was quickly expelled when it was realized that the party intended to use the alliance for its own purposes. In trying to meet the threat of the far left, which disputed its traditional claim to hegemony of the left, and to counter the obvious attractions that these groups held for the newer, less experienced members, the PCP often appeared far more leftist and adventurist than its very cautious leadership would have liked.

At the same time, the PCP had to contend with the PS, whose leaders resisted the growing strength of the PCP within various sectors of society, in particular within the armed forced and the union movement. The clash was inevitable as the two parties vied for leadership of the revolution, with two very different objectives in mind. The PS occasionally joined tactical alliances with the far left against the PCP, but as the revolution developed in 1975 it became increasingly identified with anticommunism among those social strata which most feared the PCP and which supported the PS as the best defense against communism, without necessarily believing in the social and political aims of that party. The hostility between Socialists and Communists shaped the future of Portuguese politics by effectively closing off any possibility of a strategy based on cooperation between the two major parties of the left.

The Postrevolutionary Left

After the revolution, the left continued to be dominated by the two big parties but underwent some changes. The far left attained its greatest success in the presidential elections of June 1976, with 16 percent of the vote going to the standard-bearer of the aspirations of the revolution, Otelo Saraiva de Carvalho, compared with only 8 percent for the PCP's candidate, Octávio Pato, but it has since declined as an effective force, even though its candidates continued to receive just over 4 percent of the vote until the general elections of 1983. Far-left groups continue to compete with the PCP and its supporters within the unions, but in general the PCP has succeeded in occupying most of the political space of the far left. The PS has also attracted some of the far leftists. However, despite the consolidation of the positions of the PCP and the PS within the Portuguese political system, these two parties do not represent the whole spectrum of the left in Portugal.

Both parties attract small movements and groups which refuse total integration and can therefore be considered as potential supporters, at least tactically, for other political groupings within the left. Linked to the PCP is the MDP, which officially became a political party in November 1974. As the PCP's junior partner in the APU, the MDP has generally been regarded at worst as a Communist front organization and at best a party of fellow travelers. As will be seen, the judgment needs to be qualified. Likewise, the PS also has had its own satellites, the UEDS on its left, and on its right the ASDI.

Outside the major parties, disgruntled Socialists, left-wing intellectuals, and other independents of the left, including many who supported President Eanes's bid for reelection in 1980, have shown interest in founding alternatives to the established parties. One of these was the Movement for a Democratic Debate (MAD), created in March 1983 and led by former Prime Minister Maria de Lourdes Pintasilgo. In its manifesto, known as the "document of the 199," MAD couched its general socialistic aims in humanist rather than Marxist terms, indicating the influence of progressive Catholicism on its basic ideals. Welcomed at first by the PCP as a possible rallying point for the intellectual left, it was later attacked by the Communists as it became more and more clearly identified with the presidential ambitions of its leader whom the Communist party has repudiated as a valid presidential candidate worthy of its support. Other members of the independent left, most of whom worked in the National Committee for the Reelection of President Eanes (CNARPE), focused their energies on a party headed explicitly or implicitly by Eanes. Their efforts led to the creation of the Democratic Renewal party (PRD) in 1985.

Finally, outside the political system altogether, a clandestine left has existed which believes in the value of direct action. Under its latest guise, the Popular Forces of the 25 April (FP-25), the clandestine left provided a convenient instrument for the Central Bloc government in its bid to pass a special law increasing its police powers, the Law on National Security. The mass arrests of suspected members of the FP-25, including Otelo Saraiva de Carvalho, in June 1984 put a temporary end to its more spectacular activities, though it managed to carry out some daring exploits in 1984 and 1985.

The Left and Portuguese Society

Since the elections for the Constituent Assembly in April 1975, the parties of the left have never received less than a combined vote of 49 percent at any national election. Such figures give very little information as to the reality of left-wing sentiment in Portugal or about the relations between the parties of the left. For such information, we must turn to our survey.

When asked to situate themselves on a left/right continuum from one to ten (with one representing the far left), 43 percent of the respondents placed themselves on the center left or the left, compared with 33 percent who felt they were on the center right or the right. However, when asked to identify themselves with more ideologically defined positions, they gave rather different answers, with only 35 percent identifying with clear left-wing ideological positions (Socialist, Communist, or revolutionary) and only 19 percent with positions of the right (Salazar/ Caetano, conservative, liberal, Christian Democrat, or monarchist).[6] The missing link is to be found partly in the 17 percent who proclaim themselves to be Social Democrats. Not surprisingly, the majority of these "Social Democrats" come from the supporters of the PSD, the Social Democrat party, which is generally considered to be on the center right in Portugal. But 8 percent of those who voted for the PS in 1983 also see themselves as Social Democrats, whereas this is true for less than 1 percent of those who support the Communist-led United People's Alliance (APU).

The tendency to place the CDS and the PSD on the right of the political spectrum and the PS and the PCP/APU on the left coincides very closely with the voters' perception of these parties. On a left/right continuum from one to ten (one again being furthest to the left) the CDS scored a mean position of 8.48, the PSD

7.14, the PS 4.74 and the PCP 1.77. PS supporters tended to place themselves slightly more on the left (score of 4.56), while APU voters put them further on the right (5.80). On the other hand, both Socialists and Communists situated APU less to the left (1.87 and 1.81) than did supporters of the CDS and the PSD, who put this coalition much nearer to the far left (1.44 for the CDS and 1.53 in the eyes of the PSD).

These figures already suggest that the PCP is perceived both by its supporters and its opponents as separate from the other major parties. This is confirmed by other findings. Respondents were asked to express their sympathy for the main parties on a scale of one to ten (ten expressing the greatest sympathy). The PS received the highest score with a mean of 5.46, the PSD followed with 5.28, next came the CDS with 4.09, and the PCP was well behind with only 2.83. The PCP's score is this high thanks to the sympathy expressed by APU supporters. Among the other parties, sympathies for the PCP range from 1.15 in the CDS to 2.50 in the PS. On the other hand, the PS finds its greatest sympathizers, outside its own supporters, from APU, with a score of 4.41.

When it comes to evaluating the PS and the PCP on a series of questions relating to specific perceptions of these parties, the PCP was generally viewed as being incapable of avoiding political confrontation and not particularly democratic, and it failed to win convincing support as a defender of Portugal's interests. Only as a defender of the workers' interests did the party receive an important relative majority, but even then more than 40 percent of those surveyed either refused to answer or had no opinion. On all these questions APU/PCP supporters gave enthusiastic positive responses. As can be seen from Table 3.1, PS voters were more positive towards the PCP than was the public at large.

The Socialist party is far from sharing this negative image, even among APU supporters, who only refuse to grant the PS the title of defender of the workers, which is only perhaps natural from the voters of a party which claims to be the vanguard of the working class.

Lack of sympathy or trust for APU/PCP became evident when respondents were asked to choose the best government for the present Portuguese situation. Overall, 27 percent prefered a PS or PS/PSD government. The number rose to 54 percent in the ranks of the Socialist party, and only 4 percent among APU voters. Presented with the prospect of a PCP/PS government, 7 percent of the population supported the idea, but this figure only reached this level because of 37 percent support from APU voters. Among Socialists, only 6 percent backed such a solution. Such results confirm that the notion of a leftist union between Socialists and Communists has very little basis outside the PCP and its supporters. Division of the Portuguese left represents much more than the incapacity of party leaderships to work together: it also reflects the reality of Portuguese public opinion.

Table 3.1 How APU and PS Voters Perceive the PCP

Do you believe the PCP is:	General			APU			PS		
	Yes	Don't Know/No Response		Yes	Don't Know/No Response		Yes	Don't Know/No Response	
Capable of avoiding confrontation	15	43		54	24		17	35	
A defender of the workers	38	48		72	21		42	36	
Democratic	29	41		71	22		33	34	
A defender of the country's interest	29	42		73	23		33	36	
An enemy of democracy	24	42		2	26		25	34	

Table 3.2 How APU and PS Voters Perceive the PS

Do you believe the PS is:	General			PS			APU		
	Yes	Don't Know/no Response		Yes	Don't Know/No Response		Yes	Don't Know/No Response	
Capable of avoiding confrontation	39	40		56	32		38	23	
A defender of the workers	45	39		58	32		32	21	
Democratic	53	39		65	31		52	24	
A defender of the country's interest	49	40		62	33		44	22	
An enemy of democracy	6	40		3	32		20	23	

The Communist Party

The PCP emerged as one of the big losers of the revolution. After appearing as the guiding force behind the moves to establish bureaucratic socialism in Portugal in 1974-1975, the PCP was singled out as the main enemy of democracy by those forces who considered that the revolution had gone far enough. After 25 November 1975, the Communists were eliminated from all positions of national state power. They participated actively in the drafting of the 1976 Constitution and could be satisfied that the main "conquests of the revolution" (nationalizations, agrarian reform, workers' committees, and workers' rights) were to be guaranteed in a document that also declared that one of the Portuguese Republic's objectives was to "ensure the transition to socialism." In the eyes of the PCP, the new constitution symbolized its role in leading the revolution in the right direction and guaranteed that there would be no return to the past. However, despite its support for a constitutional framework that met most of its demands, the party has remained largely outside the regime, since none of the other major parties can seriously consider it as a possible partner in a governing coalition. At the same time it has proved too powerful to be simply ignored.

In this situation, the PCP has had to fight to maintain its position within Portuguese politics. As a consequence, it has had to forge an essentially defensive long-term strategy, best understood as a "strategy of influence," which it has used to sink deep roots into Portuguese society. This strategy of influence has hidden behind claims that the party is still seeking to establish socialism in Portugal, for the sake of party militants who would otherwise lose faith in it.

This policy of "power without responsibility" has created a latent crisis within Portuguese communism as the PCP finds it increasingly onerous to assume the mantle of Western Europe's main proponent of absolute fidelity to Soviet-style socialism, while adapting to the political reality of working within a Western democratic state. This crisis is masked by the party's constant claims that its membership is always increasing, its aggressive language, and the impressive demonstrations it can usually organize. None of this can conceal the fact that the PCP's latent crisis is having an effect on every aspect of its activity, as the party struggles to maintain the essence of its identity.

The Impossible Deradicalization of the PCP

Many observers have concluded that in general West European Communist parties have not escaped the process of deradicalization. According to this view, Communist parties, like all other parties advocating radical change, must, at some time or other, come to terms with social and economic reality and moderate their demands.

Robert Tucker attributes this process to the rise of younger, less radical leaders and to the increasing size of the membership.[7] In a similar vein, the sociologist

Frank Parkin talks of the "political acculturation" of the party leadership as the main explanatory factor in the deradicalization process.[8] That implies working-class leaders of a radical party adopt more moderate norms as they occupy positions of authority within the state apparatus.

The party has done all it can to prevent the *embourgeoisement* of its leadership by maintaining the so-called golden rule of a working-class majority at the top level, though this has been more difficult to achieve at the intermediate levels. Though the leadership has become increasingly bureaucratized, it certainly has not succumbed to the charms of bourgeois democracy. The PCP's problem lies elsewhere, in its incapacity to adapt its ideology to its strategy.

With some pride, the party declares its attachment to the fundamental principles of Marxism-Leninism and publicly attacks those Communist parties which would abandon them. Any modifications to its ideological tenets are purely tactical. The PCP refuses the logic of reformism, both in its language, still very reminiscent of the Cominform era, and in its attitudes. The leadership never misses an opportunity to declare its admiration for Eastern European socialism and takes great pains to point out that the norms of West European advanced capitalism do not apply to Portugal. Objectively, according to the PCP, Eurocommunism would have no place in Portugal. On the other hand, the party insists on the need to attract middle-class members and voters and criticizes some of its activists for their sectarian attitudes toward such potential supporters. There seems little acceptance of the idea that ideological changes are inevitable if the party is to keep in step with the socio-political consequences of economic development, however delayed this may be in Portugal.

The crisis of ideology in the PCP is not so much a growing dichotomy between a radical vocabulary and a truly reformist policy as a failure to recognize the difference between ideological principles and dogma.

The Strategy of Influence

Like all Communist parties, the PCP's strategy evolves around two poles, the domestic situation and membership in the international Communist movement. All national Communist parties continually attempt to balance the demands of both. At first sight, it might be tempting to describe the PCP in terms of Ronald Tiersky's description of the French Communist party (PCF), to the effect that the *grands tournants* in the history of that party "have unfailingly reflected changes in Soviet policy and attitudes."[9] After all, the Portuguese party openly admires the Communist party of the Soviet Union and all that it stands for. However, it would be a mistake to see this as a purely emotional attachment born from the long years of exile in Eastern Europe of many of the present leaders. It also corresponds to a conscious choice made during the late 1960s when party unity was threatened. Since then it has proven a useful means for increasing the PCP's stature in the international Communist movement well beyond what a party from a small country would normally warrant. Any attempt to shy away from a pro-Soviet line would now create divisions which could only weaken the party. The PCP would therefore find it difficult to make the attitudinal or ideological concessions to the Socialist countries which are necessary if it is to make any headway among the middle classes.

According to a former member of the party, the PCP's main problem in postrevolutionary Portugal has been "the absence of a strategy for the conquest of power."[10] Such an assessment implies that the party is pursuing that particular objective. A closer examination of its behavior and policy statements demands a more balanced judgment. There is little to indicate that the PCP has really expected or even wanted to exercise power in the conditions of postrevolutionary Portugal. Its aims seem much more geared to wielding influence and veto power than to participating in any constructive way or to managing the country's permanent economic crisis. The strategy is basically defensive rather than offensive and involves both strengthening the party's position within Portuguese society and in pressuring the various institutions of government. This two-pronged strategy has also conditioned the PCP's functions within the Portuguese system, which express another facet of its present crisis.

Since 1976, the Portuguese Communist party has carefully attempted to establish its hegemony on the left. Concretely, this has meant the political elimination of the far left, maintaining control over the union movement, and pushing the Socialist party to the right. Paradoxically, elimination of the far left began with the party's biggest electoral defeat when its candidate, Octávio Pato, was badly beaten in the presidential elections of June 1976. The candidate supported by the far left, Otelo Saraiva de Carvalho, came ahead of Pato in almost all parts of the country. Otelo's relative success in 1976 marked a turning point in the party's history. Having exposed, in its view, the futility of the far-left option, the PCP had already won back its electorate by the municipal elections of December 1976. Far-left groups have remained active in certain sectors of the Communist-controlled labor federation, the General Confederation of Portuguese Workers (CGTP), and in the elected workers' commissions, but they no longer represent a threat to the PCP.

With the Socialists, the battle has taken on other dimensions. Here the party faces two contradictory objectives: to discredit the PS as a party of the left and to form a governing alliance with it. The second objective has become practically a ritual, which no one takes seriously because of the irreconcilable differences between the two parties. It can, however, affect left-leaning Socialist voters who are unhappy with the PS's centrist policies and who might be persuaded to vote for the PCP. It also keeps the party in step with the other Western European Communist parties. The PCP sounds much more convincing when it denounces the Socialist party for turning to the right and for practising rightist policies when in power. This tactic also calls for caution. If the PCP pushes too hard against a PS government, even one involved in an alliance with the Social Democrats, it runs the risk of alienating Socialist voters and of isolating itself. On the other hand, it can hope to reap benefits as the parties in power take unpopular decisions and the PCP establishes itself as the only real party of opposition. The Communists must also counter the threat of the Socialists in the union movement. Since 1979 the CGTP has had to contend with a new federation, the General Union of Workers (UGT), controlled jointly by the PS and the PSD, which has been relatively successful in the services sector. The tactic employed is very simple. The PCP has joined forces with the CGTP to denigrate the UGT and to attempt to show its collaborationist attitude towards the government and the employers.

Finally, asserting hegemony on the left involves two other areas where the party has met some success. It has established some intellectual hegemony, not by controlling the media or recruiting intellectuals but by muting public criticism of the party in intellectual circles and creating the impression that serious questioning of its policies and actions is confined to the forces of the right or their objective allies of the far left. The party has also managed to monopolize, among the civilian forces, the image of the Portuguese revolution. It has become the undisputed defender of the "conquests of April," a symbol which it manipulates at every opportunity. It knows that the working class views this as enormously attractive; there it has become a vital instrument of mobilization. It has been helped by parties to its right, including the Socialists, who have turned their back on the revolution or at least downplayed its importance. However, becoming exclusive proprietor of the "conquests of April" also has its drawbacks. As the revolution recedes in Portuguese memories, especially in the middle classes, it ceases to act as a positive force of mobilization and limits the effectiveness of another element of the PCP's strategy, the search for social and political allies.

The party has never hidden its claim to the title of "vanguard of the proletariat" and has followed the traditional Marxist-Leninist view that the industrial working class represents the driving force behind the Socialist revolution. Given the socioeconomic realities of Portugal and the relative weakness of the working class, the party has always insisted on the need for an alliance between the working class (including farm laborers) and the small and medium farmers. This policy did not succeed during the revolution, not only because of the reservations and hostility of the conservative farmers of the center and north, but also because of the sectarianism of many local Communists. After the revolution, the party attempted to increase its influence in these areas by infiltrating small-farmer organizations, but it has had to admit its lack of success in attracting small farmers into its ranks despite an increase in its electoral support in the areas where they predominate.[11]

The PCP has clearly established a political and social base of influence in the Alentejo, the agricultural area southeast of Lisbon, where agrarian reform destroyed the power of the owners of Portugal's latifundia, and in the region around the city of Setúbal. The Communists are also strong in Lisbon and have maintained an increasing foothold in the country's second largest urban area, Oporto, though they are outdistanced in both Portugal's major cities by the Socialists. They have never succeeded in scoring significant results outside their traditional strongholds. But then they have never been seriously threatened by any other party in their fortresses either.

This workers/farmers alliance forms the basis for a broader class strategy which extends to all those social groups objectively opposed to monopoly capitalism. In particular the PCP has turned its attention to a rising group among the middle classes, technicians in the widest sense of the term. Like other Western European Communist parties, the PCP has realized the importance of a social force which is by no means set in its political orientations and whose services have become indispensable. Despite attempts to attract technicians, the party's efforts have met little success. Since the publication of statistics on the composition of party membership in June 1975, the number of "technicians and intellectuals" has hovered around 5 or 6 percent of the total membership.[12] Since this figure includes teachers and artists, it can be assumed that technicians make up only a small part of that number.

The emphasis on the need for a broad social alliance has not been translated into a coherent political strategy like the Italian Communist party's "historical compromise" or the PCF's "union of the people of France." Instead, the PCP has preferred to rely on a more traditional political formula, a united front which it dominates completely and of which the APU coalition with the MDP represents the latest version. However, this classic strategy acts as an obstruction to the type of alliance policy based on a coalition of social classes, since it serves as a reminder of the PCP's limited and utilitarian view of such alliances.

Extending the party's influence throughout Portuguese society has become an essential component of a more general strategic objective, that of maintaining a decisive presence in key sectors of the economy. The revolution brought agrarian reform in the south and nationalization of large sectors of Portuguese industry. The Communists played an important part in controlling the process of agrarian reform in 1975 and have ensured a dominant role in the Collective Production Units which were created at the time. They have made it very difficult to enact any legislation that would dismantle the institutions of the reform, thereby consolidating their position in a region where they have enjoyed traditional support. In the nationalized industries the PCP has met a stronger challenge. Since appointments to managerial positions are made by the government, the party can only wield power at the level of the workers, through the labor unions and the elected workers' commissions. As has been shown, the CGTP's hegemony has been contested by the UGT, and within the CGTP far leftists have attacked the Communist-dominated leadership. There is little evidence that the PCP is losing control of the CGTP. But the CGTP leadership is finding it increasingly difficult to mobilize workers to follow its calls for strikes or for limited actions against government policy. As for the workers' commissions, their importance as instruments of control or influence within industrial firms is largely symbolic. Despite these difficulties, a strong presence in the nationalized industries remains crucial to a strategy of influence, and the party must make sure that its tacit agreement is still necessary for the smooth running of this important sector of the economy.

Although the PCP left government in early 1976, this does not mean that it abandoned its influence within the country's governing institutions. The party has strongly supported the division of powers instituted by the 1976 Constitution; this has allowed it room to maneuver and granted it the opportunity to exploit the growing opposition between the presidency and the government. In the Assembly it has acted as a constitutional opposition party and has slowly but surely established itself as the single persistent opposition force to government policies, irrespective of the party in power. This does not prevent it from playing the political game strictly according to the rules of the Constitution.

In the running battle between President Eanes and the government, the PCP always sided with the president even though he has consistently disclaimed this support. The reasons for backing President Eanes were tied to the PCP's perception of the role of the military in Portuguese politics. Before the constitutional revision of 1982, the party saw the Council of the Revolution as a major force for defending the "conquests of April" written into the Constitution. This view merely continued the position held by the PCP during the revolution. By supporting those military factions most attached to the ideals of the 25 April, whatever their attitude towards the party during the revolution, a wedge was inserted between an important part of the military and the centrist civilian governments. Ever since the events of 25 November 1975, the party has carefully avoided antagonizing the moderate left within the armed forces. During the presidential elections of 1976, it did not directly attack General Eanes and maintained a policy of benevolent neutrality toward him. When the time came to adopt a position on the presidential elections in 1980, the party hedged its bets. It never ruled out the possibility of backing Ramalho Eanes, but hesitated to come out fully in his favor. Late in October 1980 it concluded that Eanes would be the candidate most likely to beat General Soares Carneiro, the candidate of the reaction. However, the party still presented its own candidate to take full advantage of the free propaganda offered by the campaign and then withdrew a week before the election to make sure that Eanes passed on the first ballot.

With General Eanes as president, the PCP achieved at least tacit recognition of its contribution to Portuguese politics, and the president avoided a confrontation with the only party that never publicly opposed him.

The PCP's strategic choices have shaped the functions and the role of that party in the Portuguese political system and have contributed to the crisis in which it finds itself. In many ways, the situation of the Portuguese Communist party resembles that of its French counterpart, especially under the Fourth Republic. As described by Georges Lavau, the PCF has fulfilled a tribune function within French politics, that is, as a defender of those social groups excluded from the political process.[13] Not only does the party seek to become sole spokesman for these groups, but it also controls and channels their anger against the system. Paradoxically, by acting this way the Communist party also serves to legitimize in the eyes of those it defends the very system it claims to oppose. This analysis closely fits the role of the PCP, which acts much more as a party of protest than as a focus for a credible alternative to the present economic, social, or political system. It would be very difficult for the party to alter this situation. As the experience of the PCF has shown, abandoning the tribune function in favor of an alliance with the non-Communist left and participation in government does not necessarily represent a formula for success. On the other hand, the logic of the tribune function leads to the implicit renunciation of the revolution as a goal (as opposed to a myth which must be defended), and this can only contribute to the demobilization of the more militant members as they become aware of the growing contradiction between the party's official rhetoric and its more prosaic actions.

Structure and Organization

The organization of the major Communist parties of Western Europe has always impressed observers, especially when compared with other political parties. Similarly Communists have always prided themselves on their capacity to beat all their rivals in this area. So when problems of organization arise, they inevitably become the object of major concern. Within the PCP this question has remained a permanent topic of debate since the revolution.

In the months following 25 April 1974, the party faced a dramatic increase in its membership which was hard to cope with. From no more than one hundred party functionaries when the military coup took place,[14] the PCP suddenly had to train dozens of new party cadres in a rapidly developing situation. This affected the quality of the membership, its capacity to establish itself in many regions, and its control over the actions of leaders at the intermediate and local level.

Like all Portuguese parties, the PCP has been plagued by problems of recruitment. Behind the official figures, always published with a certain sense of triumph stressing the constant increase in the number of members, lie some disturbing trends for the party's leaders. For a start, the numbers given out can only offer an approximation of the real state of party membership. Without disclosing exact figures, the PCP acknowledges that there is a certain problem of turnover. The party also admits that it has no way of checking on information provided by local organizations, since many of them do not keep their files up to date. The PCP has carried out several recruitment drives since 1976 to increase membership. These successive campaigns have revealed a significant drop in the recruitment rate, which indicates that the party may soon be reaching a saturation point.

A second problem with recruitment concerns the social composition of the membership. If the party is satisfied with keeping the number of industrial and agricultural workers in its ranks at 57 to 58 percent of the total members, it has experienced disappointment in other social categories. As has been shown, neither farmers nor intellectuals constitute an important segment of the membership, but by far and away its biggest failure is to attract women. At the end of 1974 women constituted only 15 percent of party members; by the end of 1983 they still only represented 22 percent.[15] Even more worrying for the party's future is the decline in young members; both in absolute and relative terms, and the concomitant general aging of the rank and file.[16]

The PCP has also had to contend with a weakening of the efficiency of the body it considers most fundamental to its effectiveness as a working-class party, the workshop cell. Too often the workshop cell has become either just a shell or an unmanageably large unit, and in the last few years the number of active workshop cells has actually fallen off.

At the heart of the party's difficulties, according to its own analyses, lies the functioning of its middle-level organizations. In many cases, the cadres elected to direct these bodies have received insufficient training and have adopted work methods which are routine or bureaucratic. Party leaders have repeatedly denounced deficiencies in the work done by these bodies, but with little apparent success because the same complaints reappear periodically. In fact, the party suffers from the organizational problems common to all parties at some time in their evolution; activists become too involved in day-to-day tasks and have little time to exercise their imagination. Such problems tend to magnify themselves in organizations that emphasize hierarchy, discipline, and strict adherence to the party line. It is then difficult to accuse intermediate leaders of lack of initiative since the parameters within which they must work are so narrow. In addition, the practice of democratic centralism and the trend toward professionalization of many leadership posts have increased bureaucratic tendencies.

The top leadership bodies have not escaped criticism. For example, at the Ninth Congress in 1979, the Central Committee and its executive bodies (i.e., the Political Commission or Politburo and the Secretaritat) were criticized for not devoting enough study to the "collective examination of the great national problems,"[17] but this sin of omission was not serious enough to cost anybody his job. The leadership has been more concerned with ensuring that the Central Committee maintain its working-class majority and a controlled rejuvenation of its membership. In 1976 the average age of a Central Committee member was forty-eight. By December 1983, the average age had dropped to forty-one. However, on closer inspection, the process of renewal has barely touched the real centers of power within the PCP, the Political Commission and the Secretariat. True, since 1974 the Political Commission has grown from ten full members to eighteen members and seven alternates. None of the original members (almost all of whom joined the party over forty years ago) has dropped out and the voting majority remains solidly in the hands of the old guard. As for the Secretariat, it is strictly controlled by the group that lived through the clandestine era and has ruled the party since the early 1960s.

The Tenth Congress marked the beginning of a turning point with the co-opting of seven new alternates, including two women, and one full member to the Political Commission, all of whom are under forty, and a new, young woman alternate to the Secretariat. On the other hand, a new body, the Permanent Political Secretariat, composed of five well-seasoned leaders, was created, presumably with the task of supervising a smooth transition from the leadership of Alvaro Cunhal. Those younger members who have risen to the top have proved not only their capacity to carry out administrative tasks but also their attachment to the general party line as laid down by the present leadership. Elements suspected of disagreement with any aspects of party policy have automatically been excluded from any leadership body; thus the facade of unity has been preserved.

Figure 3.1

PCP Leadership Structure

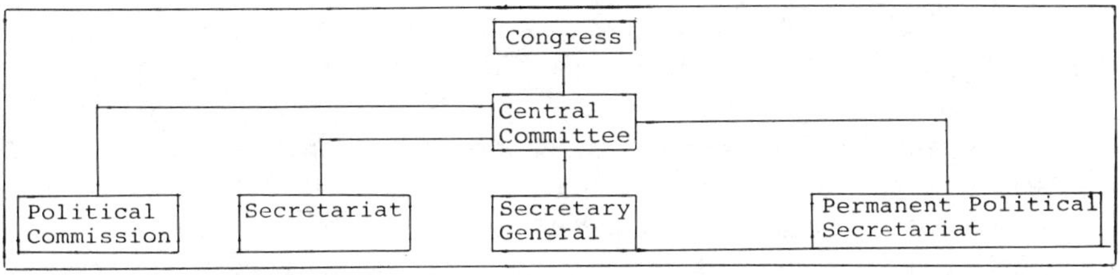

```
                    ┌──────────┐
                    │ Congress │
                    └──────────┘
                    ┌───────────┐
                    │ Central   │
                    │ Committee │
                    └───────────┘
┌────────────┐  ┌─────────────┐  ┌───────────┐         ┌────────────────────┐
│ Political  │  │ Secretariat │  │ Secretary │         │ Permanent Political│
│ Commission │  │             │  │ General   │         │ Secretariat        │
└────────────┘  └─────────────┘  └───────────┘         └────────────────────┘
```

A Crisis of Militancy

All Portuguese parties have experienced a decreased commitment on the part of their members. Disappointment with the results of political action, the availability of alternative activities on a much greater scale than before, and the impact of the economic crisis have all undoubtedly contributed to this phenomenon. The Portuguese Communist party has not escaped this general trend. Much of the problem stems from poor organization. Lack of competent cadres has meant that members have frequently been left to their own devices or never been offerred a real chance to participate in party activities. Many members do not belong to any party organization,[18] and a considerable number have no contact with the party whatsoever. As a consequence of the weak links between local organizations and their members, the party has complained continually that too many people do not pay their dues, the most elementary act of militancy. But perhaps the most telling indicator of decreasing militancy comes from the figures on the distribution of the party press. According to Alvaro Cunhal, *Avante!* sold over 100,000 copies a week by the summer of 1975 (when official party statistics claimed about the same number of members) and then dropped to a steady 85,000 a week by the middle of 1976, while *O Militante* maintained an average of 20,000 copies a month.[19] By 1979 *Avante!* was producing some 78,000 weekly copies and *O Militante's* figures had climbed to 32,000.[20]

The PCP has not put all the blame for this decrease in party activism on weak organization. It has realized that its bodies often operate in a way which does little to encourage participation except on the part of the local leadership itself. Party meetings, as reported by the PCP press, sound like excruciatingly tedious sessions where the local executive expounds party policy on a particular issue or a debate is conducted on mundane organization problems which only interest the initiated. Understandably, the average member does not feel very involved and prefers to stay at home. This situation tends to perpetuate itself as party work falls on fewer shoulders and the party itself becomes the preserve of the dedicated few.

The Portuguese Democratic Movement

For the first few months of its existence after 25 April 1974, the Portuguese Democratic Movement (MDP) appeared to be a broadly based organization bringing together Communists, Socialists, and other left-of-center movements. It soon became clear that it was firmly controlled by the PCP, a fact which was confirmed in the minds of most non-Communists when the MDP became an official political party in November 1974. This move prompted the PS and the PPD to decamp and to denounce it as an extension of the PCP. The latter's decision to respect the "autonomy" of the MDP as a political party by calling for the members of the party who also belonged to the MDP to choose between the two organizations did little to convince outsiders that anything had really changed.

Through the MDP, the Communist party was able to extend its influence in local government during the revolution, though much of the ground was lost with the anti-Communist riots of the summer of 1975. The MDP also allowed the PCP to penetrate certain segments of society, in particular middle-class intellectuals and professionals, which would have found it difficult to give direct support to the Communist party. This tactic paid off when the MDP became Portugal's fifth party in the elections for the Constituent Assembly in April 1975. Even though it only took just over 4 percent of the vote, with five deputies, to some extent it compensated for the PCP's disappointing showing of less than 13 percent of the vote.

In the postrevolutionary period, the MDP was sarcastically referred to as "PCP number two" in non-Communist political circles. It did not participate in the general elections of April 1976, its vote being split between the PS and the PCP, with rather more going to the Socialist party.[21] In the December 1976 local elections the party reappeared on the political scene to sign an agreement with the PCP to form the United People's Electoral Front (FEPU), which later became the APU. Just before the general elections of December 1979, the MDP and the PCP formed a new alliance, also under the APU banner, but with one major difference: the MDP would establish its own parliamentary group in the Assembly and could lead a separate existence, though periodic consultation between the two parties would take place. By joining this alliance, the MDP won three seats in Parliament in 1979. In the October 1980 election, the MDP lost one of its deputies, but won back a seat in April 1983.

The APU label has proved very useful to the Communist party by softening the negative impact of its own initials and broadening its social base. The extra votes brought by the MDP and the use of the APU name has proven invaluable under the d'Hondt electoral system which, as we have seen, favors large party groupings. For the first years of the APU, the MDP also believed that it could gain by throwing in its lot with the PCP because of the wide dispersion of its support throughout the country. However, every parliamentary seat it has won has been gained through hard bargaining with the PCP, and the relationship with the Communist party has come under heavy attack within the party.

Agreement to consult one another on particular issues in the Assembly has not meant that the MDP has submissively supported every position put forward by the PCP. For example, during the long, and often bitter debate on the revision of the Constitution in 1982, there were 141 split votes. On seventy-one of these occasions the MDP voted against the PCP, including fifteen times when it supported amendments which the Communist party opposed. On the final vote on the revision the MDP chose to abstain, whereas the PCP voted against. Such incidents have not convinced outside observers of any real MDP autonomy.

The Long Road to Autonomy

Analysis of the MDP at the local level reveals a heterogeneous party whose relations with the PCP depend very much on local conditions. In the southern district of Faro, a PS stronghold, MDP activists tend to be politically closer to the Socialists than to the Communists. In the Alentejo, on the other hand, the party cannot escape close assocation with the PCP, which is so strong in that region. This situation has created some resentment. The MDP in Lisbon has proved to be the most receptive to strong links with the Communist party and the most reluctant to criticize collaboration with that party. Finally, in the north where the PCP is weak and has a well-deserved reputation for sectarianism in its local organizations, MDP/PCP relations have proven very difficult and, not surprisingly, northern sections of the MDP have spearheaded the movement toward a reassessment of the whole relationship with the Communist party.

At the root of frictions between the MDP and PCP lies the concept of the APU. The Communist party has increasingly appropriated the APU label and made it synonymous with itself. Within the APU, both at the municipal and national levels, the MDP is expected to play a secondary role, subordinate to the interests of the PCP. Thus, despite its contribution to the APU vote in Faro, the MDP lost its seat there to the PCP in the 1983 general elections. In the district of Viana do Castelo in the north, where the APU has constantly been on the verge of winning a seat, the PCP vetoed a leading MDP candidate for the 1979 elections without any protest from the MDP's National Secretariat. The resentment felt at the grassroots level against PCP domination finally became public in December 1982. In Santarém the MDP refused to take part in the municipal elections of that year as a member of the APU coalition. Just over a month later, the debate on the MDP's relationship with the PCP began at the national level at a party conference held three days before the party leadership was to meet the PCP to discuss their joint actions in the coming general election of April 1983.

During the conference the various delegates introduced motions criticizing the PCP and calling for at least five seats in the next elections, if the APU got the same results as in 1980. A compromise was reached setting a minimum of three seats. The conference also supported a motion requesting that certain sectors within the PSD be included in what one leader described as a "large bloc of democratic forces" that could form the basis of a government after the elections.[22] The PCP angrily reacted to this last suggestion with a note from its Information and Propaganda Section, the first public criticism of the MDP from the Communist party. This was intended as a warning, not as a signal for a prolonged polemic, and the PCP refrained from publishing it in its official journal, *Avante!*. Presumably the MDP's demands came up during the ensuing negotiations with the PCP, but the only mention of them in the joint communiqué issued afterwards was a reference to the necessary electoral reinforcement of the APU, defined as a "rise in votes and an increase in the number of PCP and MDP deputies."[23]

The next public salvo in the battle for increased MDP autonomy came from a local organization. In early 1984, the MDP association in Braga announced that it had had enough of the party's subservience to the PCP and cited a list of grievances against the PCP's actions in the north and their negative impact on the MDP. An internal debate ensued which came to a head at the party's Fifth Congress in early June 1984.

At the Congress, the party delegation from Evora put forward a motion supporting the idea of separate MDP lists at the next legislative elections. The Secretariat countered with a more flexible proposal which would give the party the possibility to seek any alliance which the party considered advantageous, without considering any one alliance "preferential or exclusive." This rallied the support of the Congress. At the municipal level, the MDP would remain part of the APU. The party had taken an important step in redefining its relations with the PCP. Six weeks later, the Braga party association announced that it had decided to abandon the APU altogether.

The PCP remained publicly silent as the MDP sought to affirm its identity. Presumably, the debate was being carried on within acceptable limits and perhaps the PCP could see advantages to a more autonomous MDP which would appear more attractive to middle class voters who would otherwise never support the PCP or an APU alliance too obviously dominated by the Communist party. But in October 1984, the MDP began to step beyond the bounds when the party's secretary-general, José Manuel Tengarrinha, announced that he would take advantage of the Statute of Opposition Rights, passed in 1977, to seek a meeting with Prime Minister Soares. The stated aim of such a meeting was to initiate a dialogue with the government with a view to finding solutions to the country's problems based on what the MDP leader called a "democratic consensus." He also denounced the closed-minded, uncompromising attitude of certain political forces "including those of the left" (i.e., the PCP) and the Manichean approach which simplified Portugal's political divisions between left and right.[24] The MDP's conciliatory message came only two days after Cunhal had declared at a PCP meeting that the most important battle of the moment was to overthrow the government.

In Portuguese political circles, Tengarrinha's declaration had the the effect of a mini bombshell. Mário Soares immediately accepted the offer to dialogue. The Communists, on the other hand, were less than enchanted. In a speech in Oporto three weeks later, Cunhal publicly rebuked the MDP. He began by calling the decision "inopportune" and accused the MDP leadership of helping a declining, antisocial government by its lack of judgment and of weakening the unity of "democrats and patriots." He even insinuated that the MDP was seeking ministerial posts.[25]

The MDP's offer to dialogue with the government, which did not mean any form of negotiation as such, followed logically from the Fifth Congress. In an interview with *O Jornal,* Tengarrinha made it clear that the MDP was attempting to distance itself from its traditional image as a party of PCP fellow travellers. This step also represented a concrete move towards a strategy which the party had been discussing even before the 1983 elections and which was adopted in June 1984 as the "Social and Democratic bloc," a much more open alliance than the APU.[26] The Communist interpretation was much simpler. The MDP was trying to stake out a political territory of its own before it became occupied by a new political party directed by the supporters of President Eanes. As various declarations on the desirability of creating a new party showed, the MDP demonstrated little enthusiasm for a new party which could certainly influence its membership and electorate; it was more interested in finding a left-wing alternative to the PS/PSD coalition than in hanging on to the APU/PCP-style opposition at all costs.[27] At a deeper level this incident highlights one of the MDP's fundamental problems, its incapacity to establish a well-defined personality among the Portuguese electorate.

A Party in Search of an Image

The MDP sees itself situated between the PS and the PCP[28] and describes its objectives in vague terms as the "peaceful transition to socialism based on the will of the people and on the economic, cultural, social, and political changes which will foster the accomplishment of human beings, in the respect of their freedom of choice, within the context of the freedoms and guarantees of all citizens."[29] This is a statement with which the Labour party, the French Socialist party, and even the Italian Communist party could hardly quarrel. The MDP refuses to go any further and rejects the label of a Marxist party, even if it uses Marxist analyses.

At first sight our survey seems to confirm the MDP's self-image. Respondents place this party between the PCP and the PS on a left/right continuum of one to ten (one = left) with an average score of 2.34, compared with the PCP's 1.72 and the Socialists party's 4.74. However, it evokes little sympathy, except among PCP and APU supporters, and scores an even lower rating than the PCP.[30] On closer examination these figures show that comparatively few Portuguese are well informed about the MDP. This impression is borne out by other results of the survey. Only 44 percent of the respondents were aware that the MDP has any seats in the Assembly, whereas the four major parties were known by over 75 percent to be in Parliament. When it came to evaluating the characteristics of the MDP as a party, almost half of the respondents were totally incapable of placing it anywhere, and those with an opinion consistently gave it a more positive image than the PCP, except as a defender of the workers.

Although the sample of MDP supporters was small, the survey does provide indications that sympathy for this party is confined largely to the middle and upper classes. The MDP achieves its highest average degree of sympathy among upper-

and upper-middle-classes respondents (2.82 and 2.88), and both classes show much more awareness of what the MDP stands for than the average voter ("don't knows" hovered around 20 percent for the upper class and 34 percent for the upper-middle class, compared with an average of 48 percent in general) and gave it consistently higher scores than the PCP, except, once again, as a defender of the workers.

Internal party statistics show that this middle- and upper-class sympathy for the MDP is strongly reflected in the composition of its membership, which breaks down as follows: service workers, 34 percent; higher executives, 25 percent; industrial and agricultural workers, 22 percent; shopkeepers and businessmen, 10 percent.[31] In addition, 60 percent of these so-called "higher executives" (*quadros técnicos superiores* or higher technical executives) are in fact members of the teaching profession,[32] which confirms the much greater role that intellectuals, in the broadest sense of the word, play in the MDP compared with the PCP.

The MDP's determination to distance itself from the PCP could alter the landscape of the Portuguese left. The PCP's isolation would tend to increase, since the MDP is a vital part of its frontist strategy which has allowed it to extend its sociopolitical base without having to make any political or ideological concessions to its partner. Firm support for the MDP's new orientation at the grassroots level would make such a course for the PCP much more difficult. On the other hand, the MDP itself has few alternatives; this was publicly confirmed when it renewed its alliance with the PCP for the 1985 elections and maintained the coalition despite unhappiness with PCP behavior toward the party at the local level.

The Socialist Party

Within two years of its inception in April 1973, the Portuguese Socialist party had become the leading civilian force in the country's politics. Amongst its initiators were Marxists, progressive Catholics, freemasons, republican liberals, and former members of the Portuguese Communist party. As the party developed during the revolution, its ideological heterogeneity tended to grow as it attracted various moderates opposed to the PCP. Like all Socialist parties, it has experienced splits and dissension, mostly on the left of the party. These have served to reinforce the party's moderate image, but have done nothing to increase the party's ideological coherence.

During the revolution, the party established for itself a solid reputation for anticommunism and opposition to radicalized forms of socialism. By firmly establishing its identity vis-à-vis the PCP, it won support from the bourgeoisie which probably would have voted for the PPD, especially in rural areas. But it also became the prisoner of this strategic choice, since it cannot now envisage even a tactical coalition with the PCP for fear of losing its credibility and a large part of its electorate. In the short term, this probably has little consequence, since the party can hardly expect to form an alliance with a Communist party so resolutely attached to traditional Leninist tactics and so openly pro-Soviet. On the other hand, this has effectively prevented any opening of Portuguese politics on the left. The PS must either go it alone and form a weak minority government or join forces with the center and the right and give up any hope of creating democratic socialism in Portugal.

The Search for Consensus Politics

To navigate successfully between the left and the right, the Socialist party must avoid political or social bipolarization. Therein lies the key to its whole strategy since 1974, an issue which is both a question of principle and a condition of survival. As a principle, the PS believes in the moderation that has been the hallmark of its secretary-general, Mário Soares. But as a condition of survival avoiding bipolarization has become even more important. This was shown in 1979 and 1980 when the leader of the PSD, Francisco Sá Carneiro, chose a policy of direct confrontation, pitting the center right and the right against all the other Portuguese political parties and the government against the presidency. The Socialist party lost ground on both its left and right as it was forced to choose sides much against its will.

So far the PS strategy has assumed three forms. After its victory in the legislative elections in April 1976, it decided to form a minority government without contracting any alliance either on its left or right, counting on the irreconcilable differences between its opponents to stay in power. Mário Soares later admitted that this was probably his greatest political error.[33] But at the time party activists put pressure on the leadership to refuse any coalition government with the PSD. Fifteen months later, Soares's government was forced to resign. In 1980 the party tried to imitate the success of the AD by creating its own broad electoral coalition, the FRS. The strategy proved a complete fiasco and became a bone of contention within the Socialist party to which we will return later. The only viable alternative to the strategy of minority Socialist government has become that of the Central Bloc, a coalition with its nearest partner on the right, the PSD. As early as 1979, Soares had talked of forming a coalition with the PSD but these negotiations fell through when he insisted that the coalition could only become a reality after the elections. In other words, he wanted to make sure that the PS would negotiate from a position of strength. With the breakup of the AD in 1982 and the election results of April 1983, the PS/PSD alliance once again became plausible.

Whether from choice or necessity, these strategies have had a deep effect on the party's program. Like all southern European Socialist parties, the PS developed a radical language which hardly corresponded to its practice. Its declaration of principles, which remained a point of reference for the first six years, declared that the party aimed to create a "society without classes," which could only be achieved by building "workers' power within the framework of the collectivization of the means of production and distribution and of economic planning with a plurality of initiatives."[34] The party claimed to be guided by an undogmatic form of Marxism and rejected what it termed totalitarian and bureaucratic models of socialism and social democracy.

By the time the party had taken over the government in 1976, it had shifted decisively to the right and implemented very few policies that could be called socialist or even social democratic. This was acknowledged indirectly at its Third Congress in March 1979, when the party adopted its most comprehensive program with the title *Dez anos para mudar Portugal* (Ten Years to Change Portugal). The program made only brief mention of the party's experience in government, praising it for institutionalizing democracy and consolidating freedom, for creating a better social climate, and for defining the rules for the functioning of the economic system. It made no allusion to its meager achievements in social policy. With *Dez anos para mudar Portugal* the PS abandoned all official reference to Marxism. This new program, ironically drawn up by a group of younger Socialists who were later to become some of Mário Soares's most bitter opponents within the party, remained the basis of reference for all future party policy. It came closer to the type of program associated with northern European social democratic parties, in particular the Labour party, than to the one associated with a party like the French Socialist party. Thus it announced that the party's economic program would be based on recognition of the role of the private sector (but with an infrastructure based on the public sector) and judicious economic planning. Realizing that the Portuguese Socialist party had never really had any social policy to talk of, and certainly no concept of the welfare state, the hallmark of Socialist and Social Democratic parties through Western Europe, it proposed what it called a "daring policy of social reforms." However, these reforms remained rather vague despite the generosity which obviously inspired them.

Finally, a very important aspect of Socialist policy is Europe. In the 1976 legislative elections the party's slogan was "*Europa está connosco*" (Europe is with us). At the party's Second Congress in October 1976, the theme of Europe was omnipresent, and in 1977 the Socialist government applied for membership in the Common Market. Europe is above all a political rather than an economic theme within the party and is part of a larger question, the whole relationship of the PS with the outside world. Mário Soares's rule over the party has been based on the relationship with the parties of the Socialist International. Europe, and especially the European Community, play a large role in this policy. As a vice president of the Socialist International, Mário Soares has established beyond all doubt both his legitimacy as head of the party and to a certain extent his credibility. It is through Soares and his contacts in Europe and with other European Socialist parties that the PS has also received outside finance. In fact, his control of the party's external finances is undoubtedly a key element in his absolute control over the party. As he is always quick to point out, outside Portugal he is, in the eyes of the world, the Portuguese Socialist party.

Despite the various programs adopted by the party and the motions that have been overwhelmingly accepted in congresses, the policy of the Socialist party is fundamentally the policy of Mário Soares, who belongs much more to the democratic, republican tradition in Portugal than to that of socialism. Both as prime minister and as leader of the party in opposition, Mário Soares has managed to impose on the party his conception and his interpretation of the party's policies. His personality and tendency to dominate what the party stands for has been a subject of internal controversy and has created deep divisions within the party, which have never completely healed.

Support for the Socialist Party

Though the PS established itself until 1985 as Portugal's first party, its relative electoral success belied fragile support. Geographically the party enjoys, more than any other party in Portugal, an even spread of support throughout the country. Unlike the PCP it cannot count on the overwhelming support of an area like the Alentejo, nor does it suffer from almost total exclusion in certain other areas. Socialists expect at least 20 percent of the vote throughout the country, and up to 40 or even 45 percent in Faro, Coimbra, and Oporto. Likewise, more than any other party, the PS can claim to be representative of every social class. It may well be true that, as two observers have pointed out, the social basis of the party is above all an alliance between the moderate working class from the north and the urban petty bourgeoisie coming mainly from the Lisbon metropolitan area,[35] but, as our survey shows, in 1983 at least 25 percent of each social class supported the PS, with the highest support coming from the so-called lower-middle and lower class.[36]

However, this electoral support is fickle. Between the high and low points of the party's electoral results between 1976 and 1983 there is a spread of 5.44 percentage points. This is the largest range of all the Portuguese political parties and compares most unfavorably with less than 1 percent difference of its nearest rival, the PSD. This softness of the party's electoral support can also be seen from our survey which shows the PS to be one of the parties that can depend the least on the fidelity of its electorate in any future elections.[37]

Unlike the PCP and the PSD, the Socialist party has been unable to establish a real network of social contacts or institutions that would allow it to set down firm roots in Portuguese society. Until 1978, for example, the party was more or less excluded from the organized working class because of almost total Communist control over the CGTP. In that year the Socialists and Social Democrats were finally able to establish their own union federation, the UGT. As yet the unions affiliated to the UGT are primarily active in the service industries, and the PS's hold over industrial workers is still fairly weak. The Socialist party's relatively slight penetration into Portuguese society is illustrated by the lack of a well-supported party press. The PS at one time had its own daily newspaper, *Portugal Hoje*, which disappeared in 1982; it now publishes a theoretical journal, *Portugal Socialista*, which appears with great irregularity, and since 1978 a weekly paper of internal party business, *Acção Socialista*, which is strong on party propaganda and does not enjoy a wide readership. One area where the party appears to be gaining a strong foothold is at the municipal level, a fact which was confirmed in the December 1982 municipal elections when the party gained a total of twenty-one municipalities. Given the rising influence of the municipalities in Portuguese politics as a form of pressure group, this could be of some importance to the future of the party's position.

Structure and Organization

Like most Western European Socialist parties, the PS has an elaborate democratic structure with sections at the local and workplace level, regional federations, and above all a series of central organizations. In fact, and again like most of its counterparts, oligarchical and centralizing tendencies have dominated the evolution of the party structure. Theoretically the grassroots organizations can lead an active life, but in reality they only serve to mobilize support at election time and to elect delegates to the National Congress, the party's highest authority. Power within the party is concentrated in the hands of the secretary-general, especially since 1981, and he can usually rely on the support of the party's central organization. Until 1981 the Congress elected a National Commission which was periodically convened to act as a sort of legislative body between Congresses; it in turn elected an executive body, the Secretariat, with fourteen members. In 1981 the Secretariat was abolished and replaced with a Political Commission which includes both ex-officio members and forty other members elected by the National Commission. But at the very center of power around the secretary-general is the Permanent Commission of the Political Commission, a seven-member group elected on a list proposed by the secretary-general or a third of its members.

This concentration of power in the hands of the secretary-general is underlined by the fact that the party's group in Parliament must submit to the party executive and is controlled by the Permanent Commision, not just in theory, as in the British Labour party, but also in fact. Thus in 1981 when Soares was having difficulty with the majority of the party's deputies, the Permanent Commission simply decided to depose the party's parliamentary leader, Francisco Salgado Zenha, an opponent of Mário Soares and once considered the party's second-in-command, and declared that the parliamentary group would be directed by the Permanent Commission. On

Figure 3.2

PS Leadership Structure

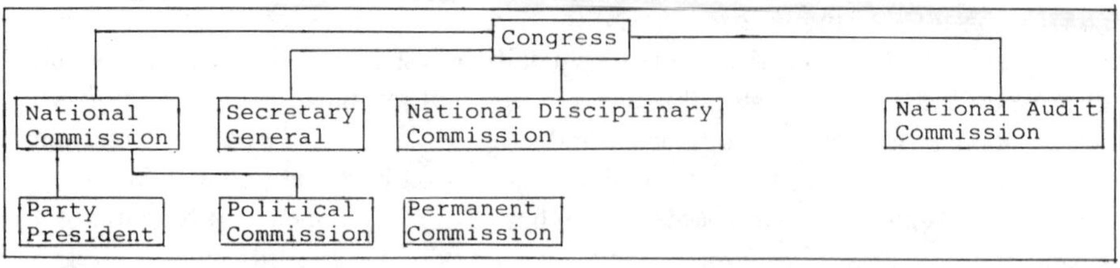

the other hand, the leadership does not expect the party executive to exercise any control over its actions in government.

One of the greatest mysteries of the Socialist party is its membership figures. During the revolution it claimed to have some 80,000 members and by May 1983 announced a rise to 130,181.[38] These figures are completely fictional; the party counts individuals who have joined the party at any time, regardless of how active they were or are, as long as they have not deliberately resigned. Most informed guesses put the party membership nearer 30,000 and, perhaps inadvertently, the party admitted figures very close to these when it organized a referendum among its members in April and May 1983 to see whether or not they would give their support for a PS/PSD government coalition. According to official party sources, all members were invited to cast their ballot and it was announced that 34,109 letters had been sent to the membership.[39]

Dissidence Within the Party

Between 1974 and 1978 at least four splits occurred within the party: three on its left and one on its right, but none had any long-lasting effects on its cohesion as a whole. On the other hand, the fight between Mário Soares and the majority of the party's executive body in 1980 and 1981 was probably the most serious divergence within the party; although it did not lead to a breakaway, it probably left deeper traces than the four previous splits. The struggle which took place during that period was in many ways peculiar to the Portuguese Socialist party, since it did not involve a right-left divergence as such, though it certainly had ideological undertones.

The roots of this difference go back to 1978 when two important events occurred. First of all, Mário Soares was dismissed as prime minister by President Eanes on the grounds that the PS/CDS coalition was no longer viable and that it was impossible to find a new party-based government within the Assembly. Soares's dismissal heralded a new, tense relationship between the two, and Mário Soares never forgave Eanes for taking such action. The second event did not appear to have much importance at the time. It involved the opening up of the party to a compact group of left-wing intellectuals who had broken with a small leftist party, the Movement of the Socialist Left (MES), in 1975 and had later formed their own small group called the Socialist Intervention Group (GIS), which naturally became known as the ex-GIS when its members joined the PS. The arrival of these fifty-odd left-wing intellectuals did not have any immediate impact within the party; however, here was a group which clearly owed nothing to Mário Soares and indicated that a new generation of Socialists had arrived.

In late 1978 Soares realized that the Socialist party was badly in need of a new image. This meant that a break would have to be made with the first generation of Socialists who had helped to consolidate the power of the secretary-general within the party. The facelift began when Soares asked a small task force directed by a young technocrat, António Guterres, to write a new party program. This group produced *Dez anos para mudar Portugal,* which the party adopted at its Third Congress in April 1979. The Congress also brought other important changes in the party.

The Third Congress introduced what Mário Soares has called *sensibilidades* (literally, sensitivities) in the Socialist party. These constituted more or less well-defined groups based on historical, personal, professional, or, in some cases, ideological affinities. They did not represent a clear left/right division, or even defined ideological schools of thought. There were the so-called *históricos,* that is, those members associated with the party before 1974, the moderates, very often close to the *históricos,* who advocated a social democratic approach to politics, the ex-GIS, and those who were called the technocrats, members who had joined the party after the coup d'etat in 1974.[40] This Third Congress must not be viewed as an open fight between factions. However, it did mark an historical moment for the party for several reasons. First of all, the party implicitly threw overboard the strategy of homogeneous minority Socialist governments. Secondly, it adopted a new program, *Dez anos para mudar Portugal,* the most comprehensive adopted so far. And lastly the Congress made changes in the party's leadership by promoting several prominent members of the ex-GIS and the technocrats who were brought into the single list of candidates for the National Commission drawn up by Mário Soares himself. This change was not well received by the party's traditional elements, and the single list for the National Commission was supported by only 68 percent of the delegates present at the Congress.

The logical conclusion of the 1979 Congress came in January 1980. A meeting of the National Commission was held in Oporto which, according to all accounts, was a tumultuous session lasting until four o'clock in the morning. The first debate was held over the party's policies and, above all, its strategy. The *históricos* lost the fight over a new strategy which, with the backing of Soares, proposed to widen the Socialist party's sphere of influence on the left and right. The logical conclusion of the debate was that three *históricos* left the Secretariat to be replaced by supporters of the new party line, giving a majority to the technocrats and ex-GIS. In the next few months, again with the full encouragement of Mário Soares, the Secretariat began to map out a strategy for the party which culminated with the creation of the FRS in the summer of 1980. Later the Secretariat complained that the FRS had been created far too late, and, indeed, it failed to make very much ground for the party in the October elections.

The defeat of the FRS heralded another change in the party. One week after the October election, President Eanes made a statement, bidding, in effect, for the votes of the right and the center right for the upcoming presidential elections in December. This created a great uproar within the PS which had already agreed to support the president. There was a strong feeling that their agreement had been betrayed. The Secretariat met almost immediately and, with the exception of one of its most prominent members, censured President Eanes for approaching the right. At that time, Mário Soares expressed his disagreement with his own Secretariat and insisted that the president should remain the party's candidate. He then asked two members of the Secretariat to see Eanes in Belém and assure him that the PS completely backed him and to encourage him to remain in the race. The next day the party's executive committee met, and Soares defeated a motion that the Socialist party should break with Eanes. Two days later the party was stupified to hear a public declaration from Mário Soares to the effect that the president had broken his agreement with the PS.[41] He was therefore going to withdraw his personal support from Eanes and temporarily step down as secretary-general of the party. The surprise within the party was understandable. At no time had Soares revealed his intentions to the rest of the leadership. So the question remains: why did Soares set out on a deliberate collision course with the majority of the Secretariat?

Conjecture still abounds as to the reason behind it. However, there are some points of agreement between whose who supported the Secretariat and those who have finally rallied to the side of Mário Soares. It is clear, for example, that since Soares's dismissal as prime minister in 1978 very little love was lost between Mário Soares and the president. It seems more than probable that Mário Soares was looking for a reason to avoid becoming involved in his reelection. It is also known that at least since 1976 Soares had been considering himself as a possible candidate for the presidency.[42] He had even met with some of his friends within the party in 1980 to consult them on the desirability of his own candidacy for the presidency. They advised him strongly against pursuing such a course. However, these personal considerations seem really secondary. Mário Soares had apparently become convinced that with the present majority in the Secretariat he no longer completely controlled the party. By withdrawing his support from President Eanes he knew that he was opening hostilities with the Secretariat, which would eventually allow him to regain control of the party.

During the next seven months the party prepared to hold its Fourth Congress. A final showdown between the secretary-general and the Secretariat became inevitable. Soares's opponents appeared to hold some very strong cards. They controlled a majority within the National Commission and the cadres at the federation level, and among the party's deputies, the leaders of its youth wing, and the party's mayors, as well as almost all the leaders of the party in the Azores and Madeira. Soares was alone and could only count on the support of some of the party's historical leaders. Yet the Secretariat lost, perhaps because it was not sure it wanted to win. Mário Soares managed to rally a majority of grassroots support, including many members who had not paid their dues for years, as the party's historical leader and the symbol of its unity. By the time of the Congress in May 1981, Soares had already won the majority of the delegates and his victory was a mere formality.

For the first time in the Socialist party's history, two reports of its activities were presented. One from the secretary-general and the other from the majority of the Secretariat. The Congress was also asked to arbitrate between different motions, one presented by the secretary-general, another by the majority of the Secretariat, and two others by two small factions within the party. Not only did Soares attack the Secretariat for its naivety and denounce the FRS as "a bad deal," but he also called for a strengthening of the role of secretary-general within the party, which meant a further concentration of his power. The Secretariat on the other hand, as well as defending its actions and the strategic choice made in the summer of 1980, also proposed changes in the party's structure that would weaken the position of the secretary-general and reduce him to a figurehead role or, at most, a coordinator. But it lost the fight and was eliminated from the new party executive, while retaining a reduced presence in the party's other leadership bodies.

The following two years prior to the Fifth Congress in October 1983 saw intensive in-fighting between the Soaristas and the group now known as the ex-Secretariat. Soares had ceased to be the party's conciliator and had become leader of the majority faction.

Ideologically, both sides admit that little separated them. Their differences centered around the question of internal party democracy, strategy, and the conception of power. The ex-Secretariat charged that Mário Soares had become an authoritarian leader and largely deprived the party of internal democracy. To which the Soaristas replied that open discussion existed and that the ex-Secretariat had failed to convince the rest of the party. On the question of strategy, the ex-Secretariat stressed at the Fourth Congress that it did not oppose an alliance with the PSD. Afterwards however, it became increasingly critical of restricting the party's options to such an alliance and advocated a more general opening to all progressive forces of the non-Communist left. It did not, despite the accusations of its opponents, advocate any union of the left with the Communist party. Finally, the ex-Secretariat appeared to view power as an instrument for transforming society and not just as an end in itself. Its members put great emphasis on the need for efficiency and a modern approach to politics. This insistence on efficiency and the political purity of their approach was strongly resented by the Soaristas who retorted that their opponents did not have a monopoly on efficiency, capacity, and political integrity.

In the period between the two congresses, the lines between the ex-Secretariat and the Soaristas tended to harden. At the same time the heterogeneous group which formed the ex-Secretariat slowly grew into a more unified group within the party. As this happened, political divisions between the Soaristas and the ex-Secretariat became more clearly defined and reached their height during the debate over the consitutional revision of 1982. On the whole, the ex-Secretariat insisted that the party respect the agreement it had made with President Eanes in the summer of 1980, which Soares and his followers had broken. This divergence led to a rather strange struggle where the majority of the party's deputies were forced to go along with a constitutional revision they did not support. They were obliged to submit to party discipline and to fall more or less under the trusteeship of the party's executive.

During this period many of the ex-Secretariat group felt betrayed by Mário Soares and badly treated. They felt they could no longer give their wholehearted support to Mário Soares, the man who had promised them so much by putting them in the party leadership in 1979 and 1980, and who subsequently let them down. In the future they could only offer support based on party interest and not on emotional attachment to a charismatic leader. However they had yet to taste the full force of their defeat, which came in the 1983 election campaign. The ex-Secretariat fought to maintain a number of deputies equivalent to their strength at the Fourth Congress.[43] The party majority seemed intent on bringing home the lesson of the Congress by obliging leading candidates from the ex-Secretariat to run in different constituencies from the ones where they had been elected before or by demoting them on the party's offical list to less favorable positions. Faced with such humiliation, the ex-Secretariat decided almost unanimously to withdraw from the election, thus leaving the PS parliamentary group almost completely in the hands of docile Soaristas.[44]

After a resounding victory at the polls, Mário Soares, realizing that his presidential aspirations also depended on reuniting the party, made some gestures towards the ex-Secretariat by offering one or two of their members a post in the Cabinet. These overtures were rejected, partly on the grounds that the ex-Secretariat did not agree with the concessions made to the PSD during the negotiations to form a new government, but also as a mark of solidarity towards the group as a whole. Between the elections in April 1983 and the party's Fifth Congress five months later, Soares made further steps towards reconciliation with the ex-Secretariat.

Before the Congress a compromise agreement was worked out, dubbed a "proclamation of principles and objectives." The Congress came as close as could be hoped to a reconciliation, although the minority made only one real gain—the inclusion of a motion supporting abortion, which the PS later adopted in Parliament as a gesture towards party unity. Members of the ex-Secretariat were again elected to the National Commission, and to the Political Commission,[45] but refused to serve in the Permanent Committee.

As the 1985 legislative elections approached, Mário Soares withdrew as the party's candidate for prime minister in favor of Almeida Santos to prepare for the upcoming presidential elections. At the same time the ex-Secretariat and the Soaristas buried their differences and prominent members of the ex-Secretariat ran for the Assembly.

Notes

1. Most estimates put the party membership at about 2,000 to 3,000 just before 25 April 1974. See Neil McInnes, *The Communist Parties of Western Europe* (London: Oxford University Press, 1975), p. 40.

2. The history of the PCP during the Salazar era has still to be written. For selected declarations of Communists arrested and tried by the regime, see *A defesa acusa. Os communistas portugueses perante a polícia e as tribunais fascistas* (Lisbon: Edições Avante!, 1975). The atmosphere within the party during the 1960s is well described by a former member in J. A. Silva Marques, *Relatos de clandestinidade: O PCP visto por dentro* (Lis-

bon: Edições Jornal Expresso, 1976). Finally, a rather special account of the hunt for Communists by Salazar's secret police, the PIDE, is given by one of the police officers in charge of this task in Fernando Gouveia, *Memórias de um inspector da P.I.D.E. a organização clandestina do P.C.P.* (Lisbon: Roger Delraux, 1979).

3. For a more thorough account of the PCP's actions during the revolution, see Alex Macleod, *La révolution inopportune: Les partis communistes français et italien face à la révolution portugaise* (Montréal: Nouvelle Optique, 1984), pp. 69-132. The most comprehensive view of the PCP during the period as seen by its leadership is contained in Alvaro Cunhal, *A revolução portuguesa: O passado e o futuro* (Lisbon: Edições Avante!, 1976). Mário Soares has given his very anticommunist version of the events in *Portugal: quelle révolution?* (Paris: Calmann-Lévy, 1976).

4. By June 1975, the PCP claimed to have over 100,000 members, "Mais de 100,000!," *Avante!*, 17 July 1975.

5. In the elections for the Constituent Assembly on 25 April 1975, the far left took less than 5 percent of the vote. However, two Maoist parties were banned from running and no far-left party presented a full slate of candidates across the country.

6. "Liberal" is understood in the meaning used in continental Europe. "Christian Democrat" is also a term used exclusively on the right in Portugal.

7. Robert C. Tucker, "The Deradicalization of Marxist Movements," *American Political Science Review*, 61 (June 1967), p. 348.

8. Frank Parkin, *Class Inequality and Political Order* (London: Paladin, 1975), p. 133.

9. Ronald Tiersky, *French Communism: 1920-72* (New York: Columbia University Press, 1974), p. 371.

10. Interview with Júlio Pinto, *Expresso Revista*, 10 October 1981.

11. A report on party organization presented in December 1983 showed that farmers still only represented 2 percent of the membership, Fernando Blanqui Teixeira, "Algumas questões sobre a organização," *Avante!/Suplemento*, 22 December 1983.

12. At the time of the Tenth Congress in December 1983, intellectuals and technicians constituted 10,458 of the claimed 200,753 members, or 5.2 percent, compared with 5.4 percent in May 1979 (ibid.)

13. Georges Lavau, "Le parti communiste dans le système politique français," in *Le communisme en France* (Paris: Armand Colin, 1969), p.18.

14. See Alvaro Cunhal, *A revolução portuguesa*, 1976, p. 397.

15. For the 1974 figures, see "As tres primeiras reuniões nacionais de organização," *O Militante*, June 1975, p. 11. For 1983, see Fernando Blanqui Teixeira, "Algumas questões," 1983.

16. In 1979, those under thirty represented 33 percent of the total membership (Alvaro Cunhal, "Relatório da actividade do comité central ao IX Congresso," in *IX Congresso partido comunista português* [Lisbon: Edições Avante!, 1979]), p. 51. By the end of 1983, this figure had dropped to 25 percent, calculated from statistics given by Fernando Blanqui Teixeira, "Algumas questões," 1983.

17. "Resolução Política," in *IX Congresso partido comunista português*, p. 332.

18. The number of members who actually belong to any party organization was given as 44 percent in 1981, and in at least one regional organization this number had only reached 15 percent, "Sobre o 11° Balanço da Organização," *O Militante*, February 1981, p. 5.

19. Alvaro Cunhal, *A revolução portuguesa*, 1976, pp. 411-412.

20. For *Avante!*, see António Dias Lourenco, "O Avante!," in *IX Congresso partido comunista português*, p. 68, and for *O Militante*, Aurélio Santos, "Propaganda e informação," ibid.

21. According to a leading member of the MDP. See Rogério Rodrigues, "MDP/CDE

de fora de Lisboa é mais crítico do PCP," *O Jornal*, 4 February 1983.
22. Interview with António Galhorda, vice-president of the MDP, *O Jornal*, 4 February 1983.
23. "Comunicado conjunto do PCP e do MDP/CDE," *Avante!*, 3 February 1983.
24. "Tengarrinha critica radicalismo de esquerda," *Expresso*, 20 October 1984.
25. *Avante!*, 8 November 1984.
26. Interview with José Manuel Tengarrinha, *O Jornal*, 26 October 1984.
27. Many MDP sympathizers apparently supported Maria de Lourdes Pintasilgo's bid for the presidency, an obvious indication of their availability for a left-wing alternative to Mário Soares, despite official reluctance on the part of the MDP leadership. See "Comunistas e MDPs apoiam Pintasilgo apenas via base de constat d'accord," *O Jornal*, 26 October 1984.
28. MDP Parliamentary Group, "Breve história do MDP/CDE em 1984," 1984, mimeo, p. 1.
29. Ibid, p. 10.
30. It may be remembered that on a scale of one to ten (one = lowest degree of sympathy), the PCP had an average of 2.83. The MDP only scored 2.57.
31. MDP, "Breve história do MDP/CDE em 1984," 1984, p. 20.
32. Ibid, p. 21.
33. "PR partidário não significa a partidarização do Estado," interview with Mário Soares in "Dez anos de democracia," *Diário de Notícias*, 24 April 1984, p. 10.
34. "Declaração de princípios," *Portugal Socialista*, 3 December 1973.
35. Maria José Stock and Bern Rother, "PS: a trajectória de um partido," *Expresso Revista*, 14 May 1983.
36. In the 1983 elections, the PS received the votes of 27 percent of the upper class, 31 percent of the upper-middle class, 36 percent of the lower-middle class and 33 percent of the lower class. Forty-one percent of the PS support came from the lower-middle class.
37. On being asked which party they would choose if they had to vote today (figure for March-April 1984, just one year after the elections) only 66 percent of those who voted PS said they would do so again, compared to 71 percent for the CDS and 83 percent for the Communist-led APU alliance.
38. Maria José Stock and Bern Rother, "PS: a trajectória."
39. *Acção Socialista*, 12 May 1983.
40. See Maria José Stock and Bern Rother, "PS: a trajectória," and Afonso de Andrade and Ana Godinho, "Viagem ao interior dos quatro congressos do PS," *O Jornal, 2 Caderno*, 30 September 1983.
41. For the agreement between the president of the Republic and the PS, see Chapter 6.
42. In 1976 the Communist party had offered to support Mário Soares for the presidency; Mário Soares, "Dez anos," in *Diário de Notícias*, 24 April 1984, p. 13. According to a member of the PS leadership at the time, Soares took this proposal back to his party's executive, which turned it down.
43. At the Fourth Congress, the Secretariat's list of candidates to the party's national commission received 34 percent of the vote, Maria José Stock and Bern Rother, "PS: a trajectória."
44. Only the PS list from Maderia was made up of ex-Secretariat supporters, inasmuch as the Socialist party could not hope to elect parachuted candidates on an island so suspicious of mainland politicians and against the wishes of a local federation dominated by the minority faction.
45. The list for the National Commission presented by the ex-Secretariat at the Fifth Congress took 32 percent of the delegate vote, and elected forty-nine of that body's 174

members. A month later the National Commission elected twelve supporters of the ex-Secretariat to its forty-member Political Commission. See *Acção Socialista*, 6 October 1983 and 3 November 1983.

4
The Parties of the Right and Center: CDS and PSD

The Social Democratic Center Party (CDS) and the Social Democratic Party (PSD, originally the PPD) are two of the four major political parties in Portugal. While they are indeed separate parties, they will be dealt with in this chapter in a parallel fashion as a number of similarities are apparent between these two parties of the right and center: both were founded after 25 April 1974, but had their origins in elements who were marginally involved in the old regime; their structures and ideologies are roughly similar; they governed together in the Democratic Alliance (AD) between January 1980 and January 1983; and both have been deprived of their founding leaders and suffer problems of leadership.

History

The PPD was founded on 3 May 1974 by the so-called *ala liberal marcelista*, the liberal wing of deputies who had been elected to the National Assembly through the official movement (ANP) of Marcello Caetano in 1969. When it became clear that liberalization within the regime was not forthcoming they resigned and left the field of active politics until after 25 April 1974. The *ala liberal* included Francisco Sá Carneiro, Francisco Pinto Balsemão, Joaquim Magalhães Mota, and Correia Cunha; when the party held its First Congress in November 1974 Sá Carneiro, former leader of the *ala liberal*, became the secretary-general. The PPD attracted an extremely heterogeneous membership in this revolutionary period as it was billed as the only viable non-Marxist option in a situation of rapid group formation and party struggle. Those individuals joining it included members of the liberal pressure group SEDES, progressive Catholics who had been members of University Catholic Action (JUC), and Freemasons.[1] While promoting a non-Marxist option, however, the party presented itself as a party on the left of the political spectrum. In its initial "Lines for a Program" it identified itself with the social democratic objectives of transformation with pluralism, and Sá Carneiro stressed in particular its option for "humanistic socialism." The party emphasized democracy and socialism, as well as a large role for the state, and the goal was to change the structures of Portuguese society and economy. Through this strategy the PPD sought to attract the center, center left, and non-Marxist left.[2] The party's stated ideology, then, was very progressive in contrast to the past political identification of most of its members and can only be understood in the revolutionary context of the period.

While the PPD was founded by the moderate opposition to the Estado Novo, the CDS was a creation of the so called new generation of the regime of Marcello Caetano. Specifically, it was founded on 19 July 1974 by Diogo Freitas do Amaral, Adelino Amaro da Costa, Xavier Pintado, and Leite de Faria. This group had anticipated a peaceful liberalization of the Estado Novo and had been involved in a certain rivalry with those who went on to establish the PPD. The CDS enjoyed the support of President Antonio Spínola after 25 April 1974 and suffered the consequences of the radicalization of politics later in that year, particularly after the attempted rightist coup and subsequent exile of Spinola after 11 March 1975 coup attempt. The CDS adopted as its ideology "personalistic humanism of Christian inspiration," but it should be noted that it was not specifically a Christian Democratic party in the traditional sense of the word. In fact, a group calling itself the Christian Democratic party (PDC) was formed in 1974 and became the main party of the ultraconservative right. The PDC was banned from participating in the 25 April 1975 elections for the Constituent Assembly for its alleged role in the 11 March coup attempt. The CDS, despite its "personalistic humanism of Christian inspiration," was identified, at least in the media which was largely controlled by the PCP and the far left in Lisbon, with the old regime.[3] The whole mood of the country at the time was strongly opposed to the conservative orientation of the "frightened right" and the party found it difficult even to have its program published in the media. The CDS founding Congress in Oporto in January 1975 came under siege from elements of the left. As the party was so far removed from the prevailing political atmosphere, many individuals who might have joined it became members of the PPD instead. It may be said that until January 1978 the CDS was in constant opposition to the revolution and all governments. In the elections to the Constituent Assembly of 25 April 1975, the CDS received only 8 percent of the vote and 16 deputies in the 250-member Assembly. It was the only party in this Assembly that voted against the Constitution when it was completed in April 1976.

If the CDS's main drawback was its inability to get in step with the atmosphere in revolutionary Portugal, and thus its very limited appeal for the political elite and the voting population, the chief initial—and long-term—problem of the PPD (continuing when it became the PSD in October 1976) was and is internal strife. As noted above, the party attracted a very heterogeneous group of individuals whose single unifying interest was undoubtedly their opposition to Marxist political parties. From its founding in May 1974 until his tragic death on 4 December 1980, the party was led most of the time by the charismatic Francisco Sá Carneiro.[4] It is significant that while the CDS held six congresses between its founding in 1975 and 1985, the PPD/PSD held twelve, including two in one year (1978), as well as fifty meetings of the National Council, its governing body between congresses.[5] From its Second Congress in Aveiro in December 1975, the congresses have been the stage for extreme dissension and personality struggles. Until his death, much of the conflict stemmed from Sá Carneiro's efforts to take complete control of the party and then, from the middle of 1978, to maintain it. This he did achieve, but at the cost of internal friction and the exodus of several important members. Probably the most significant individual to leave was Magalhães Mota in April 1979, whose departure led to the founding of the ASDI, which became a party in June 1980. It is worth noting that in one of the earlier conflicts in 1975, Carlos Mota Pinto, a future leader of the PSD, left the PPD. With so many members leaving, even founding members, the party's structures also changed. Sá Carneiro was secretary-general, but he had the statutes altered in October 1976 so that he could assume a more prestigious position as president. There have been joint leadership schemes (January-May 1977 and early 1983) and at times Sá Carneiro appealed to the bases of the party over the intermediary structures. Not suprisingly, in the media the PSD has become known as an unstable party.

Suggestive of the nature of leadership and the instability was Sá Carneiro's strategy of bipolarization. After initially attempting to involve the PS in a somewhat wider coalition, or Central Bloc, the PSD formed the AD with the CDS and the small monarchist PPM in July 1979. The idea of bipolarization was to posit opposites clearly in the political system, presumably allowing for a clear choice of options which would inevitably lead to the success of a united right against a divided left.[6] The AD assumed the form of a coalition of electoral, parliamentary, and governmental scope which applied to the elections for the Assembly on the Continent, but not on the islands of Azores or Madeira; nor did it apply to local elections. This strategy succeeded in the interim elections for the Assembly in December 1979, when the AD won 128 seats out of 250, and again in October 1980 when the AD won 134 seats. Also integral to the strategy of Sá Carneiro was the election of the AD's presidential candidate—General Soares Carneiro—in the elections of December 1980. The goal was to have "one government, one parliament and one president," not only to concentrate power but also to change the Constitution, by referendum if necessary, to a more conservative orientation. However, the presidential candidate, hand picked by Sá Carneiro with only slight prior consultation, received only 40 percent of the vote. The strategy thus failed. Three days before the presidential elections Sá Carneiro was killed in an airplane crash. There was no doubt that Sá Carneiro had run the party: he was the main founder, the secretary-general and then president, and through the numerous internal struggles had dominated the party as well as the AD itself.

Undoubtedly the main issue in the PSD since Sá Carneiro's death has been that of leadership of this diverse and split party which has been in government in one form of coalition or another since January of 1980. After Sá Carneiro's death Francisco Pinto Balsemão took over the presidency of the party and subsequently became prime minister; he endured extreme pressure in his party until resigning as prime minister of the AD government in December 1982 and as president of the PSD two months later. He quit without leaving a logical successor for either position, which led to the final collapse of the AD. Whereas the PSD was allied with the CDS and PPM in the AD between July 1979 and January 1983, after the elections on 25 April 1983 a new agreement was worked out and the PSD and the PS formed a Central Bloc government in June 1983, which collapsed two years later. The PSD, then, has governed in coalitions formed with parties to its right, in the bipolarization strategy of the AD, and to its left, in the Central Bloc. It should be noted that the principal architect of the Central Bloc strategy was Carlos Mota Pinto. This strategy, as all others, was contested internally.

This same flexibility or pragmatism in coalition partners has characterized the CDS. The CDS remained an opposition party until January of 1978 when it joined a tactical coalition with the PS of Mário Soares, which had formed a minority government since August 1976. It must be recalled that the PS still defined itself as Marxist and had played a key role in drafting the Constitution. The CDS had been set up by elements previously involved in the Estado Novo, was popularly considered to be on the right, and had voted against the Constitution in 1976. In the elections to the Assembly on 25 April 1976, the CDS had increased its margin substantially over 1975, winning some 16 percent of the vote and 42 deputies (two more than the PCP). When the PS government fell on a vote of confidence in December 1977, the CDS was willing to join a coalition with a party far to its left, although this leftism had increasingly eroded during the sixteen months of government. It was eager to enter government in order to gain greater legitimacy and to become a viable actor in a political system with which it had been out of tune. The government was very much a PS government, however, as the CDS with its 42 deputies (compared to the PS with its 107) received only three ministries and five subsecretaries of state. The CDS broke its agreement with the PS in July of 1978 because it correctly perceived that the PSD, in which Sá Carneiro had consolidated control, was drawing support from the right. The CDS was not able, however, to influence the formation of another government, and its main problem lies in the fact that it cannot presume or hope to be a senior party in a coalition; it has never been able to nominate the prime minister. On the collapse of the AD, the PSD, whose vote remained intact, was able to join with the PS in the Central Bloc. The CDS had no such alternative. In addition, it suffered seriously from its involvement in the AD and from internal troubles. Not only did it lose its main strategiest—Amaro da Costa—in the same plane crash in which Sá Carneiro died, but its founder and leader—Freitas do Amaral—quit as party leader in January 1983. In the Assembly elections on 25 April 1983 the party received 13 percent of the votes, 3 percentage points less than in 1976, and only 30 deputies (12 fewer than 1976, 13 fewer than 1979, and 16 under 1980, when it was in the AD).

Both the PSD and the CDS continue to suffer serious problems. The PSD was in government for five of the nine years between 1976 and 1985, but is characterized by severe internal tensions and major conflicts over issues of program and personality. It remains an unstable party and is considered necessary but unreliable in governments. The CDS is almost eclipsed today and is not racked by more internal strife only because it is in opposition and at the present has little "vocation for power".

Structure

The formal structures of the PSD and CDS are highly disparate. The structure of the party has been of minor concern to the CDS, which has variously been characterized as "a party of individuals," "a party of notables," and "a party with a head and no body."[7] The party has a membership estimated by one source at approximately 30,000. However, the party lists have not been updated and it is difficult to know for sure.[8] The CDS has never built up its local organization. It was formed by a group of "notables" at the top, and, while in government in 1978 and again between 1980 and 1983, it did not build up the grassroots.[9] It remains a party of the elite without strong structures of support at the bottom. What is more, the elite hold positions of prestige in other areas (the university, professions, and business) and attempt to transfer this prestige to the party for political purposes. Maria José Stock's analysis of the parties found that the strength, or power, of the party is located in its structures at the national level. For example, 42 percent of the party Congress is composed of delegates who are present ex-officio, with emphasis on members from all of the national structures. (The comparable figure for the PSD is 20 percent). This same representation through ex-officio status applies as well to the National Council and the Political Commission.[10] The party elite, however, is painfully aware of the need for more elaborate, democratic, and mobilizing structures to build up and strengthen the bases of the party. At the present it is very personal, structurally weak, and does not even publish its own party weekly.

This is not the case with the PSD. It not only has its own publication—the

Figure 4.1
PSD Leadership Structure

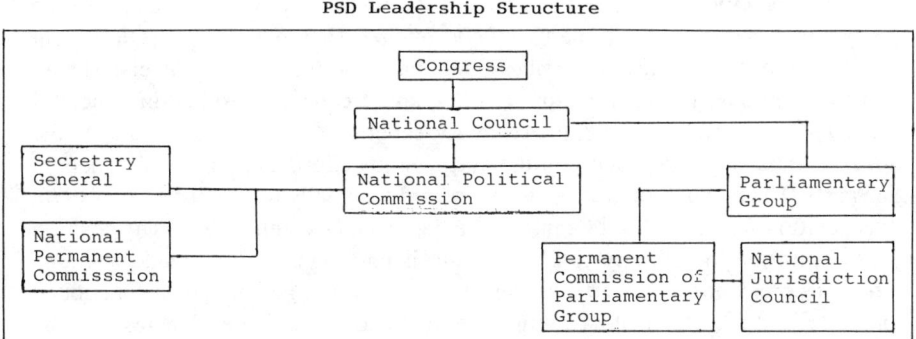

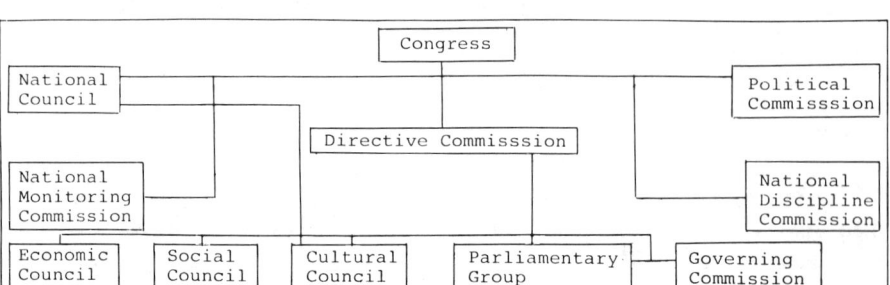

Figure 4.2

CDS Leadership Structure

weekly *Povo Livre*—but it has strong grassroots organizations, well integrated with the upper levels of the party. It claims some 80,000 members and its structure is decentralized. Journalists and scholars generally agree that the PSD has the most thoroughly developed grassroots of any party but the PCP. Indicative is the fact that structures at the local level elect 60 percent of the party Congress (versus the 20 percent who are there ex-officio), and in general there is little co-option and more positions are elected. In the 1983 Congress the referendum for important decisions was also introduced and utilized in early 1985 to select the party's presidential candidate. The importance of the grassroots organization is illustrated by the disproportionate number of local offices held by the PSD in comparison to its vote for the Assembly. For example, in the local elections in December 1982 for the 305 municipal councils, the PSD held the greatest number of majorities. The PSD won majorities in 88, or 29 percent, of the municipal councils; to this must be added its share in the AD which had a total of 48, or 16 percent. These compare to 55 (18 percent) for the APU; 27 (9 percent) for the CDS alone; and 83 (27 percent) for the PS.[11] The 29 percent for the PSD, then, was the highest for any party, although its share of the vote for the Assembly in the elections of 25 April 1983 was 27 percent against the 36 percent of the PS.

The PSD must be viewed in terms of the ongoing structural changes in the party, its character as a party of *baronatos* (barons), and the different socioeconomic character of members and leaders at the different levels. The almost continuous struggles within the PSD have frequently resulted in structural changes. From the beginning, the secretary-general, Sá Carneiro, appealed to the local memberships, especially in the north, in his conflicts with other leaders in the party. The position of president was created especially for Sá Carneiro in 1976; this position was occupied by Pinto Balsemão from December 1980. The position was eliminated in February 1983 when a troika arrangement was made with one honorary president and three vice-presidents. This arrangement never functioned properly, and the March 1984 Congress eliminated the vice-presidencies, and the party's leader, Carlos Mota Pinto, became president of the National Political Commission. Also, in the 1984 Congress it was decided that the secretary-general was no longer to be elected at large but on the same slate as the National Political Commission. In effect, a great deal of attention has been focused on the party's structure since its founding in 1974, due to conflicts among the elite. The Congress is the paramount body in the PSD. It should be noted that the leader from early 1983 until early 1985, Mota Pinto, was president of the National Political Comission but lacked a majority in the National Council, which is supposed to be responsible for the development and implementation of the political program of the party.

The PSD is decentralized and is well organized at the grassroots. It is, however, a party of *baronatos*. This means that between eight and a dozen notables operate at the national level but have their own local bases of support. They include such figures as Angelo Correia, Amândio de Azevedo, Eurico de Melo, and Helena

Table 4.1
Profession or Occupation of Members of the PSD and CDS in 1983

Socio-Professional Groups	PSD	CDS
High level administrators and liberal professions of high technical competence	5.9%	8.8%
Middle-level administrators and liberal professions of medium technical competence	18.5	17.1
Lower-level functionaries and clerical workers	19.7	16.9
Rural salaried workers, fishermen, domestic workers, and nondefined workers	2.9	2.5
Skilled workers	13.5	6.8
Industrialists	3.8	7.8
Businessmen in commerce	1.5	6.8
Farmers	8.5	7.3
Students	11.5	5.3
Housewives	7.1	14.1
Retired or unemployed people	2.5	3.3
Not specified	4.5	-
Owners	-	3.3
TOTAL	100.0	100.0

Table 4.2

Distribution of Members of the PSD and CDS by Socio-Professional Strata

Socio-Professional Strata	PSD	CDS
I - Higher	9.9	17.3
II - Upper Middle	30.8	33.9
III - Lower Middle	55.4	43.6
IV - Lower	3.9	5.2
TOTAL	100.0	100.0

Roseta. They hold power not because of positions in the formal structures but due to their local bases and their personal relationships within the party. This means that the formal leader, the president, or more recently the president of the Political Commission, cannot assume that he controls the party. His power is constantly questioned and built-in tensions are apparent. The barons do not necessarily represent sharply defined ideologies but rather different tendencies which are constantly shifting. Past and present leaders in the PSD indicated the difficulty of leadership, and of governing, due to the constant pressures from this group with their shifting coalitions.[12] During his period of consolidated rule, from mid-1978 until his death, Sá Carneiro was able to deal with them by his unquestioned charisma and his appeals to the grassroots during and even between Congresses. Pinto Balsemão found it more difficult and finally resigned. Mota Pinto fared no better and quit, as did his successor, Rui Machete, who only survived three months.

The CDS is a party of the elite, whereas the PSD is a party with well developed grassroots but in which a restricted elite, the barons, play a predominant role. Table 4.1 shows the data for membership of the two parties by profession or occupation. Table 4.2 reflects these same data, but according to a class division based on these professions or occupations.[13]

What stands out is the higher class background of the members of the CDS, compared to the PSD. In the former more than 50 percent are in higher- or higher-middle-class professions, compared to about 40 percent for the PSD. These data are in line with the perceptions the party elites hold of their memberships, a fact which was confirmed in our interviews. Specifically concerning the PSD, Table 4.2 indicates that the single largest class group is that of the lower middle, with 55 percent. This corresponds roughly to the petty bourgeoisie in Portugal, an image conveyed by a party leader who indicated that the members already have a certain status and are on their way up as qualified workers, white collar workers, and the like. He also reported that there was a problem in that the party leadership is not

Table 4.3 Profession or Occupation of Leaders of the PSD and CDS in 1983

Socio-Professional Groups	PSD National Leaders	PSD Deputies	CDS National Leaders	CDS Deputies
High level administrators and liberal professions of high technical competence	78.7	56.0	51.3	83.9
Middle-level administrators and liberal professions of medium technical competence	16.4	32.0	14.1	9.7
Lower-level functionaries and clerical workers	–	4.0	–	3.2
Rural salaried workers, fishermen, domestic workers, and nondefined workers	–	–	–	–
Skilled workers	–	–	–	–
Industrialists	3.3	–	2.6	3.2
Businessmen in commerce	–	1.3	1.3	–
Farmers	–	–	1.3	–
Students	1.6	4.0	1.3	–
Housewives	–	–	3.8	–
Retired or unemployed people	–	2.7	1.3	–
Not specified	–	–	23.0	–
Owners	–	–	–	–
TOTAL	100.0	100.0	100.0	100.0

quite the same; they have already "made it" and might not share the same aspirations as their members. For him the problem was not the lack of articulation through the many party structures, but rather the gap in aspirations and style.

These observations correspond closely to the figures displayed in Tables 4.3 and 4.4. Here the data are derived from the same profession or occupation categories as were used for the members.[14] If the data in Tables 4.2 and 4.4 are compared, what stands out is the exclusively upper- and upper-middle-class professional or occupational background of the party elite in both cases. A very small percentage of deputies belong to the lower-middle class but they are not as important in this system as the party elite in any case. This holds for both the PSD and the CDS, although one might anticipate a somewhat broader representation for the PSD than the CDS. In sum, there is a very large gap between party elite and mem-

Table 4.4
Distribution of Leaders of the PSD and CDS by Socio-Professional Strata

Socio-Professional Strata	PSD National Leaders	
	Higher Levels of the Party Apparatus	Parliamentary Group
I - Higher	80.7	58.9
II - Upper Middle	18.5	34.9
III - Lower Middle	0.8	6.2
IV - Lower	-	-
TOTAL	100.0	100.0

Socio-Professional Strata	CDS National Leaders	
	Higher Levels of the Party Apparatus	Parliamentary Group
I - Higher	78.2	85.5
II - Upper Middle	21.8	11.3
III - Lower Middle	-	3.2
IV - Lower	-	-
TOTAL	100.0	100.0

bers in terms of professional or occupational class background. While this would be anticipated in the CDS, which has made no secret of its character as a party of notables or its weakness at the local level, it is somewhat surprising for the PSD. This distance in background aggravates the ongoing tensions and instability within the PSD.

Program and Ideology

It should be noted that during the revolutionary period of 1974-1975, all of the four major parties except the PCP defined themselves further to the left than their leaderships and social bases would suggest. Thus a gap has existed from the beginning between the ideological positions and the actions of the parties. In the CDS the leaders have always declared themselves on the right of the political spectrum and appealed, at least initially, to the "frightened right." In the ten years since its inception the CDS has given different emphases to different aspects of its ideology, although it has remained a party of the right. From 1975 it declared itself Christian Democratic and joined the European Union for Christian Democracy. The party maintains the Christian Democratic theme today but with less emphasis. In its Second Congress in July 1976, the party broadened its program, calling itself "popular and European." In the Third Congress in December 1978 it again emphasized its Christian Democratic theme but added as well a liberal (i.e. a proponent of free enterprise) element. Between the Third and Fifth Congress, which was held in February 1983, this liberal theme was given increased emphasis. With the change in leadership in February 1983 and the coming of Lucas Pires as president, "liberal nationalism" was emphasized. The party was to be liberal modern and European. Further, there are at least three tendencies within the party. One stresses Christian Democracy; another economic liberalism; and yet another locates itself within the political right. Finally, party leaders admit, its ideology is not particularly different from that of the PSD. It is a party of the right; its particular themes or emphases vary depending on which tendency predominates at a particular time and on the political context of the period.

Recently the CDS has shifted its emphasis from ideology to a broader appeal, in order to win more than the 13 percent of the votes received in April 1983. One of the key issues it raised was revision of the Constitution. The CDS of course participated in the AD during the period of revision in 1982. At that time the political sections were revised, with a decrease in the powers of the president, but the economic sections were left alone. The CDS has once again taken up revision of the Constitution. This time it has demanded revision of the economic sections and an increase in the powers of the presidency. At the present time the CDS is a relatively small party in which ideology is not particularly important; it is seeking to define and capture an issue in order to regain some strength. So far it has not found it.

In the period immediately following its founding the PSD emphasized "socialistic humanism." Its goals were to create a free and democratic socialist system in Portugal, which would transform all sectors of society.[15] It defined itself as a Social Democratic party and attempted to join the Socialist International (SI). However, its application was vetoed by the PS which already belonged to the SI. From at least late 1975 the party, under the leadership of Sá Carneiro, emphasized its anti-Marxist stance. It has opposed not only the PCP's orthodox Marxism but also the PS, formal commitment to Marxism. The PSD's frequently primitive anti-Marxism has been particularly important in appealing to some of the party's local supporters. Probably more important than ideology or program have been its strategies which vary according to the political context and whichever group is predominant in the party at a particular period.

The PSD has been in government, in one coalition or another, since January 1980. It is thus ironic that during this period it has demanded "change," "structural reforms," and "projects" as though it had always been in the opposition.[16] This is due to a certain formalism in programs, a flexibility in ideology, and a strong tendency to internal factions. These factors allow the PSD to be simultaneously in the government and in the opposition, and to generate a great deal of attention. While this applies to the CDS to a much lesser degree, if only because it is smaller and out of power, the observation of Marcelo Rebelo de Sousa would seem to apply to both. "Reviewing the political functions of the political parties, what stands out is the programmatic rigidity that they reveal, contrasted with their strategic and tactical flexibility, and with the ideological vanguardism, which increases the internal factionalism."[17] The parties have much more to do with power and less to do with ideological or programmatic purity, although they are in fact distinguished one from another by general orientations.

Despite the internal factions and the ideological positioning and repositioning of the PSD and CDS, our 1984 survey revealed what appears to be a fairly accurate location of the parties according to general programs. The respondents were asked to locate the political parties on a left-right continuum of one to ten, where left was one. As Table 4.5 shows, the respondents locate the four main parties according to general programs. Of particular importance is the proximity of the PSD, with 7.1 and the CDS with 8.5; ideologically, as suggested above, there seems to be little distinguishing these two parties, at least in comparison to the PS not to mention the PCP.

Table 4.5

Left-Right Positions of the Four Main Parties

CDS	8.5
PSD	7.1
PS	4.7
PCP	1.8

Personalities: Leadership and Tensions

The issue of personalities has been less serious in the CDS than in the PSD. The party was led fairly consistently from its founding in 1974 to 1983 by Diogo Freitas do Amaral. It did suffer with the death of its main strategist, Amaro da Costa, in December 1980, but was able to continue to function as a party. However, with the unexpected departure of its historical leader, Freitas do Amaral, in January 1983, the party underwent a difficult period exemplified by the low 13 percent received in the Assembly elections on 25 April 1983, which dropped to under 10 percent in the 6 October 1985 elections. Freitas do Amaral most likely left the party in order to broaden his basis of appeal for a possible bid in the presidential elections in early 1986. To be identified only with the CDS (which never won more than 16 percent of the vote) would not be a strategy likely to win the presidential elections in which he and Mário Soares would fight for the votes of the center. The relations between Freitas do Amaral and his successor, Lucas Pires, have been good and they meet at least once a month.

There are the three tendencies in the CDS, as noted above, and in the Fifth Congress in February 1983 the orientation of Lucas Pires—"liberal nationalism"—won out over a more traditional political conservativism and Christian Democracy. It was not at all clear that this orientation would come out ahead, and it required the support of one of the most traditional of the political conservatives, Adriano Moreira, minister of the *Ultramar* (overseas) in the Caetano government, to assist Lucas Pires. The result was that Lucas Pires became president and Adriano Moreira chairman of the National Council, the second position in the party. The same arrangment was maintained at the Sixth Congress of the CDS in Aveiro in February 1985. Tensions emerged over the presidential elections in late 1985. The CDS had to decide whether or not to support the candidacy of Freitas do Amaral after some two years of a defined distance between him and the party. The situation was further complicated by talk within the party of the possible candidacy of Adriano Moreira. A split could occur, with the more traditional political conservatives supporting Moreira and the other tendencies supporting Freitas do Amaral. The situation becomes yet more complicated by the strange behavior of Lucas Pires in April 1985. Despite the support of some elements in the party for Moreira's candidacy, he at first reported that it made sense for the CDS to support an independent military candidate—Firmino Miguel—who was also backed by sectors of the PSD. At the same time Lucas Pires sent a letter to Mário Soares suggesting a trade of an immediate revision of the Constitution for support of the PS candidate for the presidency. The CDS, then, has not been racked by personality conflicts largely because it has been out of power with no immediate expectation of being in the government.

Personalities, and the conflicts among them, is the defining characteristic of the PSD, at least since the death of Sá Carneiro in late 1980. Some commentators have characterized the PSD as a federation of parties or an association of barons. Sá Carneiro was the leader since its founding in 1974, and his personal juggling and strategies explain much of the instability in the PSD between 1974 and 1980. For example, the new position of president of the party was created for him in October 1976 but in January 1978 he refused to reassume the position. However, he returned to this position with the bipolar strategy in July 1978. This strategy caused problems within the party and tended to polarize politics in general, but it did lead to the AD governments with the CDS and PPM. With his death in late 1980 the question of leadership became the key issue in the party.

Pinto Balsemão was elected to the presidency of the party, and then to the position of prime minister, by the National Council and the Political Commision of the PSD in December 1980. Balsemão was one of the founders of the party. He enjoyed the support within the party of a group known as the moderates and was opposed by the conservatives, which included Eurico de Melo and Anibal Cavaco Silva. The former favored a more active role for the party in the labor movement, simultaneous holding of party and government positions and less conflict with President Eanes. The latter group differed with the moderates on at least these three issues. Balsemão was annoyed with this internal squabbling over leadership and resigned in August 1981, thereby forcing a vote of confidence within the party which he won. In 1981 the party held two congresses in which Balsemão attempted to consolidate power. Following a relatively minor decrease in the AD's vote in the local elections in December 1982, and still very much under pressure from the opposition in the party, Balsemão resigned as prime minister in December 1982 and as president of the party at the Tenth Congress in February 1983. With his departure none of the original founders of the party were left: Sá Carneiro was dead, and Magalhães Mota had left the party to found the ASDI.

At the Tenth Congress a new leadership arrangment was attempted, which included an honorary president and three vice-presidents. This troika did not work and Carlos Mota Pinto emerged as the most important vice-president and then as leader of the party at the Eleventh Congress in March 1984. While there was general agreement that there should be firm leadership, Mota Pinto was president of the Political Commission and opposition groups held a majority in the National Council. Perhaps the PSD could be best compared to a feudal system: Sá Carneiro was a king who kept the loyalty of the barons and if necessary could appeal to the local membership to gather more power. With his death no comparable king has appeared, and the barons are fighting among themselves. Aside from material benefits, there has yet to emerge wide support for any of the three or four tendencies or for a unified program, let alone ideological position.

The AD

A brief review of the experience of the PSD in the AD and then the Central Bloc may help clarify the issues of personality and programs. The AD was a coalition for elections, the Assembly, and the government. Following it, the PSD entered into the Central Bloc with the PS from June 1983 until June 1985. Sá Carneiro assumed the initiative to form the AD, and, along with his party, maintained the leading position in the coalition because the PSD had more deputies than the CDS (80 versus 43 for the CDS and 5 for the PPM in 1979), the PSD had increased its vote in the local elections in December 1979, and Sá Carneiro projected a strong image as prime minister. He normally took the initiative in most activities of government during the AD. Because of the stability of the vote since 1976 no single party has received a majority of deputies in the Assembly. After the attempted efforts at minority governments between 1976 and early 1978, it was generally understood that President Eanes would require a majority in the Assembly before recognizing a government.[18]

Following the December 1979 interim elections, the AD won a vote on its programs by 128 to 113 in the Assembly on 18 January 1980. Most of 1980 was given over to preparations for the regular elections to be held in October 1980 for the Assembly and in December for the presidency. The following period, which was to be a time of revision and governing, was cut short by Sá Carneiro's death. Even if he had lived, there is no guarantee that the AD would have survived or been effective, since Sá Carneiro indicated that he would resign his office if President Eanes was reelected. His death exacerbated the ongoing instability in the PSD, and in hence the AD, over the issue of leadership. Thus constitutional revision did take place but it required a two-thirds vote in the Assembly, which necessitated the support of the PS. In effect, the AD coalition was not a long-term solution to political stability and government performance, mainly because of the nature of the PSD as an unstable and conflictual party. The AD collapsed because of difficulties and rivalries between the parties as well President Eanes's opposition to Balsemão's replacement as prime minister, Vítor Crespo, which led to new elections for the Assembly. The PSD did not want to renew the AD, and while neither the PSD nor the PS indicated that they would form a coalition it was clear that this would be the case if they received a sufficient number of votes.

The Central Bloc

The PS and PSD signed an agreement regarding policies for the Assembly and the government on 4 June 1983, approximately a month and a half after the elections. The agreement was supposed to last for the four years of the Assembly and contained extensive details on policies as well as an additional protocol on social and economic matters.[19] The issue of the presidential elections in 1985 was touched upon but left open for further elaboration. This Central Bloc was opposed from its inception by a group within the PSD headed by Marcelo Rebelo de Sousa who preferred the bipolarization strategy of Sá Carneiro.[20] In terms of support within the Assembly, where the PS had 101 deputies and the PSD 75 out of 250, no one doubted that the Bloc should last the envisioned four years. However, while Mário Soares has managed to help keep control of the PS, the issue of leadership remained polemical and contested within the PSD. This conflict assumed many different facets centered around a variety of issues, but at its core is the fact that the party is divided and rarely agrees on any issue.

Three areas were particularly sensitive within the PSD and with its relations to the PS in the Central Bloc. These concerned the composition of the government, the need for structural reforms, and the question of the presidential elections in late 1985. Tensions were obvious shortly after the Bloc was formed in mid-1983 and continued until its collapse in June 1985. From late 1983 there were general discussions, negotiations, and difficulties over the composition of the government, and plans were supposedly being elaborated for a major shuffle. The discussions increased in the spring, and the turnaround was supposedly imminent. Finally, no changes were made and the government held instead a vote of confidence, which it won, to demonstrate its legitimacy. What is important is not the ongoing tensions over government composition, nor the inability to move various individuals or ministers, but rather the reasons for not having the shake-up. As reported to us by a high PSD official, the causes were fundamentally the lack of involvement of the party leaders, Mário Soares and Carlos Mota Pinto, in the preparation for a shuffle. This suggests that more elements within the PSD were promoting it than anyone else, and the fact that for political reasons it was impossible to remove some key individuals, without which it made no sense to have a shake-up. In effect, these individuals were barons and thus inviolate.

The next issue was the so-called structural reforms. As noted previously, since 1980 the PSD has acted as if the government was against it; it the supported constitutional revision of 1982 and criticized it afterwards. During the two years of the Bloc the PSD frequently threatened to leave it if certain structural reforms were not implemented. This led to a great deal of negotiation and debate, and finally in December of 1984 the PS and PSD came to an agreement for a timetable for some forty-seven reforms which were to be implemented. The significance of the agreement, the tensions, and the final terms lay in the fact that different individuals and factions within the PSD could manipulate these issues and attempt to terminate the agreement with the coalition partner. Sufficient cause to create a great deal of confusion was always evident, and little agreement existed within the PSD on the priority and extent of implementation required for these structural reforms. By May 1985 they included such key areas as the labor laws, the electoral laws, agrarian reform, and constitutional revision. None of these were easy to pass in the Assembly, let alone implement, and they provided an ongoing tension in the coalition as the internal problems of the PSD were projected nationally.

Undoubtedly the most divisive issue within the PSD and in its relations with the PS was the presidential elections of early 1986. It was obviously disastrous for any party to fail to put forward a candidate for the presidency; its overall credibility as a political party would thereby have been open to doubt. Mário Soares had made no secret of his intention to run for the presidency. If the PSD had presented a candidate while still in a coalition with the PS, this would have necessitated disassociating the party from the PS and attacking it in order to prepare the way for the PSD's own candidate. There were lines of division, unclear at that, within the PSD over the desirability of running its own candidate, the issue of whether or not the candidate should be a member of the party, and the timing of making a decision.

Much of the politics of 1984 and 1985 was given over to precisely this issue. It overshadowed the Congress in March 1984, various meetings of the National Council, and the Congress in May 1985. In the March 1984 Congress, Mota Pinto and his group passed a motion to delay a decision until early 1985 and then to have the decision made by the National Council on the recommendation of the Political Commission. This position was opposed by two other tendencies within the party led by Mota Amaral and Marcelo Rebelo de Sousa. Between March 1984 and February 1985, however, the situation was not resolved. Finally, after months of being criticized for inaction and allowing Mário Soares to all but win the presidential election, Mota Pinto presented in February 1985 the name of General Firmino Miguel, deputy chief of staff of the army, as a possible presidential candidate for the PSD. He was contested in the National Council and, with the opposition tendencies joined, lost a motion of support; he thus resigned as head of the party. Following on this the PSD held a referendum on the nature of the party's presidential candidate. A bare 36 percent of the members responded, but generally supported an independent candidate. The Political Commision and other key PSD figures met and selected General Firmino Miguel as their likely candidate. However, the strong disagreement within the PSD over the candidacy, the uncertainty that the CDS would lend its support, and the demands for unspecified items in a "contract program" for structural reforms caused the potential candidate to withdraw from the race in early April 1985. The PSD, then, was left without a candidate and was, if possible, even more split. The next shift was to ignore the referendum at a Political Commision meeting and to decide that the PSD Congress of May 1985 would pick a PSD militant.

At the Twelfth PSD Congress in mid-May 1985, the key issue was precisely what strategy the party would follow in the presidential elections to be held later in the year. The option that won in the Congress was led by Anibal Cavaco Silva who had served as minister of finance in the Sá Carneiro government, but who left politics on the death of the president of the PSD. In the Congress he openly supported the candicy of Freitas do Amaral as president, thus favoring the recreation of a coalition of the right and an opposition to the Central Bloc. The denouement was not long in coming. In June the PSD presented its Central Bloc partner, the PS,

Table 4.6
Which Governments or Regimes Governed, or Govern, the Country Best?

1978	
Salazar	7%
Marcello Caetano	28
Palma Carlos	1
Vasco Goncalves	8
Pinheiro de Azevedo	3
Mário Soares	9
(First Constitutional government)	
Don't know	31
No Response	13

Table 4.7

Which Governments or Regimes Governed, or Govern, the Country Best?

	1984
Salazar	11%
Marcello Caetano	24
Palma Carlos	–
Vasco Goncalves	5
Mário Soares	4
(First Constitutional Government)	
Marío Soares and Freitas do Amaral	0.5
(Second Constitutional Government)	
Nobre da Costa	0.4
First Government of Presidential Inspiration	
Mota Pinto	0.2
Second Government of Presidential Inspiration	
Pintasilgo	8
Third Government of Presidential Inspiration	
Sá Carneiro and Freitas do Amaral (AD)	13
Balsemão and Freitas do Amaral (AD)	0.5
Mário Soares and Mota Pinto (Central Bloc)	6
Don't know and None	19
No response	7

with a list of demands which were politically and probably constitutionally impossible, and left the coalition on 13 June. The PSD is a split and conflict-ridden party which, by being a swing party, has transferred its own characteristics into the political system in general.

Public Opinion and Electoral Support

It may be useful to compare public opinion concerning the various governments, including those in which the PSD or CDS have been involved. Both the 1978 and the 1984 surveys included identical questions on what governments or regimes governed, or govern, the country best. The data from the 1978 survey can be found in Table 4.6 and from 1984 in Table 4.7. What is impressive about these two surveys, six years apart, is the continuing positive view of the Salazar and Caetano governments with an amazing 35 percent in both surveys responding that they governed best. After this important fact is the high evaluation given to the first AD government in which Sá Carneiro was prime minister as well as president of the PSD. It should be mentioned that the first AD government was in power less than a year, or half as long as the second AD government of Balsemão, and approximately the same amount of time the Central Bloc government had been in power at the time of the survey. The main point of these data is the importance of the leadership of Sá Carneiro which has not been matched by any leader in any government since.

In order to attain a sense of the potential of the different parties, the 1984 survey included a question as to which political tendencies the respondent identified with most. The data are found in Table 4.8. These data suggest that the CDS has a likely potential of 10 percent, which could be expanded considerably if the party could capitalize on those identifying with Salazar or Caetano. The Social Democrats and the present constituency for the CDS have slightly less than the PS but could, if a new AD were formed, undoubtedly form another majority government. It should be emphasized that there are regional variations with, for example, the 7 percent overall for the Communists increasing to 16 percent in the Alentejo.

Tables 4.9 and 4.10 reflect the data on opinions of the PSD and CDS voters on the two parties. It is clear, particularly regarding the PSD, that the voters for these two parties do not distinguish much difference between them. The opinions concerning the CDS are somewhat more definite, with the CDS voters, as one might anticipate, having a more positive view of their party. These data suggest, at least in terms of opinion on these five themes, that the voters do not hold very divergent opinions on the PSD and that even the CDS does not generate great diversity of feeling. Indeed, in the elections of 6 October 1985 the CDS lost heavily to the gain of the PSD. This contrasts to the opinions regarding the PCP as discussed in the last chapter.

In sum, the two main parties of the center and right, the PSD and CDS, are parties formed after the revolution from diverse groups. They quickly defined their programs and became identified in the public opinion with particular orientations, although both have been flexible in orientations and there are different tendencies within both parties. Their organizations are similar, although more tensions are apparent in the PSD due to the gap between members and the elites. The PSD, particularly with the death of its main founder and leader, Sá Carneiro, has been wracked by strife which continues today. The parties have their own regional bases of support and it seems as likely, given public opinion and past voting tendencies, that an AD strategy is as possible as that of the Central Bloc.

Table 4.8

Political Tendency Identified With?

Salazar/Caetano	9%
Conservatives	2
Liberals	2
Christian Democrats	6
Social Democrats	17
Socialists	28
Communists	7
Revolutionaries	0.4
Monarchists	0.1
None	25
Don't know/No response	5

Table 4.9

How PSD and CDS Voters Perceive The PSD

Do you believe the PSD is:	General		PSD		CDS	
	Yes	Don't Know/No Response	Yes	Don't Know/No Response	Yes	Don't Know/No Response
Capable of avoiding confrontation	34	42	47	38	43	32
Defender of the workers	34	41	54	37	54	31
Democratic	50	40	64	35	67	30
Defender of the country's interests	46	41	61	36	60	31
An enemy of democracy	10	41	-	37	10	30

Table 4.10

How PSD and CDS Voters Perceive the CDS

Do you believe the CDS is:	General		PSD		CSD	
	Yes	Don't Know/No Response	Yes	Don't Know/No Response	Yes	Don't Know/No Response
Capable of avoiding confrontation	21	42	30	40	51	31
Defender of the workers	21	41	32	40	55	30
Democratic	42	40	58	37	70	29
Defender of the country's interests	38	41	53	38	67	30
An enemy of democracy	13	41	2	39	6	29

Notes

1. For the background of the party see Maria José Stock, "PPD/PSD: trajecto de uma década," *Expresso Revista,* 5 May 1984. On SEDES see Norman Blume, "Sedes: An Example of Opposition in a Conservative Authoritarian State," *Government and Opposition,* Summer 1977, pp. 351-366.

2. On the ideology of the PPD see Maria José Stock "A base social de apoio e o recrutamento dos lideres do PSD e do CDS" (paper presented to Coloquio: Formação e Modos de Acção de Grupos Sociais em Portugal Depois de 1950, Bad-Homburg, 12-15 December 1983), p. 10. For the programs and ideologies of the major parties see João António de Salis Gomes, "Ideologia política—Ideologias dos partidos parlamentares," *Prospectivas,* 2 and 3 (July-September 1980); 4 and 5 (October 1980-March 1981).

3. Salis Gomes, "Ideologica politica," 2 and 3, pp. 33-35; Maria José Stock, "A base social," p. 10.

4. For his positions and ideology see Francisco Sá Carneiro, *Textos,* 3 vols. (Lisbon: Editorial Progresso Social e Democracia, 1981 and 1982).

5. For a review of some of these congresses see PSD, *Dez congressos: Dez anos de vida* (Lisbon: Editorial Progresso Social e Democracia, 1984).

6. For a defense of bipolarization see, José Duraõ Barroso, "Elogio da bipolarização," in Pedro Santana Lopes and José Durão Barroso, *Sistema de governo e sistema partidário* (Lisbon: Livraria Bertrand, 1980), pp. 113-116 and passim.

7. Maria José Stock, "A base social," p. 22. The organizational charts for the parties are taken from the Anexos of this manuscript. See also her "CDS: retrato em familia," *Expresso Revista,* 4 August 1984, p. 34-41R. In the latter article she also gives a number of these characterizations.

8. Maria José Stock, "A base social."

9. This point is made in the internal party document, "Intervenção do presidente da comissão política na C.P. em 25 de fevereiro 1984," p. 5 (mimeo).

10. Maria José Stock, "A base social," pp. 22-23.

11. *Eleições para os orgãos das autarquias locais, 1982* (Lisbon: Secretariado Técnico dos Assuntos Para o Processo Eleitoral, 1983), p. 577. For analysis of the data see Jorge Gaspar et al., *As eleições para as camaras municipais* (Lisbon: Instituto Damião de Gois, 1982).

12. The characteristic of barons is noted in Maria José Stock "PPD/PSD: trajecto," p. 17.

13. Maria José Stock, "A base social," pp. 33-34.

14. Ibid., pp. 39 and 42.

15. Salis Gomes, "Ideologia politica," pp. 35-40.

16. This is a common criticism of the PSD in the media as well as in interviews with leaders of other parties. The youth wing of the PSD, the JSD, distinguishes itself from the older generation in the party by its interest in ideas and ideology.

17. Marcelo Rebelo de Sousa, *Os partidos políticos no direito constitucional portugûes* (Braga: Livraria Cruz, 1983), p. 631.

18. Ibid., pp. 569 and 574.

19. See *Diário de Notícias,* 4 June 1983, for details.

20. For arguments against the Central Bloc see, Conceição Monteiro et al., *Contra o bloco central* (Lisbon: Cognitio, 1983).

5
The Political Role of Groups and Associations

The Estado Novo was a conservative, authoritarian and avowedly corporatist regime. In it the National Assembly played a very minor role and the Corporative Chamber was merely advisory. Numerous studies have demonstrated in great detail the manner in which the regime co-opted potentially politically significant elements, controlled rural and urban workers, and established a network of groups and associations to involve the population in a regime-directed web which would oppose autonomous organizations or participation. The rural population was caught up in a system of *grémios, casas de povo*, etc., which Joyce Riegelhaupt describes as follows:[1]

> Villagers were marginal actors in the Portuguese political system; they were integrated into a political process which granted them a minimal role of apathetic acquiescence. The Estado Novo prevailed for almost fifty years by enforcing apathy; it permitted only the articulation of private goals and provided no means for the presentation of communal goals. Peasants individually and severally were made powerless in a system that gave little to them, but also asked little in return.

Urban workers in commerce and industry, but not civil servants, were included in *sindicatos* (unions). The unions were in fact part of the public administration and, as such, were controlled by the government which sought to implement its ideology by encouraging a cooperative relationship between owners and workers. The unions were recognized and regulated by the Ministry of Corporations and Social Welfare, thereby making them dependent upon government for both important (such as selecting leaders) and unimportant issues.[2]

The system of co-option and control did not apply only to urban and rural workers. Instead, it pervaded the whole economy and society, and while property owners and businessmen did indeed benefit they too were included in a system of regulation and control. Through such measures as the *Lei de Condicionamento Industrial* of 1931 and the *Lei de Fomento e Reorganização Industrial* of 1945, the state was directly and indirectly involved in all aspects of the economy. As Elizabeth Leeds demonstrates, this resulted in the formation of a limited number of *grupos económicos* or cartels.³ These large, integrated, and somewhat diversified groups controlled most of the economy and, with the cooperation of the state, discouraged competition—thereby becoming even less competitive. Marcello Caetano, among others, criticized these groups, but it would seem obvious that the corporatist system, in tying up so much of society, would naturally result in such a situation.⁴ Also the Catholic Church became a de facto part of the regime, discouraged internal innovation even after the Second Vatican Council of 1962-65, and was not active in seeking to increase its influence in society. It, like other groups and institutions, was incorporated into the system and discouraged the free formation of other movements, groups, or associations.⁵

The composite definition by Philippe Schmitter of corporatism captures nicely the sense of the system:⁶

> Corporatism can be defined as a system of interest representation in which the constituent units are organized into a limited number of singular, compulsory, non-competitive, hierarchically-ordered and functionally differentiated categories, recognized or licensed (if not created) by the state and granted a deliberate representational monopoly within their respective categories in exchange for observing certain controls on their selection of leaders and articulation of demands and supports.

By the early 1970s this system of control and co-option was in disarray. The corporatist system was increasingly recognized as anachronistic, economic groups were split over Europe versus the colonies, workers' demands were escalating and illegal strikes took place, and the Church was deeply divided over the regime and pastoral obligations. Still, group formation was controlled and attempts at autonomous formation and mobilization were repressed. When the only institution capable of overthrowing the regime, the military, made the coup on 25 April 1974 the authoritarian regime and its security and corporatist underpinnings collapsed quickly and thoroughly.

In the epilogue to his *Corporatism and Public Policy in Authoritarian Portugal,* Philippe Schmitter observed that the corporative complex "has been replaced by a veritable beehive of autonomous, voluntaristic, competitive, overlapping, non-hierarchic associational activity. Portugal has suddenly become one of the most pluralistic polities in existence . . ."⁷ Indeed, within a year of the coup, some fifty political movements or parties had been founded, union activity exploded, *comissões de moradores* (neighborhood committees) sprang up spontaneously, firms were taken over by workers and managed by cooperatives or workers' committees, and in some rural areas peasants formed their own organizations. The associational wasteland of the Estado Novo was replaced rapidly by a wild, unbridled and somewhat anarchic proliferation of groups, movements, and associations, seeking to find new forms of participation and to articulate their demands. There was even an attempt to install and implement in mid-1975 a political system of popular power which "envisaged a decentralization of both political and executive power to neighborhood and workers' committees and to local and regional 'people's assemblies,' with a national people's assembly as the supreme revolutionary body. Had it come anywhere near implementation, it would have made Portugal a revolutionary state unique in the Western world (with the possible exception of Cuba, from which most of its inspiration was derived)."[8]

This system was obviously not implemented, but rather was replaced by a liberal democratic regime in which the political parties have assumed the predominant roles in politics. While many legacies of the revolutionary period exist, such as the paramount role of the state in the economy and the politicization of the media, the ongoing proliferation of groups is not one of them. Groups and associations are not actively discouraged by the system in place since 1976, and in fact the Constitution of 1976, as revised in 1982, actively supports the formation of organizations in both rural and urban areas.[9] What is evident, however, is a relatively low level of group formation, as indicated in our survey data, and a continuing process of disorganization, conflict, and monopolization by the political parties of the available space for influence in the political system.[10] Groups and associations seem to have a relatively minor role in influencing government policies and implementation in Portugal. The groups are not created and directed from above, as they were in the Estado Novo, and opportunities exist for their formation, but they have not assumed prominent roles in the current political system.

Our surveys of 1978 and 1984 included questions on membership and involvement in groups, associations, and organizations in general. In response to the first question on whether during the last year the respondent was involved with, or participated in, the activities of groups and associations, it was found that whereas in 1978 11 percent reported affirmatively, by 1984 this had increased to 15 percent.[11] On the face of it, then, it would appear that a slight increase in group involvement occurred. However, if we look to Table 5.1 on the data from responses to the follow-up question on the type of groups, associations, or organizations we are forced to further consider the issue of group membership. In the first place, a total of only 11 percent in 1978 and 15 percent in 1984 belonged to any group or association. The vast majority of the population did not belong to any group or associa-

Table 5.1
Which Type of Group or Association Are You Involved With?

	1978	1984
Recreation/sport	40%	50%
Neighborhood Association	7	5
Union	31	13
Professional Association	10	6
Religious Association	4	6
Cultural Association	15	22
Student Association	2	5
Workers' Committees	4	0.5
Humanitarian Association	–	8
Parents' Association	–	2
Other	6	6

tion. The trends in the data seem clear enough: There is an increase in the more social and cultural organizations (from 55 to 72 percent, and up to 80 percent if we include the humanitarian associations) and a decrease in the more political types of organizations. Leaving aside for the moment the obviously dramatic decrease in union membership, which will be dealt with later, we see a drop from 11 to 6 percent for the neighborhood and workers' committees. It seems fair to conclude that the groups and associations that emerged in the revolutionary period have by and large not been consolidated. Rather, while memberships in social and cultural organizations have increased slightly, the overall trend is for a decrease in the more politically defined types of organizations.

The Labor Unions

The unions emerged as active participants in the early stages of the revolution but it remains to be seen whether they can exercise any autonomous influence within the political system when their links with the parties are so strong. To some extent, the Portuguese labor movement has followed the dominant trend of the rest of southern Europe where ideology so often determines union actions and rhetoric. But it has surpassed even France, Spain, or Italy, since in Portugal union leaders also can run for Parliament under a party label (with the certainty of being elected, given the present voting system) and hold office in their respective parties' decision-making bodies. These practices are by no means restricted to the PCP. PS and PSD leaders also get elected to top union positions. Politicization of the unions is further reflected in their actions and demands, which are frequently directed toward the state and therefore assume immediate political signification. And the state cannot afford to ignore them. On the contrary, governments have attempted to come to terms with the unions and to institutionalize union-government-employer relations, with, as yet, only moderate success, since the country's main union federation will have no part in what it considers to be mere instruments of class collaboration. Yet, despite their highly ideological nature, Portugal's unions also act as pressure groups intent on defending fundamental interests of their members and of the working class in general. Before assessing the role of the unions as pressure groups, we must understand the development of the country's two union federations, the CGTP and the UGT.

The Revolution and the Rise of the Union Movement

In the period immediately preceding the coup d'etat of 1974, there existed side by side in Portugal the official, vertical union organization which was completely discredited and a parallel semiclandestine movement called Intersindical, created in October 1970, in which the Communists played a fairly important role. With the revolution, Intersindical rapidly occupied the space left by the old regime and the battle was then joined by the Communists on the one hand and far leftists, often tacitly supported by Socialists, on the other, for control both of Intersindical in particular and the labor movement in general. In its battle for hegemony, the PCP fought on three fronts. First, it struggled to emasculate the far leftists, and to a lesser extent the Socialists, in the various unions and in the growing number of workers' committees. At the same time, it tried to channel workers' demands on the government in an attempt to control and moderate them. This very often brought the PCP into conflict with the workers themselves, especially in the early months of the revolution, since the Communists opposed what they considered excessive demands on the part of the workers and even actively fought against what the party considered to be adventurous strikes. Finally, it tried to assert its leadership through legal means, by forcing the passage of a bill that would give union monopoly to Intersindical. This touched off the battle for *unicidade,* or official recognition for a single union federation, Intersindical, a concept supported only by the PCP and a slender majority of the MFA leadership. All the other political forces, led by the Socialist party, responded by calling for *unidade,* or united actions between unions of different political persuasions. In the short run the Communist party won, since in April 1975 a law was promulgated giving Intersindical complete control over the union movement. However *unicidade,* came to an end with the adoption of the new Constitution in 1976, as its Article 57 ensured pluralism within the labor union movement.[12]

The Constitution also set down other principles governing union organization and the scope of union activities. No worker could be forced to join a union, a measure which has effectively outlawed the practice of the closed shop. Unions were to be organized democratically with "regular elections to their governing bodies by secret ballot" (Article 57/3). Two other principles were interpreted by unions in a very flexible way: their independence from "employers, the state, religious denominations, parties and other political associations" (Article 57/4) and the right to form "tendencies" within unions. Most unions have remained formally independent of the parties, but no one seriously believes that the parties have no connection with the unions or that they do not exercise some form of control. As for the right to form tendencies, neither Intersindical nor its successor, the CGTP, has allowed the establishment of minority tendencies, and the 1976 Constitution did not oblige unions to provide forums for the expression of different internal tendencies. The right to form tendencies was included in the 1982 revision.[13] The CGTP complied with this new provision in its revised statutes of 1983 but without actually implementing it.

The Constitution also provided specifically for union participation in the decision-making process. According to Article 58/2 (57/2 in the 1982 revised Constitution), unions have the right to be involved in the drafting of labor legislation, to participate in the management of social security organizations and "other organizations whose aim is to satisfy the interests of the workers," and to supervise the implementation of economic and social plans. Obviously unions cannot be forced to participate. Nor is it clear whether the government distinguishes between participation and consultation. On this issue its task has been somewhat simplified by the attitude of the CGTP.

The CGTP

At its Second Congress in January 1977, Intersindical officially adopted the title of the National Confederation of Portuguese Workers—National Intersindical (CGTP-IN). Until 1979 the CGTP enjoyed a virtual monopoly over the Portuguese labor movement, though many unions still remained outside it. At the same time, the Communist party extended its control. However, Socialist members within Intersindical challenged Communist domination from early 1976 onwards through a movement known as the *Carta Aberta* (open letter) movement. Having met with little success as an autonomous, recognized tendency within the CGTP, *Carta Aberta* gradually developed into a rival union federation which finally was confederated in January 1979 as the General Union of Workers (UGT).

With a claimed membership of some 1,380,900 and 149 affiliated unions out of a total of 293 unions in the country,[14] the CGTP holds the undisputed first place in the Portugal's union movement and completely dominates the industrial sector. Despite its claims to total autonomy, the CGTP's policies and actions have closely paralleled those of the PCP. It practices the politics of total opposition, of confrontation and hard-line rhetoric, and refuses any collaboration with the government. It organizes strikes and demonstrations whose explicit aims are often political and coincide with the declared objectives of the Communist party, which in turn invariably supports its actions.

The overwhelming strength of the PCP at all levels of the CGTP cannot conceal the fact that non-Communists within the federation have resisted the more blatant forms of external control. Far-leftist elements have been able to take over the leadership of some individual unions and non-Communists have been elected to the federation's governing bodies. At the CGTP's Fourth Congress in March 1983, one representative of the Maoist UDP was elected to the union's top decision-making body, the National Council, albeit as a nonvoting alternate, and eighteen other members of this seventy-one member body were openly identified with non-Communist left-wing parties or union tendencies, including the PS. At that Congress, the CGTP adopted new statutes formally recognizing the right of minorities to establish tendencies; however, even these minorities did not ask for any immediate follow-up for fear of being isolated within the federation and of losing the representation they had been tacitly awarded by the majority. In the months after the Fourth Congress, various minority representatives within the National Council and the Executive began asking for greater freedom of expression, as a logical sequel to the recognition of tendencies, and even organized meetings among themselves to coordinate their demands.

Like the PCP, the CGTP's aggressive rhetoric hides behind a defensive not an offensive strategy, and it acts as a tribune for discontent which it channels and controls. With the deepening of the economic crisis after 1981, the contradiction between the union's radical slogans, which have become monotonously summarized into calling for the government of the day to be thrown out, and its modest achievements has not escaped the workers, who appear increasingly unwilling to be mobilized for purely political purposes. There is no lack of issues, be it security of employment, inflation, or unpaid wages; however, the CGTP's attempts to organize demonstrations or strikes in 1984 and 1985 met with very poor response.

Officially, the CGTP refuses to acknowledge the existence of any crisis within the Portuguese labor movement, but it obviously realizes that the unions have come under pressure and that the old tactics are no longer producing the desired results. Signs of a new approach began to appear at the Fourth Congress, when one of its most influential leaders, José Luís Judas talked of the possibility of some form of dialogue with the government on the union's list of demands.[15] The Congress also adopted a program that referred to the necessity of attracting professional groups other than the traditional supporters from the industrial and agricultural working class and in particular technicians and white-collar workers, heretofore the preserve of the UGT.

In the first half of 1984, the apparent opening of the CGTP was not translated into concrete action; instead, it reverted to more conventional methods and concentrated its attacks on the PS/PSD government and on publicly refusing any form of collaboration. The CGTP flatly rejected the government's attempt to institutionalize a form of socioeconomic consultation between the government, the employers, and the unions through its Permanent Council for Social Coordination (CPCS). By autumn 1984, the CGTP had modified its tactics, following the meeting of the National Council at which the minority tendencies had vented their grievances. It organized a round table in Lisbon to discuss a variety of political and social issues, without rigging it in advance with prepared texts and final motions, and invited some one hundred and twenty lawyers to come and participate freely. This conference followed a two-day seminar on tax policy which was sponsored for economists of different political backgrounds. But the most spectacular and successful operation organized by the CGTP was the campaign in favor of workers whose wages had not yet been paid, just before Christmas 1984.

The problem of unpaid wages was a phenomenon that plagued the Portuguese economy as the economic crisis deepened. Bankrupt public companies could no longer pay their workers, but inasmuch as they could not legally close down, the workers continued to work there for fear of losing their jobs. To pressure the government, the CGTP joined forces with several other organizations to carry out twelve days of demonstrations, an exhibition, the drafting of an appeal from sixty-seven leading personalities representing various shades of the left (all using the CGTP's allotted time on television to concentrate on this single issue), a silent vigil around the Assembly of the Republic, and the publication of a black book on misery and hunger in Portugal. Such tactics in no way implied that the CGTP had foresaken its traditional methods or softened its demands. However, it showed that it could adjust to new situations and that an evolution had begun.

The UGT

From the date of its First Congress in January 1979, there was never any doubt about the link between the UGT and the political parties. It came into being with an agreement negotiated between the PS and the PSD at the highest level, a relationship that was institutionalized in the union's top decision-making body, the National Secretariat, where the PS and the PSD had equal representation until March 1984. The secretary-general has always been a Socialist, while the presidency has gone to a member of the PSD. Although the UGT has attempted to follow an autonomous line, it has inevitably reflected both the rivalry between the PS and the PSD and the quarrels within the PSD factions.

This situation does not mean that the UGT has found it impossible to act as a union first and to let defense of its members' interests override party rivalry. During the lifetime of the AD government, when the PSD was in power and the PS in opposition, the PSD leaders in the UGT supported the conservative candidate for president, General Soares Carneiro, whereas most of the Socialists publicly favored General Eanes. The political question did not create any noticeable rifts. At the same time, the UGT as a whole opposed several government measures aimed at revising labor legislation, and the Social Democrats within the UGT went along with the Union's decision to join forces with the CGTP in a transport strike in April 1980. With the advent of a PS/PSD government, the UGT has shown its willingness to cooperate with the government, but, as will be seen, not at any price.

The Socialist tendency within the UGT leadership has displayed surprising unity, despite the internal wrangling of the PS. With the Social Democrats, it has been a different story altogether. Until the UGT Third Congress in March 1984, the PSD was offically represented by the Social Democratic Reformist Union Tendency (TESIRESD), though there existed also another group, the socio-professional workers, which advocated closer ties with the PSD and accused TESIRESD of acting as an independent pressure group within the PSD promoting the interests of its own leadership. Things came to a head in 1983-1984, when the PSD began organizing a congress of Social Democrat workers aimed at uniting the two factions and bringing them under stricter party control.

TESIRESD itself was split over how it should react to this initiative. Eight of the fifteen PSD members of the UGT Secretariat and the president of the UGT, Miguel Pacheco, supported by the TESIRESD National Council, convened an extraordinary congress in November 1983 which confirmed the refusal of the majority of the TESIRESD to attend the scheduled PSD congress. An important minority within the organization, including the seven remaining PSD members of the UGT Secretariat, ignored this decision and went ahead with preparations for the coming congress of Social Democrat workers.

Selection of delegates for the congress gave an overwhelming majority to the socio-professional workers, 209 of the 300 delegates, with the rest going to the TESIRESD dissidents. At the congress itself in January 1984, the real battle came not over the question of tighter party control of union members but over representation within the new PSD union body. The majority of delegates rejected a carefully worked out agreement which gave the former TESIRESD supporters somewhat more seats than warranted on the basis of their numbers elected to take part in the congress. A meeting was required between the leaders of both sides to reach a workable arrangement whereby both factions agreed to present joint lists of delegates for the UGT's Third Congress, under the name of the TSD (Social Democrat Union Tendency), and to have equal representation in all UGT governing bodies. The TESIRESD was left out of the negotiations altogether, and the PSD officially sanctioned the new union structure two months later at its congress in Braga.

At the UGT's Third Congress, the TSD and the Socialists compromised and put an end to PS/PSD parity in the federation's leadership, confirming PS supremacy within the ranks of the UGT.[16] In exchange, the Socialists agreed to postpone any reference to the 1985 presidential elections and accepted the elimination of the TESIRESD from the UGT leadership, including the presidency, which had been held by Miguel Pacheco since 1979.

With a claim of forty-nine affiliated unions in 1983,[17] the UGT has solidly established itself in the tertiary sector. Since 1981-1982, it has gained increasing influence among blue-collar workers, especially in the textile and chemical industries and in the transport sector. It still remains far behind the CGTP, but its strength has been growing in traditional CGTP sectors, a situation which has only exacerbated the conflictual relationship between the two federations. Parallel unions exist in almost every sector, vying for members at a time when union membership is generally down, with each attempting to obtain more favorable settlements than its rival. The ideological style of their actions and the highly politicized nature of their relations have harmed the effectiveness of both the CGTP and the UGT as representatives of workers' interests.

The Unions as Pressure Groups

The CGTP has adopted a deliberate strategy of confrontation which has emphasized political objectives over bread-and-butter issues. However, it could not remain the country's first union federation if its actions were confined to the overtly political. Above all, it pursues a policy of defending the rights acquired through the revolution and has thus succeeded in wielding a form of veto power which has become critical for Portugal's working class as successive governments have come under internal and external pressures to change labor legislation and to dismantle the public sector. Despite appearances to the contrary, the CGTP has exercised a controlled response to any apprehended attacks on the labor status quo.

The relative moderation of the CGTP's defensive policy is indicated by the number of strikes, most of which were led by the CGTP, since 1976. Until 1981, there were never more than 378 strikes (reached in 1979) in any given year.[18] The AD government's reelection in October 1980 altered the whole atmosphere of labor relations in Portugal. The government attempted to put a ceiling on wage settlements that was below the rate of inflation and announced plans to amend labor legislation to make it easier to dismiss and lay off workers. At the same time, the economic crisis became increasingly felt after a year of artifically induced expansion by the first AD government as it prepared for the elections. The number of strikes rose dramatically, from 280 in 1980 to 700 in 1981, and stayed above 500 in the next two years. There was also a hardening in strike strategy as the CGTP launched two one-day general strikes in 1982, with varying degrees of success. Because of the openly political aims of these actions they failed to receive UGT support, but the UGT also hinted that it was prepared to advocate a general strike if the government remained unresponsive to union pressure to shelve its intended attacks on acquired rights. However, the strike (with a success rate of less than fifty percent) has proved an ineffective weapon for obtaining specific workers' demands.[19]

Unions are ill-equipped to sustain long strikes since they lack strike funds. Strikes are therefore mainly symbolic, aimed at mobilizing workers and at demonstrating the unions' potential strength to employers. They rarely last more than two to three days. One sector of the economy, public transport, has been particularly hard-hit by frequent strikes, especially in Libson. This movement began in earnest in 1979, and only slowed down in early 1984 when the transport workers themselves began to resist calls for strikes from the CGTP. Between January 1979 and January 1983, Lisbon's commuters had to live through ten bus strikes and fourteen work stoppages on the subway, for a total 147 and 327 hours, respectively.[20] The actual length of these strikes has varied from ninety minutes to seventy-two hours, and bus and subway strikes have usually not coincided. The reasons behind this movement can be traced to the general problem of the governments' insistence on wage increases below the level of inflation and the delays frequently incurred in renewing annual collective agreements. The economic causes, which even brought the CGTP and the UGT together briefly in April 1980, only tell part of the story. UGT/CGTP rivalry tells the rest, as competition for members and hegemony in the public transport sector has increased. For the same reasons, failure to stop the subway from operating normally in February 1984 was interpreted as a sign of a decline in CGTP influence.

The UGT's approach to union strategy reflects its political origins. It was originally founded as a counterweight to the CGTP and its policy of confrontation, and, as such, the UGT has been wary of using the strike weapon or organizing demonstrations except as an ultimate form of pressure to back up its socioeconomic demands. It emphasizes collaboration with the government and negotiation rather than confrontation wherever possible. This attitude has been expressed in its calls for a social contract to be signed between the unions, the employers, and the government.[21] Not surprisingly, the UGT agreed to join the PS/PSD government's new Permanent Council for Social Coordination, which the CGTP had vigorously denounced in January 1984.

Despite their conflictual relationship, both union federations support what they consider to be fundamental acquired workers' rights and collaborate tacitly to defend them. Employers may lament the rigidity of Portuguese labor legislation, but any government that tried to change it in any important way would find itself in a serious battle which would almost certainly consolidate both union federations. These issues cover the constitutionally recognized right to strike,[22] the recourse by employers to short-term contracts to avoid the complicated process of offical dismissals, and layoffs. The UGT made its position clear at its Third Congress and announced that it would launch "a total offensive, leading to direct opposition to the present government" should it insist on changing either the law on dismissals or the law on strikes; it added that such action would provide grounds for declaring a national strike of all its unions and for leaving the CPCS immediately.[23] The CGTP has adopted a similar stance.

As much as the government might like to change Portugal's labor laws, it knows that it cannot move without consulting the unions. This was offically acknowledged by the Central Bloc government when it presented a decree-law on layoffs in November 1983 and announced that it had amended its original bill after meeting with the unions; as a consequence, it agreed that the unions had to be consulted before a firm could start laying off workers.[24]

Portugal has not remained immune to the general crisis that has shaken the union movement throughout Western Europe, reflected by a declining membership, a growing passivity on the part of unionized workers as they feel helpless before the economic crisis, and a less tolerant attitude towards labor disruptions and union demands on the part of the public. Our survey shows that almost 40 percent of the adult Portuguese population feels no sympathy for either of the two national trade union federations. Where sympathy is felt, it goes overwhelmingly to the UGT.[25] The main reason for this attitude, which indicates a disavowal of the CGTP's strategy of confrontation, would seem to be weariness with strikes. Out of sixteen suggested reasons for the economic crisis in Portugal, strikes came third, behind the world economic crisis and the lack of harmony between the political parties.[26] Forbidding strikes came first as the best way to solve the crisis out of nine measures proposed.[27] These findings do not mean that the vast majority of the population sees the unions as the source of all Portugal's ills, nor that it wishes to ban strikes. They do indicate, however, that unions cannot count on automatic public support for strike actions, which rarely achieve concrete results, in an atmosphere of uncontrolled inflation and fear of unemployment.

The Owners' Confederations in Industry, Commerce, and Agriculture

Prior to the coup of 25 April 1974, and especially before the nationalizations in the spring of 1975, the economy was dominated by the seven large economic cartels. With the extensive nationalizations, takeovers, occupations, and departures of owners, these groups were dismantled and so far have been unable, and probably unwilling, to reconstitute themselves. Their role has to some extent been taken over by the state which assumed ownership in some cases and control in others of large and key sectors of the economy.[28]

It must be remembered that the Estado Novo provided a large place for the state in the economy, with extensive legislation that both protected and controlled economic activity. This situation allowed the large cartels to grow and, particularly with the role of the colonies, heavily protected the national firms both individually and as a group. If the owners sometimes found the legislation onerous and bothersome, they could feel secure and could sell to and import from the colonies on favorable terms; also, the labor movement was kept under control and wages stayed low.

It is probably no exaggeration to say that the owners as a class, with the exception of the seven largest cartels, were weak even relative to the low level of industrialization and overall underdevelopment of the economy. The revolution was made against the old regime which protected these economic actors and it had a strongly anticapitalist bent. The Constitution includes a number of anticapitalist themes and articles and the overall tenor of the basic document is prolabor and prosocialist. Since the revolution, then, owners have tended to be on the defensive. Weak before, and attacked during, the revolution, they are now finding the context defined by the Constitution not to their liking and are trapped in a context of ongoing recession and economic constraints. Within this situation, owners' associations have attempted to function and to influence government. It should be noted at the outset that one of the key themes for these economic actors has been revision of the economic section of the Constitution; this section was not amended in 1982, which implies the minimal influence of these actors as formal groups.

The AIP and CIP

The Portuguese Industrial Association (AIP) was founded in 1860 and has sought to work at the national level in training, information, and general promotion of entrepreneurial activities. The AIP was formed, and continues to function, according to pre-1974 legislation which provided for the right of association but not the right of organizing owners. Some 1,400 firms of varying sizes from all areas of industry and services in the private and public sectors, as well as mixed enterprises and cooperatives, belong to the AIP. It has functioned mainly to promote technical advancement, sales, etc., with a minimal emphasis on a social or political role. It has been able to assume an image of moderation and realism and has not actively contested governments in the post-1976 regime. However, since the AIP was not prepared for the revolutionary context, another organization was founded to promote a more clearly political role for business in dealing with the government, with the objective of having the economic sections of the Constitution revised and legislation improving the climate for private owners in industry passed.

The Confederation of Portuguese Industry (CIP) was founded three months after the coup. Today it claims to represent 47,000 firms grouped together in associations, federations, and unions, or some 75 percent of Portuguese industry across all sectors. Despite a fairly intense publicity campaign, however, it is widely acknowledged that the CIP is an elite organization which is still searching for roots at the local level. From about 1976 its claims of influence have been recognized as shallow. It has made statements and issued documents in favor of private initiative, against the nationalizations, about government coalitions, and regarding particular needs, but there has been a widely acknowledged gap between wishes and implementation. Its strength, such as it is, has been the strength of owners who have engaged in passive resistance by failing to invest or expand rather than a political strategy that can influence governments, at least in the short run. Its obvious weakness despite its claim to represent a majority of industrial owners has been attributed to financial problems, a lack of stimulus for small firms, and a lack of leadership. Successive governments have been frustrated in their search for a counterforce to the CGTP and have looked for other possibilities among the owners.

Since 1978 the AIP has partially filled this vacuum. It could do this as it assumed control of the Lisbon Trade Fair which has brought in substantial funds. Further, it has been genuinely representative and has been more cooperative and less antagonistic to the governments. The fact that two associations of owners in industry exist concurrently has created a certain amount of competition between them; the main legal difference is that the CIP has exclusive power of representation in the area of labor conflicts and collective contracts. At the present time both associations are headed by relatively young and active leaders, which makes even more manifest the competitive views and antagonistic positions of these umbrella organizations.

The CCP

Whereas much activity and hostility are visible in the area of industries, the situation in commerce is much more pacific. The Portuguese Confederation of Commerce (CCP) was founded in November 1976. It is composed of older associations, bringing together the wholesale and retail trade. Today these two organizations exchange the presidency of the CCP. While the CCP is relatively cooperative, this does not mean that it is any more effective than the AIP or CIP. It has worked very little in the public realm. It seeks instead to influence government directly. However, the very high rates of interest, extensive legislation constraining commerce, and the overall drop in turnover indicates that it may not be effective in a context of economic austerity.

The CAP

The Confederation of Portuguese Farmers (CAP) was formed in 1975 in order to resolve collectively and politically the heated issue of agrarian reform; since then it has only slightly diversified its areas of operation. Due to the context of its founding, the organization's strength is greater in the south, where there was greater involvement in agrarian reform, than in the north, which has caused antagonisms within the CAP. However, even in the south not all owners in agriculture feel that the CAP represents them. The interests of CAP associates are frequently divergent now that agrarian reform has peaked and the conflicting interests of the rural owners have become manifest: the seventy-two organizations associated with CAP are heterogeneous in respect to specialization, territory, and whether they are cooperatives or private holdings. In addition, the CAP manifests the weak and underdeveloped situation of agriculture in Portugal. Even so, it has exerted some influence with the Ministry of Agriculture, perhaps because its general secretary since its founding, Manuel Casqueiro, has provided much stability and a high level of intervention.

The CAP is contested by the Secretariat of Collective Units of Production, close to the PCP, and the National Confederation of Farmers, which claims to represent the minifundia owners in the north where the CAP is only marginally influential. Thus even in the relatively weak economic area of agriculture there is no single umbrella association to represent the owners.

The CNEP and CNAE

The divisions within and among the owners' associations become more manifest when it comes to forming an association to bring them all together. The government of the center-right, the AD, which presumably represented the interests of owners, attempted to encourage the formation of such an association. However, it has been impossible to form one organization even with government support. The *parceiros sociais* (social partners) of the CIP, CCP, and CAP created the National Council of Portuguese Entrepreneurs (CNEP), and the *parceiros económicos* (economic partners) of the AIP, together with the Commercial Associations of Lisbon and Oporto, created the parallel and competing organization of the National Council of Entrepreneurial Associations (CNAE). It should be noted that the Oporto Industrial Association dropped out of the CNAE in October of 1984. The small, weak, and still defensive owners in industry, commerce, and agriculture are divided among themselves, a situation that carries to the highest levels of their associations. These formal organizations have little coherence and apparently slight influence at all levels of government.

This does not mean that all business interests in Portugal are unrepresented in government. They are represented, but by more informal and direct intervention by individuals and larger firms through the various ministries, and particularly the Ministry of Finance. Influence and power is indeed exercised but not through the divided and competing formal associations.[29]

The CPCS: An Effort to Square a Fragmented Circle?

The creation and functioning of the Permanent Council for Social Coordination (CPCS) by the Central Bloc government provides an illustration of the problems created by the ongoing splits among the various economic actors. Unlike Spain during the transition from dictatorship to democracy, Portugal lacked economic pacts between labor, owners, and government. However, in 1983 the serious economic situation necessitated approaching the IMF at mid-year and implementing a recessionary austerity program. In January 1983 the Socialist party initiated a series of meetings with the "social partners" including the CGTP, UGT, CIP, CCP, and CAP. On 12 February, President Eanes met with most of the leaders of these organizations, excluding the CAP but including the AIP and Oporto Industrial Association. These meetings reflected government and industry's realization that cooperation would be necessary to face the economic crisis. The institutionalization of an ongoing dialogue was proposed by the government at the end of 1983, the first instance of a social dialogue in Portugal after the revolution. This proposal led to the creation of the CPCS, which began to function on 20 March 1984. In the initial discussion and subsequent negotiation, the CIP was successful in having the planned Council modified according to its purposes. The original proposal stipulated that the CPCS be composed of the *parceiros económicos,* but in the final formulation this competing association was excluded. Indeed, in order to ensure CIP participation a number of fairly serious modifications were introduced, and the result was an organization to deal more with the overall political economy of the country and less with specific issues of labor and society.

The Council is a consultative body that functions at the level of the prime minister's office. It is a tripartite organization which coordinates representatives of labor, management, and government to encourage dialogue. It gives opinions on the overall political, social, and economic situation of the country; suggests solutions in the economic area; and must be consulted when the government proposes legislation relevant to its general area of concern. It is made up of the prime minister; the ministers of finance, labor, agriculture, and industry and commerce; three representatives from the CGTP; three from the UGT; and two each from the CIP, CCP, and CAP. Formally, the composition is at a high level; government members must be ministers and their replacements must also be members of the government, and all other organizations are represented by their leaders.

Thus far the CPCS has not functioned well. Of all the owners' associations noted previously, only the CIP, CCP, and CAP have participated. Significantly, the members of the CNAE, and particularly the AIP, do not belong. The CGTP has refused to cooperate from the beginning as it considers the Council, and its functions, as generally illegitimate. After a mere three months of operations, in June 1984, the CIP, CCP, and CAP refused to participate in a meeting and threatened to boycott the Council entirely. They demanded a commitment by the government for major changes in the economy, and insisted that without these changes there was no purpose in a dialogue. However, most of these changes involved aspects of the economy in which change was not acceptable to labor (and through the UGT, not acceptable to the PS), such as indemnity payments to former owners for nationalized enterprises, or were unfeasible, such as streamlining of the public sector. Generally, of course its possibilities are circumscribed as it has but an advisory

Table 5.2

Do You Consider Yourself Religious?

Religious	86%
Atheist	3
Indifferent	9
Other	2
No Response	0.3

role, and it can be argued that the government has the predominant role in the Council.

The Catholic Church

The Catholic Church is an historic institution in Portugal. It is identified with the founding of the country and has been involved for good or ill at all important junctures of its history. Today, 96 percent of the Portuguese are baptized Catholics and 80 percent of all marriages are celebrated in the Church. Our survey asked a number of questions concerning religion and attitudes towards the Church, and showed that the vast majority of the people considered themselves religious (Table 5.2). We then asked if they in fact practiced a religion and found that 80 percent reported that they did, 19 percent did not, and 0.9 percent did not respond. Of those practicing a religion, 97 percent reported that they were Catholic. In sum, 67 percent of our sample reported that they were practising Catholics.

We know from our own and others' research, that at least in this century the political influence and associational life of the Church has been weak.[30] The Church was not threatened during the Estado Novo. It acted as a central institution in the regime and provided legitimation but was controlled in its political and even social role by Premier Oliveira Salazar. Innovation was discouraged, many active and progressive elements left the Church, and serious splits occurred among the hierarchy. Earlier studies have showed that there was little associational life centered around the Church during this period, in contrast to other ages and other countries.[31] It is thus interesting to look at the data displayed in Table 5.3 dealing with religious activities of those who indicated that they practiced a religion (69 percent of the respondents). What is of particular interest here is the very low—less than 3 percent—membership in religious associations of the 69 percent who indicated they practiced religion. However, this figure is still higher than the 6 percent shown for the total sample in Table 5.1. In any case, the survey shows that the level of involvement on a regular or active basis with religious associations is extremely low, a finding in line with our earlier studies which conclude that the Church's level of influence was low and the pastoral, beyond the cult, very shallow.

Immediately after the coup of 25 April 1974 until approximately 1976, the Church was either confused about responses in the political realm or extremely defensive. Since then, as demonstrated by Luís de Franca, the Church has been supportive of the democratic system but somewhat unclear as to how to proceed.[32] De França also indicates the areas of priority for the Church hierarchy by reviewing the statements of the Bishop's Conference for the ten years after 1974. These areas include education, Rádio Renascença, abortion, and questions relative to the family and birth control. The issue of abortion became particularly important when the Assembly passed a law in mid-1984 decriminalizing abortion in certain cases (rape, malformed fetus danger to the health of the mother). The law passed with the support of the PCP and PS and the opposition of the PSD and CDS. The Constitutional Court declared the law constitutional and the president proclaimed it rather than bringing on a major institutional crisis by introducing a referendum. The Church hierarchy and some Catholic groups and individuals spoke out strongly against the government, calling for civil disobedience and not voting for deputies who supported the law. On a key issue, then, the Church, as in other European countries, could not intervene with any degree of success.

A better understanding of some aspects of the Church's influence may be gained from data collected in our 1984 survey. We asked whether the Church had influence in Portugal. Sixty-seven percent responded that it had much or very much, 18 percent indicated that it had some, and 7 percent thought that it had none. We then asked whether the respondent thought that this influence was positive or negative, and we found that the overall average was 6.6, where 1 is very negative and 10 is very positive. In effect, the population thinks that the Church has influence and that this influence is generally positive. Even so, the abortion law passed, the potentially unstable Central Bloc coalition survived its passing by another year, and no public demonstrations have occurred about it since its proclamation.

We asked a number of questions on abortion. In response to a question on whether it should be permitted or not, we found that 45 percent responded yes, 50 percent no, and 6 percent did not respond. Of those responding no, some 50 percent said that it should never be permitted. Thus 25 percent of the overall sample thought that abortion should never be permitted. Another 49 percent thought that it could be permitted under certain conditions, which, upon verification, are precisely those provided for in the law. The law as passed received the support of 75 percent of our sample. The Church's influence may be relevant to some issues or cases, but the abortion law was based on fundamental, if quiet, support among

Table 5.3

Which of These do you Practice with a Certain Frequency?

Pray at home	49%
Attend mass every week	54
Attend mass from time to time	29
Belong to a religious association	3
Give money for Church works and activities	17
Participate actively in the mass and religious activities	5
Don't practice much	9
No response	1

much of the population. The political leaders were aware of survey results on these issues and in retrospect have not suffered from the opposition of the Church.

What seems clear from this review of groups and associations, as well as the Church as an institution, is the relatively limited role that they play in Portuguese politics. Few people join groups; those with the most obvious political implications, such as the unions and owners' associations, are split; and the Church is limited in its political role. There must undoubtedly be some other, more informal, means for groups to have access to government but it is not clear what these are. The CPCS would appear to be symptomatic of how interests are represented, indicating that the process is constrained and largely ineffective. The political system in Portugal today is one in which the party system is structured, and monopolizing, while the interest groups remain unformed after the Estado Novo corporatism and the revolution.

Notes

1. Joyce Firstenberg Riegelhaupt, "Peasants and Politics in Salazar's Portugal: The Corporate State and Village 'Nonpolitics,'" in Lawrence Graham and Harry Makler (eds.), *Contemporary Portugal: The Revolution and Its Antecedents* (Austin: University of Texas Press, 1979), pp. 187-88. For a perceptive and detailed analysis of how the system worked in the rural areas see José Cutileiro, *A Portuguese Rural Society* (Oxford: The Clarendon Press, 1971).

2. Mário Pinto and Carlos Moura, *As estruturas sindicais portuguesas* (Lisbon: Gabinete de Investigações Sociais, 1973), pp. 6-8.

3. Elizabeth Leeds, "Salazar's 'Modelo Económico': The Consequences of Planned Constraint," in Thomas Bruneau, Victor Pereira da Rosa, and Alex Macleod (eds.), *Portugal in Development: Emigration, Industrialization, the European Community* (Ottawa: University of Ottawa Press, 1984), pp. 23-29.

4. On the groups see Maria Belmira Martins, *Sociedades e grupos em Portugal* (Lisbon: Editorial Estampa, 1973). For Marcello Caetano's comments see his *Depoimento* (Rio de Janeiro: Distribuidora Record, 1974), pp. 113-121.

5. On the Church see Thomas Bruneau, "Church and State in Portugal: Crises of Cross and Sword," *Journal of Church and State*, vol. 18, no. 3 (Autumn 1976), pp. 463-490, as well as Silas Cerqueira, "L'église catholique et la dictature corporatiste Portugaise," *Revue Française de Science Politique*, 23 June 1973, pp. 473-513.

6. Philippe C. Schmitter, *Corporatism and Public Policy in Authoritarian Portugal* (Beverly Hills: Sage Publications 1975), pp. 8-9.

7. Ibid., p. 62.

8. Insight Team of the Sunday Times, *Insight on Portugal* (London: André Deutsch, 1975), p. 255. For a description and analysis of several of these innovations see the chapters by Bermeo, Downs, and Logan in Lawrence Graham and Douglas Wheeler (eds.), *In Search of Modern Portugal: The Revolution And Its Consequences* (Madison: University of Wisconsin Press, 1983).

9. For example under Article 9 on Fundamental Tasks of the State, Item c is to "Defend political democracy and ensure the organized participation of the people in the resolution of national problems." Article 46 on the Liberty of Association guarantees the right of association with certain limits on paramilitary groups and fascist groups. And throughout the Constitution are guarantees of participation (Article 48), the right to form workers' com-

mittees (Article 54), to form unions (Article 57), and to create cooperatives (Article 61), including in the rural areas (Article 100).

10. For a comparative analysis of participation see Sidney Verba, Norman Nie, and Jae-On Kim, *Participation and Political Equality: A Seven Nation Comparison*.

11. Nonresponse was slight, with 2 percent in 1978 and less than 1 percent in 1984.

12. Article 57/1 of the 1976 Constitution (Article 56/1 in the 1982 revision) stipulates that: "Workers shall be free to form trade unions, a condition and safeguard for the building of their unity in defence of their rights and interests." The PCP and MDP abstained on the vote on this paragraph.

13. The PCP abstained on the 1976 version of the right to form tendencies. It rejected the more restrictive revision of 1982.

14. Figures for 1983, provided by the CGTP itself (Nuno Pacheco, "Desafiar o poder à sombra do passado," *Expresso Revista*, 19 March 1983). As this author points out, these figures are obviously inflated as is the UGT's claim to have 981,000 members, (ibid.). A more realistic estimation puts the CGTP and the UGT's respective membership at 900,000 to one million and 450,000 to 500,000 in 1984. These figures put the rate of unionization in Portugal well below the often touted claim of 60 percent or more.

15. See Alberto Antunes, "Caderno reivindicativo pode condicionar as negociações com o futuro governo," *O Jornal*, 18 March 1983.

16. At the Third Congress the PS had 733 of the 1,148 delegates, the TSD 255 and the TESIRESD 160 (Nuno Pacheco, "O princípio do fin de uma aliança," *Expresso Revista*, 7 April 1984).

17. Nuno Pacheco, "Desafiar o poder à sombre do passado." There were forty-one in 1979 (ibid.).

18. The figures given here are based on the statistics of the Ministry of Labor as given in José Pedro Castanheira, "Dois anos de greves ofensivas e oito de defensivas," *O Jornal*, special supplement on the unions, 1974-1984, 9 March 1984. In the same year (1979), there were 2,080 registered strikes in Britain, 3,121 in France (excluding those in the public sector), and 2,000 in Italy (*Year Book of Labour Statistics* International Labor Organization: Geneva, 1984, pp. 765-766).

19. According to a report of the Ministry of Labor (1979), quoted in José Pedro Castenheira, "Dois anos de greves." There is nothing to indicate that the rate of success has increased since.

20. Nuna Pacheco, "A estranha 'guerra' dos transportes", *Expresso Revista*, 12 February 1983.

21. The social contract would be a nationally negotiatied collective agreement covering a whole host of issues such as wages, social security, holidays, labor legislation, etc., based on the Scandinavian model. See *O que é a UGT?* (Lisbon: Fundacão José Fontana, 1981), p. 27.

22. Article 58 of the 1982 Constitution not only guarantees the right to strike but also declares that it is up to the workers "to define the scope of the interests to be defended through the strike, and the law may not limit that scope." It also outlaws lockouts.

23. III Congresso UGT, *Proposta da UGT para os proximos 4 anos*, March 1984, p. 7.

24. Decree-law no. 398/83, *Diário da Republica*, 1st series, no. 252, 2 November 1983, p. 3,739.

25. To the question: For which union federation do you feel most sympathy? the response was: CGTP-IN, 19 percent; UGT, 32; percent, neither, 40 percent.

26. The world economic crisis was cited in first or second place by 35 percent as responsible for Portugal's own economic crisis, lack of agreement between the parties by 20 percent, and strikes by 18 percent.

27. Fourteen percent placed outlawing strikes at the head of measures which would

best solve the economic crisis (respondents were asked to name only one method). Denationalization came a close second with 13 percent.

28. For a description of what was taken over by the state see M. Belmira Martins and J. Chaves Rosa, *O grupo estado* (Lisbon: Edicões Jornal Expresso, 1979).

29. It should be noted that the associations have many other roles, such as training, negotiations, foreign trade, hosting of conferences, and publishing of analyses.

30. In addition to the sources cited in note 5 above, see the chapter on Portugal in Thomas G. Sanders, *Secular Consciousness and National Conscience: The Church and Political Alternatives in Southern Europe* (Hanover, New Hampshire: American Universities Field Staff, 1977).

31. IPOPE, *Estudo sobre liberdade e religião em Portugal* (Lisbon: Moraes Editores, 1973), p. 40.

32. Luis de França, "Igreja, sistema social e político depois do 25 abril de 1974" (paper for colloquium on Formation and Modes of Actions of Social Groups in Portugal After 1959). Bad-Homburg, 13-15 December 1983.

6
The Constitution of 1976 and its Revision in 1982

The democratic political system achieved by early 1976 was codified and defined in a constitution which was approved by the Constituent Assembly on 2 April and promulgated by President Francisco Costa Gomes on 25 April of that year. This long and comprehensive document of 312 articles, reputedly the third longest in the world (after Yugoslavia and Uruguay), specified in great detail the economic, political, and social systems to be achieved and consolidated in postrevolutionary Portugal. The Constitution reflected the context in which it was drafted, being laced with references to socialism, a socialist economic system, and extensive rights for workers. For example, under Fundamental Principles, Article 2 stipulates that "the Portuguese Republic . . . has as its objective the assuring of the transition to socialism by means of the creation of conditions for the democratic exercise of power by the working classes."

The Constitution

The Constitution was elaborated by the Constituent Assembly elected on 25 April 1975. Six parties had representatives elected to the Assembly, but the dominant orientation was given by the PS and the PCP which together had won 50 percent of the votes in the elections. In the 250-member Assembly the PS had 116 deputies and the PCP and its ally, the MDP, had a combined total of 35, or more than a majority. Revolutionary enthusiasm pervaded the country, and indeed the whole nature of the political regime was in question for much of the time the Constitution was being elaborated. Most specifically, not only because of the the pact between the MFA and the six main parties but also to recognize the role of the MFA in the overthrow of the old regime, the authors of the Constitution ensured that the military would continue to have a role in government with the Council of the Revolution.

The Council of the Revolution (CR) was a military organization growing out of the MFA; its role was specified, for a given transition period. It was included in order to involve the military in guaranteeing the new democratic regime. Specifically, its role was defined in terms of an advisory council for the president, a court for judging the constitutionality of laws, and a decision-making body for the armed forces. The CR was meant to disappear at the end of the period of transition, after the revision of the Constitution which would become possible after 15 October 1980 when a second Assembly of the Republic would be elected.[1] Only the CDS, with its sixteen deputies, refused to ratify the Constitution, though it took full part in the debates.

Even as the Constitution was going into effect, several politicians declared their intention to amend it. Sá Carneiro, leader of the PSD, even went so far as proposing a new Constitution in January of 1979. From its inception, then, the basic charter of the new democracy was considered in extremely political terms as it represented an economic, political, and social model which was agreed upon at one time in a specific context but was not seen as permanent in the face of political change and the dynamics of party governments. In the words of José Durão Barroso, a colleague of Sá Carneiro, the PCP favored the socioeconomic model but not the political model of the Constitution, while the PSD and the CDS accepted the political but not the socioeconomic model.[2]

It is important to keep in perspective the main issue concerning the possible revision of the Constitution of 1976. While very elaborate details defined the particular socioeconomic model desired in Portugal, they proved to be more hortative than accurate descriptions of the fact. In particular, Part Two on the economic organization and the socialization of the economy saw little real implementation.[3] The grave economic crisis after decolonization and the revolution, the serious problems with the balance of payments, and the necessity of approaching the International Monetary Fund and a consortium of rich countries in 1977-1978 proved to be more important than the articles in the Constitution. Professor Jorge Miranda has demonstrated that four levels of implementation (or non implementation) of the Constitution were in fact operative. Those sections that were carried out most fully concerned the establishment of a liberal democracy and rights and guarantees to maintain such a system. Those that were least enforced involved the transition to socialism.[4] Within a short time after promulgation, then, it became obvious that large parts of the socioeconomic sections were not particularly relevant. However, this did not prevent the theme of constitutional revision from becoming *the* political issue for at least eighteen months between April 1981 and September 1982; indeed, revision was discussed from 1978 and continued to be considered in mid-1985 despite the revision in 1982. This was the case for a number of reasons; the following are among the most important:

First, the Portuguese approach to politics has been defined largely in terms of constitutional law. Political science hardly exists as a discipline, and lawyers dominate all aspects of national politics. For these reasons there is a strong tendency to identify constitutional law, and thus constitutions, with politics. Political problems (and even short-term issues of political struggle) tend to become constitutional issues.

Second, one of the roles of the CR was to judge the constitutionality of laws passed by the Assembly. As shall be seen, the CR vetoed several laws dealing with the delimitation of economic sectors. It became clear that this body would indeed have to disappear if these laws were to be passed.

Third, the give and take of Portuguese politics between 1976 and 1980 brought a number of politicians, mainly the party leaders, into conflict with President Eanes, who was elected in 1976 and reelected in 1980. In order to limit his freedom of action and further restrict the socioeconomic model of the Constitution with which Eanes was identified, a change in his powers would be required. To implement that change, the Constitution would have to be revised, which would be possible after elections for a second legislature. But revision also needed a two-thirds vote in the Assembly. No provision existed for a presidential veto over constitutional revision. Revision then, was solely up to the political parties; the general population had no voice in the matter, not even through a referendum.

Due to the balance of forces between the presidency and the government, revision of the definition of powers sections of the Constitution was politically important. The 1933 Constitution, which had been written by Premier António de Oliveira Salazar, had strongly concentrated power. The government was not responsible to the National Assembly, while the premier was formally responsible to the president whom he had chosen. In reality the system became very much a "presidentialism of the premier."[5] The authors of the 1976 Constitution wanted to avoid too great a centralization of power in one body or individual, and the resultant system has been termed either semipresidential or bipolar in that power is shared by a popularly elected president and a popularly elected Assembly from which the government is formed.[6]

The survival of a government depended on the confidence of the Assembly *and* the president. Because of the fairly stringent conditions for voting out a government (however easily formed, even as a minority government), the confidence of the Assembly was less significant than it might have been. It should be noted that the PS, which from 1975 has been the party with the greatest number of votes but never a majority, played a key role in defining these requirements. The president derived his legitimacy not only from popular and national elections (61 percent of the vote in 1976), but also from his role as commander-in-chief of the armed forces and chairman of the CR. It was understood at the time of the revised party pact in February 1976 that the president would be a military officer.[7] The president held few independent executive powers except to chair the CR, which held exclusive powers regarding the armed forces. However, his powers over the formation and dismissal of governments were crucial, as the president could dismiss the prime minister after consulting with the CR and nominate the prime minister after taking into consideration the results of the elections. His leeway in forming and dismissing governments was formally substantial, as was his role in dissolving the

Assembly. He had the right of vetoing legislation on constitutional grounds and disposed of a de facto pocket veto as neither the Assembly nor the government could force him to promulgate laws. Through these and related powers, the president could exert substantial control over the political system. The president would not necessarily utilize these powers, but his conduct would depend upon the political parties and their relationships in the Assembly.

Revision

Even before the formation and success of the AD in the elections of 1979 and 1980, the parties forming it advocated constitutional revision. Both the PSD and CDS opposed the socioeconomic model defined in the Constitution and criticized the balance of power between the structures of government. During the period of minority governments (1976-77) or governments of presidential inspiration (1978-79), President Eanes's de facto powers expanded substantially.[8] Further, in its capacity as a constitutional court, the Council of the Revolution found four instances of unconstitutional legislation on the delimitation or opening of the economy to private involvment in certain restricted sectors. The AD, then, put constitutional revision high on its list of priorities. However, even with the 134 seats won in the October 1980 elections, the AD lacked sufficient votes for the two-thirds majority required in the 250-seat Assembly to revise the Constitution. To get around this difficulty, Sá Carneiro decided to run an AD-sponsored candidate in the presidential elections of 7 December 1980. If his candidate, General Soares Carneiro, won, he would revise the Constitution by referendum (although this was not provided for in the Constitution). However, the AD candidate came in a poor second, with 40 percent of the vote against President Eanes's 56 percent. The death of Sá Carneiro just prior to the elections avoided a constitutional crisis, for the former had stated that he would not form a government if Eanes were reelected president. It did not, however, resolve the issue of constitutional revision to which the AD, now under the leadership of Pinto Balsemão, was committed. With its 134 votes, the AD still required the support of the PS to obtain the 167 votes necessary for revision.

In opposing the AD in 1979 and 1980, the PS had framed an agreement with the president in July 1980 in which the former would support Eanes in exchange for certain commitments on his part. The most important of the seven points of the agreement are as follows:[9]

1. Constitutional revision would only be allowed on the basis of two-thirds of the deputies.

2. There would, then, be no referendum.

3. The nomination of the prime minister would be according to election results although the president might form a minority government.

4. The president would give up his role as chief of the General Staff.

5. The PS would not limit the powers of the president in a revision of the Constitution.

As indicated earlier, Mário Soares withdrew his support for President Eanes between the elections for the Assembly in October and the presidential elections in December 1980. Despite Eanes's clear victory at the polls, revision went ahead since both the AD and the PS had their own reasons for restricting power of the president and Eanes did not control any of the parties.

From late 1980, revision became constitutionally possible and in the spring of 1981 the matter was introduced in the Assembly. Each of the four major parties, as well as the MDP, presented proposals for revision. More than a year later, on 12 August 1982, the Assembly approved the revision with the votes of the AD and the PS, together with those of the ASDI and the UEDS. The PCP with 39 votes and the UDP with 1 voted against, and the MDP abstained. The president, who had no option in any case, promulgated the revised Constitution on 5 November 1982.

The revision required the support of the PS of Mário Soares; thus his influence on its outcome was predominant. As shall be seen, the powers of the president were substantially reduced, which suggests that the PS reneged on its agreement of July 1980. The PS argued, however, that the abolition of the Council of the Revolution necessitated a redistribution of powers so that the president would not accumulate too many. After promulgation, the president publicly criticized the revision, indicating that while the debate had presumably dealt with the socioeconomic model, in fact the real changes concerned the distribution of powers. Those pertaining to the presidency were diminished, while the Assembly and government increased in powers. An examination indicates that this was indeed the case.

Several of the more ideological statements were removed or revised (Articles 80, 81, 83, 91, and 185), and Article 2 on the transition to socialism was modified to emphasize pluralism and participation. Part Two on the Economic Organization was only slightly modified, and possibilities for change were left to legislation.[10] This was undoubtedly due to the crucial role of the PS which did not want to amend this section.

The real change concerned the balance of powers. The greatest effect of revision undoubtedly lay in an increase in the role of the parties in the political system. As noted in Chapter 2, the Constitution of 1976 allotted a large role to the parties. With the elimination of the CR, the Council of State and Constitutional Court were created to take over some of its functions. The Law on National Defense set up a Higher Council for National Defense to assume its remaining functions.

The Council of State is a consultative body for the presidency. Its members include the president, president of the Assembly, prime minister, president of the Constitutional Court, attorney general, and the presidents of the regional governments of the Azores and Madeira. Also members are ex-presidents elected since 1976, five persons designated by the president, and five persons elected by the Assembly on the basis of proportional representation of the parties in the Assembly. Members identified with the political parties thus have an absolute majority in this seventeen-member body.

The predominance of the parties is even clearer in the two other bodies. The Constitutional Court has thirteen members; ten are appointed by the Assembly and it co-opts the other three. The Higher Council for National Defense is composed of the president, the prime minister; the deputy prime minister; the ministers of national defense, foreign affairs, internal security, finance, industry and energy, transport and communications; two deputies elected by the Assembly; the four chiefs of staff; the two ministers of the Republic appointed by the government to the Azores and Madeira; and the presidents of the two regional governments. At least twelve of its members, then, are identified with the parties.

The president's power to dismiss the government was formally diminished to "when necessary to assure the regular functioning of the democratic institutions and consulting with the Council of State"; the pocket veto was abolished; the Assembly cannot be dissolved during the six months immediately following its election or during the last six months of the President's term; and the *political responsibility* of the government to the president was reduced to mere *responsibility*. The government now depends principally on the Assembly. While somewhat ambiguous on the actual role of the president in dissolving governments, the overall thrust is clear. The Assembly and the government, and thus the political parties, are much more important and the president less so. According to one constitutional lawyer, active in politics and in favor of diminishing the powers of the president, six articles in the revision strengthened the presidency and twenty-one weakened it. The former are both quantitatively and qualitatively less important.[11]

Public Opinion and Constitutional Revision

Revision of the Constitution was the meat of politics for much of 1981 and 1982. It would appear, however, that the Constitution and its revision were not especially relevant topics for the general population. Our 1978 survey asked questions on the Constitution and found that 52 percent of the respondents did not recognize phrases characterizing the document and another 12 percent got them wrong; only 32 percent were able to correctly identify these phrases. In a survey done in early 1983, 36 percent percent were aware that the Constitution had been revised, 6 percent reported that it had not, and 58 percent simply did not know.[12] In our survey of early 1984 we again asked a number of questions on the Constitution. Fifty-nine percent recalled that they had heard of constitutional revision, 38 percent had not heard about it, and only 2 percent did not respond. However, this was followed up by an open question concerning elements in the Constitution that had been revised and while only 3 percent did not respond, 68 percent could not recall, and another 12 percent gave the wrong answers. Thus less than 20 percent of the initial 59 percent who had heard about revision gave the correct answers. In effect, while some general awareness of revision was apparent, there was general ignorance of detail.

Based upon this survey, and supported by earlier work, the Constitution and its revision do not interest the general population very much.

Results of the Revision

Constitutional revision did not have quite the results anticipated by its opponents and proponents. While the economic sections were not revised and remained an element of political debate, the elimination of the CR as a constitutional tribunal has allowed for change in the delimitation of economic sectors so that the public sector was opened to private investment on 5 July 1983. This has allowed the banks, which were nationalized in 1975, to be open to private initiative as well. In addition, the loss of powers of the president were not as great as anticipated, at least in the short run, because of a political crisis in late 1982 which saw the AD government of Prime Minister Pinto Balsemão disintegrate, the CDS leader in the government, Freitas do Amaral, resign, and the president refuse the AD's nominee for a new prime minister. To solve the constitutional impasse the president called early elections for 25 April 1983 which resulted in the formation of the Central Bloc government. Thus in the period immediately after revision until mid-1983, there was either unstable government or a government in crisis, and the president acted essentially as he had in the past to dismiss one government and then recognize a new one. The ambiguity of the revision was used by the president to ensure that a government with sufficient support could be formed.

Incredibly enough, a mere eighteen months after the revision of the Constitution in late 1982, new calls began to be heard in early 1984 for another revision. The lead was taken by the CDS, now in the opposition, to finish the revision by modifying the economic sections of the Constitution and strengthening the powers of the president. This initiative found an echo in the PS. Later Pinto Balsemão, prime minister at the time of the first revision, also called for a revision in which the powers of the president would be increased.[13] Many journalists and scholars have wondered if the attention given to revision—to blaming the Constitution for political and economic problems and thus revising it to resolve these problems—is not a kind of alibi for immobility that has its sources elsewhere.

Our 1984 survey included a question as to whether the respondent thought that the Constitution should be changed or revised. Fifty-seven percent did not know, 4 percent did not respond, and of the remaining 39 percent there was a division of 25 percent in favor and 15 percent against. In short, the population does not have strong feelings about revision of the Constitution. Of the 25 percent responding yes, most thought that it was the economic section that should be changed. The spread, however, was so broad that none of the points in this open-ended question were particularly convincing. In sum, the population continued to lack an opinion concerning the revision of the Constitution.

Constitutional revision in Portugal since 1981 seems to be mainly a matter of political activity without a great deal of external importance. It is clear from the survey data that the population is not very well informed or particularly interested in this subject. At the level of the political elite, revision is something that is discussed, debated, and argued about, but when it comes to working out the details the short-run political considerations prevail over larger issues. Even without revision, for example, the economic sections were implemented in a manner different from the statements in the Constitution. The president continued to act in governmental crises, even though his powers were intentionally limited on precisely this point. Maybe the most accurate short statement is that the revision took away positive powers from the presidency and transfered them to other organs, dominated by the political parties, which have been unable to utilize this power effectively.

Notes

1. On the status of the Council of the Revolution, see in particular Jorge Miranda, "Do conselho da revolução ao conselho da república," *Prospectivas,* April-June 1980, no. 2, pp. 56-63.
2. Pedro Santana Lopes and José Durão Barroso, *Sistema de governo e sistema partidário* (Lisbon: Livraria Bertrand, 1980), p. 124.
3. This is dealt with in some detail in Marcelo Rebelo de Sousa, *Direito constitucional* (Braga: Livraria Cruz, 1979), pp. 338-43.
4. Jorge Miranda, *Manual de direito constitucional,* vol. I (Coimbra: Coimbra Editora, 1982), pp. 330-31.
5. *Manual de instrucçō cívica do cidadão português* (Lisbon: Terra Livre, 1980), pp. 91-2.
6. On the model of the semipresidential system see Maurice Duverger, "A New Political System Model: Semi-Presidential Government," *European Journal of Political Research,* 8 (1980), pp. 165-87; for the bipolar model see Werner Kaltefleiter, *Die Funktionen des Staatsoberhauptes in der parlamentarischen Demokratie* (Koln: Westdeutscher Verlag, 1970). For a legal analysis in the Portuguese context see Jorge Miranda, "O sistema semipresidencial português entre 1976 e 1979," text presented at international conference on semipresidential regimes, Centre d'Analyse Comparative des Systèmes Politiques of Université de Paris, 20 January 1983.
7. Jorge Miranda, "A ideia de direito legitimou a mudança e a lei fundamental," *Diário de Notícias,* 24 April 1984, p. 31.
8. On these powers see Part One of Santana Lopes and Durão Barroso. See also the institutional (II part) and political (III part) analysis of Emídio da Veiga Domingos, *Portugal político: Análise das instituições* (Lisbon: Ediçoes Rolim, 1980).
9. For the full terms of the agreement see *O Jornal,* 15 November 1980. See also the discussion of the agreement, and its neglect by Mário Soares, in the interview with the then parliamentary leader of the PS, Francisco Salgado Zenha, in *Diário de Notícias,* 23 October 1981.
10. On this economic section see A.L. de Sousa Franco, "A revisão da constituição económica," *Revista da Ordem dos Advogados,* 42 (September-December 1982), pp. 601-87.
11. Marcelo Rebelo de Sousa, *O sistema de governo português antes e depois da revisão constitucional* (Lisbon: Cognitio, 1983), pp. 36-40. On this point see as well, Jorge Miranda in *Diário de Notícias,* 24 April 1984, pp. 32-33. For a somewhat different interpre-

tation see Luís Salgado de Matos, "Significado e consequências da eleicão do presidentepor sufrágio universal—o caso português," *Análise Social* XIX (1982-83), pp. 235-259.

12. See *Expresso,* 19 February 1983.

13. See *Expresso,* 24 November 1984, for the position of Balsemão and an editorial in favor of increasing presidential powers.

7
The Quest for Stable and Efficient Government

All constitutions drafted in Western Europe since 1945 have reflected an overriding concern with ensuring governmental stability. In some cases, as in Italy and in the French Fourth Republic, complicated constitutional provisions were introduced to prevent governments from falling easily, though these safeguards often proved ineffective. Others have imposed stronger constitutional guarantees, such as in West Germany where Parliament can only overthrow a government if an alternative is already in the offing. More recently the trend has been towards "streamlining" parliament, the most visible example being that of the French Fifth Republic. In a "streamlined" parliamentary system, much greater weight is given to the executive, a parliamentary majority in support of the government is assumed, and important restrictions are put on parliament's power to bring down the government and on parliamentary obstruction. Portugal has followed this trend. However, despite a conscious desire to break completely with the Salazar-Caetano system, the authors of the Portuguese Constitution did not begin from scratch.

For almost fifty years Portugal's system of government was heavily weighted in favor of the executive. Many of the practices of that period have continued. For example, the Cabinet still retains the right to make laws without referring to Parliament. The new Constitution also bears the obvious influence of the French Fifth Republic, in particular its separation of functions between the executive and the members of the Assembly,[1] and the rule that a government will only fall if a motion of censure receives support of an absolute majority of all members of the Assembly. The authors of the Constitution did not, however, follow the French example of making the president the undisputed head of the executive and met with less success than the French in finding a formula for stable government.

The fear of concentrating power in the hands of one man caused the framers of the Constitution to divide executive power between the president and the government, which created an immediate source of conflict. But, above all, the Constitution could deal only imperfectly with the reality of party politics.

A President with Potential Executive Powers

During the Estado Novo it appeared as though the president held the most power of any figure in the political system. Until 1959 he was directly elected, since 1933 he was a military man, and the government depended on him not the National Assembly. Appearances were deceptive, and in fact the premier, António de Oliveira Salazar, ruled the country from 1930 until his incapacitation in 1968. A gap was apparent between the laws and the reality of political power in the Estado Novo: "The abdication of the President of the Republic and of the Government to the advantage of the Chief of the Government, and the consequent concentration of powers, constitutes an unequivocal demonstration of the divergence existing between the constitutional facade and the concrete reality."[2] After the founding of the new regime and the promulgation of the Constitution in 1976 a more precise separation of powers has become apparent, but an ambiguous situation still exists which the revision of the Constitution in 1982 did little to clarify.

Between 1976 and 1986 the country had one president, General Ramalho Eanes, who played the key role in putting down the attempted military coup from the left on 25 November 1975 and as chief of staff of the army introduced major reforms to professionalize it and link it more closely to NATO. Elected to the presidency in 1976 with 61 percent of the vote in a four-way race, he also gained popular legitimacy to which were added important powers as chief of the General Staff of the Armed Forces and president of the Council of the Revolution. His legitimacy in key areas of the military and his popular support were crucial in ensuring stability in the new democratic system. While the powers of the president in forming and dismantling governments are large in the 1976 Constitution, they are relatively slight in terms of governing in the executive sense of the word. A review of the president's vetoes, his statements, his meetings with ministers and other officials, and his trips both inside and outside Portugal between 1976 and 1982 indicate a role that expanded or contracted depending upon the stability of governments. When more or less stable governments were in power (such as the first constitutional government of mid-1976 until late 1977 and the AD governments of early 1980 until late 1982), the president's role in executive-type matters was slight. With unstable governments it increased, confirming the observations of Marcelo Rebelo de Sousa.[3]

The president is elected for a five-year term and can only be reelected once (Article 126 & 131). Article 127 of the Constitution of 1976 stipulated that candidates for the presidency be put forward by between 7,500 and 15,000 registered voters, while only the parties could present candidates for the Assembly. These provisions were not changed in 1982. In theory, then, a presidential candidate need not have any agreement with the political parties. In 1980, President Eanes was supported by the National Committee for the Reelection of President Eanes (CNARPE), and his campaign program emphasized that the "President is the President of all the Portuguese" (as opposed to the president of one party or another).[4] As noted in Chapter 6, President Eanes signed an agreement with the PS and re-

Table 7.1
Who or What Institution Really Governs the Country?

(multiple answer possible)	1978	1984
President of the Republic	39%	31%
Cabinet	20	23
Prime Minister	26	25
Assembly of the Republic	14	19
Council of the Revolution	11	–
Council of State	–	4
Nobody	2	6
Don't know	30	19
No response	3	2

ceived unsolicited support from the PCP. In neither case did he make policy commitments to the parties, a factor which allowed him to maintain total independence.

The 1982 revision sought to reduce President Eanes's capacity to intervene in government, which caused him to lament that "the president of the Republic does not have the means whereby he can be co-responsible for governmental action since in the text of the Constitution he is only to be informed by the prime minister concerning matters of internal and external politics."[5] Or, as he stated in the same speech: "I can, then, say that I do not believe it is appropriate for the present and future needs of the political system that the president of the Republic, elected by direct and universal suffrage, does not have the political means to defend his election program nor even have a clear link of political responsibility in relationship to the executive."

The president repeated his criticism of the restrictions of his powers to implement policies and influence national politics in his interview in the *Diário de Notícias* on the tenth anniversary of the revolution.[6] He complained that powers had been divided in such a way that nobody quite knew who was responsible for what; the division of powers in the revised Constitution decreased those of the president but also made them less clear.

Unlike the parties running for the Assembly, the president must win a majority, in two ballots if necessary. President Eanes won both of his elections handily. And, as Salgado Matos has shown, the electoral support of the president was not only greater than any of the four parties, but also more evenly distributed.[7] On the face of it, then, President Eanes's claim that it makes no sense to have limited his powers with the constitutional revision of 1982 is at least partially accurate. In the present situation it would seem to create ambiguity and confusion.

This ambiguity is recognized by the respondents to our survey. We asked a question on who or what institution really governs the country (see Table 7.1). The broad spread of the responses indicates that the respondents are not sure who is in fact governing.

These data suggest a number of points. The "don't know" is down significantly as the institutions had been around eight instead of two years; the Council of State is correctly perceived to be less important than the Council of the Revolution; the perceived importance of the president has decreased; and while the totals for cabinet and prime minister are about the same (46/48 percent), the Assembly total has increased. These perceptions are probably accurate. Most important is the spread between the presidency on the one hand, with the largest single attribution, and the three elements of the parliament on the other. It is, then, a division of legitimacy, as might be expected in a semipresidential system; however, in this case it is one in which the powers of the presidency have decreased.

The president's view that he should have more power is generally supported by our respondents. The response to a question on whether the president should have more, less, or equal power in comparison to the government is given in Table 7.2.

Thus while some two-fifths thought the present distribution of powers was right, eleven times as many respondents thought the president's powers should be increased as those thinking they should be decreased. The same general sense is found throughout the questionnaire with the president receiving greater sympathy than any of the other nine political figures listed.

The support for greater presidential power is not thought to be a tendency towards dictatorship. The responses to a question on what institution has contributed most to defend liberty and democracy in Portugal is reflected in Table 7.3, which shows that the president is thought by twice as many respondents as chose the next institution to have contributed most to the defense of democracy and liberty in Portugal. It might be recalled that President Eanes did play a role in 1975 and 1976, but so did Mário Soares, prime minister at the time of the survey. In sum, an increase in presidential powers is generally favored, the president is thought to have played a role in defending liberty and democracy, and the present division of powers is not clear to much of the population.

An obvious solution to the ambiguity of powers resulting from constitutional revision would be the founding of a party by the president himself. In his interview to the *Diário de Notícias* on the tenth anniversary of the revolution President Eanes

Table 7.2

In Comparison to the Government: Should the President have More, Less, or Equal Power?

More	33
Equal	38
Less	3
Don't know	21
No response	5

Table 7.3

Which of These Institutions Have Contributed Most to Defend Liberty and Democracy in Portugal?

President of the Republic	41%
Cabinet	5
Prime Minister	9
Assembly of the Republic	20
Others and none	8
Don't know	28
No response	3

made it clear that a president who headed a party could have great powers. Not only could his party undoubtedly hold a majority in the Assembly, but through the party he could have a high level of influence in the three bodies that replaced the CR. In his view these powers would be enormous, maybe even excessive. For Eanes this implied that it would be difficult, if not impossible, to elect nonpartisan presidents in the future.

President Eanes often declared his opposition to the semipresidential form of regime as defined in the French Fifth Republic. It must be remembered that Portugal was a dictatorship for almost fifty years with a similarly high concentration of powers. He did not, then, publicly encourage proposals for the founding of a party or movement. These proposals, which emerged as early as 1979, came from a wide variety of political, military, and even lay movements and from a spectrum of ideological angles. The "presidential party" would be one solution to the lack of presidential powers but would produce a number of problems, not the least of which would be the high concentration of power. Another consideration would be whether the party of the president would also receive a majority in the Assembly; if it did not then policymaking might well be paralyzed.

Despite these obvious impediments, well known to President Eanes and his advisors, he made a number of statements in 1984 indicating that he might support such a party. In the speech at Coimbra celebrating the third anniversary of his reelection he stated that "there is reason, place, and necessity even for new parties in a society where not everything functions in an overall satisfactory manner." And later in Viseu on 10 June 1984, celebrating the Day of Portugal, he questioned the capacity of the parties to represent the people in the political institutions as they were supposed to do. This party finally took shape in the spring of 1985 as the PRD but without the formal support of President Eanes. However, the presence of his wife, Manuela Eanes, at its founding convention and the prominent role she played on its behalf during the 1985 legislative election campaign made it clear that it had his implicit backing. President Eanes has not lacked opportunities to intervene in the workings of government. But both the Constitution and practice since 1976 make it clear that decision-making power resides first and foremost in the government.

A Government with Sweeping Powers

Articles 200 to 204 of the Constitution lay down the powers and duties of the government and the Cabinet. As under Salazar, the powers of the government have been divided into three types: political, legislative, and administrative. The government's political and administrative powers correspond roughly to those of other parliamentary governments, but the Portuguese system is unique in including the government's so-called legislative power. Under the present Constitution there are in fact four types of legislative power. The Assembly has, according to Article 167 of the Constitution, exclusive powers in some thirteen areas. Secondly, the government, according to Article 201, alone has legislative jurisdiction for all matters concerning its own organization and functioning. A third series of topics, covered by Article 168, belong to the Assembly but can be delegated to the government with specific authorization. Finally, there is a concurrent residuary power for both the government and the Assembly. Laws made by the government, without any reference to Parliament, are called decree-laws and constitutionally have exactly the same value as laws passed by Parliament.[8]

Careful distinction must be made between delegated legislation and parliamentary authorization. Delegated legislation in Portugal, as elsewhere, can be made by the government based on enabling legislation or framework laws, even on topics which belong to the exclusive jurisdiction of the Assembly. On the other hand, Parliament can authorize the government to make decree-laws within the so-called relative reserved domain of the Assembly. This constitutes more than just giving the government the right to make delegated legislation. It amounts to a surrender of Parliament's right to legislate.

The existence of concurrent residual lawmaking powers sometimes leads to confusion, since the government can, very often by accident, cancel legislation already made by Parliament. Moreover, since the legislative process in the Assembly tends to be slow—it can take from four to six months to get a law through Parliament—governments increasingly resort to decree-laws. Governments may also use emergency procedures to rush any measure through the Assembly. Article 172 provides for parliamentary ratification of decree-laws other than those made under exclusive jurisdiction of the government. Ten deputies may, within ten sitting days of the publication of the new law, request that such laws be amended or withdrawn. The realities of a majority government have made this possibility more or less inoperative.

The Heavy Machinery of Government

The Portuguese Constitution provides few guidelines for the structure and functioning of the government. Article 186/1 of the revised Constitution boldly states that "the government shall comprise a Prime Minister, the other ministers and the secretaries and undersecretaries of state." The Constitution also distinguishes between the Council of Ministers, which includes the prime minister, any deputy prime ministers, and other ministers and corresponds closely to the British Cabinet, and the rest of the government. Otherwise, the government can decide for itself how it will be organized and how it will function. This means that no government need feel bound to follow the rules of operation of its predecessors. A very broad model of structure and functioning, based on widely accepted practices (some dating from the previous regime) has emerged, but with an extraordinary range of variations. What has evolved is a very unwieldy, poorly coordinated body hampered not only by the normal vicissitudes of interparty and intraparty rivalries but also by structural problems, reinforced by the mutual distrust between politicians and the civil service.

When a government is formed, it immediately adopts a decree-law determining its structure and principles of operation. The Cabinet itself is usually a small body, consisting of between fifteen and eighteen members. Unfortunately, little attempt has been made to transform the Cabinet into an efficient policymaking body. Structurally, no provision exists for interdepartmental committees at the ministerial level, with one exception that goes back to the previous regime—that is the creation of a specialized Committee for Economic Affairs. The Constitution allows for the creation of "councils of specialist ministers . . . for particular subjects" (Article 187/2) and governments have interpreted this strictly as ad hoc committees for immediate problems.

Prime ministers have also tended to refrain from creating formal "inner cabinets," preferring to meet senior members of the government on an informal basis. There has been one exception. Prime Minister Sá Carneiro adopted a very British approach to the appointment of the members of his governments and created a formal so-called "political committee of the government" which acted as a true political planning committee. It was composed of himself; his deputy in the SD, Pinto Balsemão; and the two leading ministers from the CDS, Freitas do Amaral, deputy minister and minister of foreign affairs, and Amaro da Costa, minister of defense, and the secretary of state to the Cabinet.[9]

One of the main problems of the Portuguese Cabinet has been coordination. Under Salazar and Caetano, power was concentrated in the hands of the Presidency of the Council of Ministers, which acted as "the nucleus of administrative bodies and services which, by their nature or for practical convenience ought to be common to the whole government or to be separate from the existing ministries."[10] It also became an instrument of interministerial coordination. The presidency of the council became the symbol of the concentration of power under the old regime; as a consequence, it was reorganized after the revolution into a "small staff unit at the service of the Prime Minister."[11] It now has a general secretariat which serves as a sort of coordinating body of administrative services within the government, as an information and documentation service for the Presidency of the Council, and as the organizer of the presidency's personnel, but it does not act as a Cabinet secretariat. This role is played by a special secretary of state to the Cabinet who organizes Cabinet meetings, sets the agenda, distributes papers, and takes minutes. As the secretary of state is a politician, not a civil servant, he can be changed at will and normally leaves the government when it falls, depriving the Cabinet of any real administrative continuity.

A form of coordination is provided by the Ministry of Finance. This practice goes back to the early days of Salazar, who established his own political supremacy over the government through this office in 1928. One minister indicated to us that the Ministry of Finance has become a monster that attempts to control all government spending. Thus, the decree establishing the structure and functioning of the PS/PSD government of 1983 declared that "all government acts which involve the increase of expenditure or the decrease of receipts have to be referred necessarily to the Ministry of Finance and Planning."[12] In practice, the efficiency of the Ministry of Finance's control over departmental spending depends on the personality of the minister of finance himself. The more skillful minister who wishes to make expenditures in his department without passing through the control of the Ministry can usually do so by ensuring that his department has set aside a small margin of credit which can be spent without drawing the attention of the bureaucrats of the Ministry of Finance or the minister himself. Some ministers can also make use of so-called autonomous funds, such as the Fund for Unemployment, which are not included in the general budget presented to the Assembly, and which the less scrupulous minister can dispose of liberally, with little or no control, as an instrument of patronage.

Inevitably, the Ministry of Finance's attempts to supervise the spending of other departments can lead to clashes, which the Cabinet or the prime minister must arbitrate. During the preparation stage of the 1985 budget, the head of the department responsible for the nationalized industries (the Ministry of Industry and Energy), demanded that some $280 million more be allotted for the public sector of the economy. He finally had to settle for less than half, but not before the minister of finance had threatened in turn to resign if it was not guaranteed that he could exercise stricter control over how various departmental budgets were used, especially over monies going to the public sector. The Cabinet gave him satisfaction with the creation of a Permanent Secretariat for Public Enterprises, directly responsible to the Committee for Economic Affairs, which in effect would put the public sector more directly under the control of the Ministry of Finance.

Politicians and observers alike have bemoaned the fact that Portugal lacks a well-respected civil service. Top civil servants are reputedly not only inefficient but also motivated basically by partisan interests. The ministers tend to mistrust permanent heads of departments, called directors-general, appointed by their predecessors and usually transfer them to other posts and appoint their own nominees.

They also follow the French practice of appointing a cabinet or personal staff, usually headed by a member of their own party, thereby creating a sort of parallel administration which sooner or later comes into conflict with the permanent civil service within the department. One of the most glaring examples of this practice was provided by the PSD secretary of state for employment appointed to the PS/PSD government in 1983, who created a personal staff of some forty-one members, most of whom were from the PSD, though normally he only had the right to a staff of five plus a number of so-called assessors, while the prime minister's office had only some thirty members. As for the actual operation of the civil service, it still tends to act much as it did under the old regime.[13]

Most of the ministers' complaints appear to be justified. They cannot always depend on the civil service to implement their decisions and are obliged to spend much time following up to make sure that decisions have actually been carried out. Enforcing government policy is made all the more difficult by the fact that the prime minister is theoretically responsible for seeing that Cabinet decisions are implemented. He has no adequate staff to ensure that this function is fulfilled, as not even the general secretariat of the presidency of the council is expected to play this role.

The Cabinet's functioning confirms this picture of a structurally inefficient government. The heart of the problem lies in the Cabinet's role as a lawmaking body. Since it enjoys sweeping legislative powers, in a context of notoriously slow legislative procedures in the Assembly, no Cabinet can resist the temptation to bypass Parliament. On the other hand, as there are no interministerial committees to deal with legislation or policy, almost all of this legislation must go through the full Cabinet. In addition, ministers jealously guard their privilege of being kept informed of all legislation that goes through the Cabinet. Cabinet meetings inevitably get bogged down in discussions of details that should have been debated elsewhere. During the revolution, these meetings could sometimes last twelve hours or more, until three or four o'clock in the morning. They have since been reduced to more manageable proportions, but even today they can go on for nine or ten hours. Sá Carneiro was the exception with short meetings which usually began at nine in the morning and ended in time for lunch.

Cabinet sittings also take time because of the general rule, followed by all prime ministers, that decisions should be made on the basis of consensus and not by majority vote. However, consensus often depends on how the prime minister interprets it. A resolute individual like Sá Carneiro will decide for himself when a consensus has been reached. When the prime minister is personally less decisive or, as is more likely the case, lacks authority over his ministers, discussions may become interminable. Under Prime Minister Pinto Balsemão, for example, differences of opinion would very often be thrashed out in long cabinet discussions which occasionally, especially toward the end of his second government, would end in a vote. The amount of time spent on debating legislation in the Cabinet has reduced the latter's role as a collective policymaking body.

The government's own legislative process remains unwieldy. No particular administrative body exists to help ministers draft legislation; they must either rely on their parallel services or on their own ability to do it themselves. Generally, once a bill has been drawn up it goes to the secretary of state to the Cabinet which checks its formal correctness. It is then circulated among the other ministers for their comments or objections. They send it back to the secretary of state and the minister concerned to be passed on to the Cabinet for adoption. Obviously, when differences arise between ministers over legislation involving them and their jurisdiction directly, a compromise will be sought before it goes to Cabinet. However, even if a bill remains contentious it will still go to Cabinet to be debated there; obviously, this is a time-consuming process.

Periodically, a minister will suggest ways of streamlining this procedure, and sometimes these ideas will actually be implemented, but only for the lifetime of that particular government. During the short-lived Mota Pinto government in 1978, the secretary of state to the Cabinet proposed the distinction between secondary or noncontroversial legislation and major bills likely to raise criticism and objections. The first would usually be passed *pro forma* by the Cabinet after circulating among the ministers. In the second case, the secretary of state would attempt to iron out differences of opinion between ministers. If this effort was unsuccessful, the debate would continue in Cabinet. The Sá Carneiro government abandoned this custom. Prime Minister Pinto Balsemão tried to overcome disagreements between ministers by creating a council of secretaries of state to prepare the way for controversial bills before the Cabinet met to discuss them. This institution met with little success. Finally, the first minister of justice in the Central Bloc government, Rui Machete, well placed to assess poorly drafted legislation, criticized the whole process and put forward his own suggestions in an interview with the weekly *O Jornal*.[14] Machete agreed that ministers did not have enough time to evaluate the "avalanche of bills" which circulated, adding that there was too much legislation perhaps "because people continue to measure the activity of a department by the quantity of bills it produces." He proposed following a procedure that is standard in many countries, setting up a legislative policy office within the Department of Justice to make sure bills respected the Constitution and other existing texts.

As these three examples show, reforms have been piecemeal and have never gone beyond tightening up existing practices. As long as ministers insist on their right to have their say, there is little hope of any effective change in the way Portuguese governments work.

The Politics of Making Governments

The president's role in the appointment and dismissal of the government shows how far Portugal has shifted from the so-called semipresidential system of the French Fifth Republic. According to Article 190 of the Constitution, the president must consult the parties represented in the Assembly and consider the election results before appointing a prime minister.[15] With the exception of the "governments of presidential inspiration" in 1978 and 1979, and the rather chaotic situation created with the fall of the second Pinto Balsemão government in 1982, choice of prime minister has been fairly clear.

Since 1976, the creation of governments has followed a very standard pattern. The president appoints the acknowledged leader of the largest party in the Assembly, who then negotiates with his coalition partners. During these negotiations agreement is reached on the future government's program and on the ministerial portfolios to be distributed among the various members of the coalition. Once the government has been formed, the prime minister is officially appointed by the president. He then has ten days in which to present his program before Parliament. Debate on the government's program lasts a maximum of three days. During the debate the opposition parties can present motions calling for the rejection of the program; if such motions are supported by an absolute majority of the members elected to the Assembly the government must resign. Until now, only one government has failed to gain parliamentary support for its program, the first government of presidential inspiration headed by Alfredo Nobre da Costa in 1978. The other two presidential governments were able to remain in power because the motions of rejection against them never received the support of an absolute majority of the members. The government of Sá Carneiro, appointed in January 1980, created a precedent by presenting a motion of confidence on his program, a procedure which has been followed by every government since and which was formally introduced into the Constitution with the revision of 1982.

The president can at best exercise a form of negative discretionary power in the choice of a prime minister. In December 1982, with the fall of the Pinto Balsemão government, President Eanes made it clear that the PSD's choice of Carlos Mota Pinto as future prime minister was unacceptable. This was thought to be a factor in Mota Pinto's final refusal to be the PSD's candidate for that position.[16] The ensuing government crisis put the president in a delicate position. The head of the junior member of the coalition, the CDS, had resigned both from the government and from the leadership of his party. The PSD had put forward the name of a former minister of education, Vítor Crespo, for prime minister, a candidacy which had provoked little enthusiasm either in the PSD itself or in the CDS. If the president refused to appoint Crespo, he could be accused of interfering directly in the internal affairs of the crumbling AD coalition. The following legislative elections would then be fought on the issue of the government versus the president. Only when it became evident that a Vítor Crespo government offered little likelihood of stability, and the threat of dissolution could not force the PSD and the CDS to solve their differences, did the president decide to call for new elections.

Until the legislative elections of December 1979, partisan rivalries affected the composition of governments in a limited way. Mário Soares had formed his first government just with members or supporters of the PS. As the uncontested leader of his party, he only needed to concern himself with balancing internal tendencies. From the collapse of the PS/CDS government in July 1978 until the elections of December 1979, Portugal was in the hands of essentially nonpartisan governments formed on the initiative of the president with little reference to the political complexion of the Assembly and which managed to hold on to power as long as no concerted opposition existed in Parliament.

With the election of the AD, Portugal began the era of coalition governments, which have now become the norm. The parties must now negotiate the composition of the government; this gives rise to problems that affect both government efficiency and stability.

When Francisco Sá Carneiro won the elections in 1979, he attempted to set a pattern of strong government similar in style and method to British practice. Rather than negotiate the division of ministerial offices with the leader of the CDS, Sá Carneiro met with Freitas do Amaral and they jointly formed a government where competence apparently took preference over partisan affiliation.[17] Sá Carneiro also temporarily gave up the presidency of his party to concentrate on the premiership. No prime minister since has enjoyed the unchallenged authority of Sá Carneiro over his parliamentary majority and the free hand to choose ministers and secretaries of state at will. Governments now result from hard bargaining between the parties of the prospective coalition. Party leaders must first take into account pressures within their respective parties and the relative weight of the various factions.

Unlike successive leaders of the PSD, Mário Soares has not suffered the threat of open rebellion since his victory over the ex-Secretariat in May 1981. However, he was unable to totally ignore internal party rivalries. He had to insist that two senior members of the PS leadership, Jaime Gama and António de Almeida Santos, both serious contenders for his succession, join the government for the sake of party unity. Gama had indicated his desire to stay out of the government so that he could strengthen his personal position with the PS, and Almeida Santos, one of the regime's most experienced ministers, reacted by threatening to do the same thing.

Mário Soares could not afford to dispense with the services of two well-seasoned ministers, as he was fully aware that he would have difficulty in replacing them. While party leaders attempt to iron out internal difficulties, they must also give consideration to finding competent people to fill the available posts. The combination of the necessary political and administrative or technical skills to carry out ministerial functions does not come easily in the top echelons of the Portuguese political parties. Faced with this dilemma, government leaders have tended to emphasize technical or formal professional capacity in their choice of ministers and secretaries of state before political ability, with less than satisfying results.[18] Parties usually also seek to fill the posts of heads of ministeral staffs with party members and sympathizers, thus compounding the problem.

Given the relatively small pool of technically competent party leaders, governments have had to look for ministers outside the parties. Thus each government has appointed a certain number of so-called independents, usually identified to some extent with one of the parties of the coalition. Choosing independents also allows the negotiating parties to avoid difficult issues. This happened when the PS and the PSD could not agree on a candidate for the important post of minister of finance and opted for a highly respected civil servant, Ernâni Lopes, Portugal's representative to the EC in Brussels, who enjoyed the doubtful pleasure of being attacked by both the PS and PSD while in office.

Persuading independents to join the government often involves negotiation with the prospective ministers as well. Since they know that government leaders call upon them only out of necessity, they can set their own conditions. When Pinto Balsemão was forced to shuffle his government in the summer of 1982, his new minister of education insisted on choosing his own secretary of state as a condition of acceptance, and the new minister of foreign affairs demanded the right to name his own appointee as the new ambassador to Washington and the creation of a Secretariat of State for Cooperation and Development. The prime minister was then criticized by the PSD's Political Commission for appointing far too many independents at the expense of his own party members.

The bargain between coalition partners also includes the appointment of secretaries and undersecretaries of state, the equivalent of junior ministers, who have the task of assisting the minister at the head of their department. Ministers themselves have little to say in the matter, which can cause tensions when they and their hierarchical subordinates come from different parties, differ over questions of jurisdiction, or are simply personally incompatible. The prime minister, who has little control over the nominees selected by the other parties in the coalition, appoints and dismisses secretaries and undersecretaries of state, who, in turn, cannot resign at will. On the other hand, their term officially ends when their minister leaves office.

During the first year of the PS/PSD government headed by Mário Soares, several departments suffered from the clash between ministers and secretaries of state, but none more than the Ministry of Agriculture, a very important department in Portugal. From the beginning the minister of agriculture, Manuel Soares Costa of the PSD, did not see eye to eye with his PS secretary of state for forestry, António de Azevedo Gomes, who had irritated his own civil servants by moving around various heads of services against the wishes of his minister. Within three months of his appointment, the minister had refused to delegate to Azevedo Gomes the necessary power to implement the government's forestry program, and he followed this action up five months later by systematically cancelling the secretary of state's memos with memos of his own. Azevedo Gomes retaliated by sending bills to the Cabinet without telling his minister, which the Cabinet was forced to ignore. In the meantime, Soares Costa also managed to alienate two of the three other secretaries of state appointed to his department. In the last two months of his office, the minister preferred to avoid the tense atmosphere of his department by working exclusively from his home and stopped signing departmental memos altogether. For almost a year effective operation of agriculture policy came to a halt, including an important agrarian reform bill.

When the governments appointed since 1976 are scrutinized, it becomes rapidly apparent that Parliament has not represented a prime recruiting ground for members of the government. True, the great majority of ministers come from the Assembly or at least have been elected before being appointed, but most secretaries of state have come either from the party ranks or from the civil service without ever serving in the Assembly. In addition, it is rare for ministers and secretaries to continue serving in successive governments. Even the three AD governments in office between January 1980 and December 1982 showed little continuity in ministerial appointments. Furthermore, a junior minister can rarely hope for promotion to a higher position on merit or for reasons of experience. The situation certainly does not contribute to government efficiency.

How Governments Fall

Article 198 of the 1976 Constitution set down three clear causes of automatic government resignation: if the Assembly rejected its program; if it failed to obtain approval for a motion of confidence; or if an absolute majority of the total membership of the Assembly adopted two motions of censure within thirty days of each other. Otherwise, the prime minister could not offically resign of his own accord but had to request dismissal by the President. The 1982 revision simplified this process by allowing a prime minister to resign. It also decreed that the death or the physical incapacity of a prime minister would imply the resignation of the whole government, as would the inception of a new legislature. Now only one motion of censure, supported by an absolute majority of all members of the Assembly, is necessary to bring down the government.

Only two governments have been forced to resign under the circumstances prescribed in the Constitution. The government led by Mota Pinto was dismissed by the president after failing to get approval for its budget and before standing the test of two motions of censure. The government led by Maria de Lourdes Pintasilgo had been appointed with the sole task of preparing early elections. As for the government of Francisco Sá Carneiro, it effectively came to an end with the prime minister's untimely death. All other governments have fallen because of internal difficulties, either between coalition partners or within the party of the prime minister.

As noted, in 1978 the president took the controversial step of dismissing Mário Soares from office on the grounds that he was no longer capable of forming a government that could command a majority in the House. To forestall any possible arbitary move on the part of the president to remove a government he did not like, the authors of the 1982 revision of the Constitution added the following paragraph to Article 198: "The president of the Republic may dismiss the government only when it becomes necessary to secure the regular functioning of the democratic institution and after the Council of State has been consulted."

It is debatable whether such vague terms, which leave the president to decide when the "regular functioning of the democratic institutions" has ceased, have clarified anything. It would certainly not have prevented President Eanes from acting as he did in 1978. As for the Council of State, the president only has to publish its opinion; he does not have to abide by it.

The president's position on this question was clarified during a meeting of the Council of State in January 1985, following a contentious speech on New Year's Eve in which President Eanes not only offered his traditional wishes to the nation for the coming year but also attacked the government for its ineffectiveness. The Council confirmed the obvious: the president might only dismiss a government when the normal functioning of the country's institutions was threatened, and he alone should judge when the point had been reached.

Saving the Government by Shuffle

Under the British Cabinet system, government shuffles usually herald important policy changes, a reordering of policy priorities, or an attempt to improve a particular government's public image. With the advent of coalition governments in Portugal, shuffling has become the ultimate means of solving Cabinet crises without the actual resignation of the government. At the same time, this practice has increased the president's capacity to intervene in the government-making process.

In the summer of 1982, Prime Minister Pinto Balsemão decided to shore up a government sorely weakened by internal squabbles by carrying out a sudden shuffle without informing the president, who learned of the move through the newspapers. Constitutionally, the president could have refused these changes.[19] Upset at this departure from established practice, President Eanes let it be known at the swearing-in ceremony of the new ministers that he considered the shuffle unnecessary.

The president had another opportunity to remind the prime minister of his constitutional powers over changes within a government when Mário Soares was forced to undertake a shuffle after Carlos Mota Pinto, his deputy prime minister, lost the presidency of the PSD in February 1985. The president informed the prime minister that he would not necessarily accept any further shuffle before he lost his constitutional power to dissolve the Assembly, which would normally occur on 14 July 1985. This threat of possible dissolution and ensuing elections put added pressure on the two coalition parties to put aside their public differences for at least five months.

This shuffle forced on a reluctant Mário Soares throws some light on party relations within coalition governments in Portugal and the nature of party politics. An important faction within the PSD put pressure on the party leadership to renegotiate the coalition agreement in favor of PSD policies, such as increased privatization of the public sector and constitutional revision. Given the problems inherent in appointing new ministers, dismissing others, and changing portfolios, which demand a delicate balancing between the parties and finding people with the appropriate qualifications (not to mention the unnecessary upheavals caused within the affected departments), Mário Soares understandably resisted making any major changes in his government.

Events within the PSD gave the prime minister the opportunity to change his government without taking the initiative himself. The defeat of Mota Pinto at the party's National Council meeting in February 1985 implied the resignation of all PSD ministers identified with him. With one exception, the prime minister only had to deal with outgoing ministers from the PSD, including the unpopular minister of education, José Augusto Seabra, who took advantage of the situation to quietly resign before being ousted. However, the PSD insisted that one of the most influential members of the Motapintista tendency, Eugénio Nobre, should only leave his post as secretary of state for public works on condition that his minister, the Socialist João Rosado Correia, go as well. The PSD had been trying to get rid of Rosado Correia for months, partly because he had disavowed his Social Democrat predecessor,[20] but mostly because he had built up a solid following in the north through the largesse of his department and was in a key position to further his own party in the December 1985 local elections. Soares thought he had found the solution to a dilemma which would make him look as if he was punishing a successful minister under constant attack from the PSD and in conflict with a hierarchical subordinate. He would simply switch Rosado Correia with another Socialist, the minister for the sea. Two hours before the swearing-in ceremony Rosado Correia refused the deal and left the government. Rosado Correia's virtual dismissal raised a storm of protest from PS municipalities, many of which sent telegrams of support. Some local Socialists threatened not to campaign for Mário Soares at the presidential elections if Rosado Correia was not reinstated, and one local party even put the flag over its headquarters at half-mast. The unhappy prime minister could only stand by his decision or risk losing some already very unreliable PSD support.

The Problems of Caretaker Governments

When the government falls or resigns, it automatically becomes a caretaker government until a new one is formed. This happens in most parliamentary systems. However, in Portugal the 1976 Constitution was vague on this point, and the concrete problems posed by at least two caretaker governments forced politicians to seriously consider this matter. Article 189/4 of the 1976 Constitution merely stated that if a government resigned or fell "the members of the outgoing government will remain in office until the election of the new government." Nothing was said about its powers, and no mention was made of a government that had been dismissed by the president. The second problem was solved when Mário Soares was dismissed in 1978. The presidential decree confirming the dismissal simply reiterated the wording of Article 189/4 and set the precedent. Practice has also made it clear that a new government exists from the moment a prime minister is formally appointed by the president; however, that government only acquires full powers when its program has been approved by the Assembly. Up to that moment the government is also considered to be in a caretaker position. As for the powers of a caretaker government before the 1982 revision, there seems to be general agreement that it could only undertake those measures that were strictly necessary for the continuance of government and including decree-laws. It could not ask Parliament for any form of legislative authorization, could not present laws before Parliament, nor could it appoint higher civil servants or negotiate international treaties.[21] The 1982 revision elucidated some of these points by adding to Article 189 a clause indicating that the prime minister is to hold office as soon as he is inducted. The same article also declares "before its program has been judged by the Assembly of the Republic or after dismissal, the government shall limit itself to those acts which are strictly necessary to ensure the management of public business."

In 1979 when it was realized that governments of presidential inspiration simply were not feasible and the state of the parties in the Assembly could not produce a viable majority, President Eanes decided to dissolve Parliament. After decreeing dissolution in July 1979, the president then appointed a government to carry out day-to-day business and prepare the elections. The government, headed by Maria de Lourdes Pintasilgo, had to go through the process of being approved by the Assembly, even though it had been dissolved. Was this a caretaker government or not? Observers assumed it was, yet by no stretch of the imagination can one say that this was a government which strictly carried out the day-to-day affairs of the nation. It also embarked on a series of ambitious social programs, including improving old-age pensions. For such presumptions it was criticized by all parties except the Communists. Offically the Pintasilgo government became the Fifth Constitutional Government since 1976, and had received parliamentary approval, though in a negative fashion since a CDS/PSD motion calling for the rejection of its program did not get the support of an absolute majority of the members of the Assembly.

The fall of the Pinto Balsemão government in December 1982 posed another problem. As we have seen, the president attempted to find another acceptable prime minister before making the decision to dissolve the Assembly. In the meantime, it was realized that the government had fallen before its budget could be approved by the Assembly. There would be no question of leaving the country without a budget during the two and a half to three month election campaign. The Constitution clearly precludes caretaker governments from presenting new legislation in Parliament, and yet according to Article 108 of the revised Constitution the budget must be presented by the government and voted by the Assembly. The problem was solved by a series of negotiations between the prime minister and the president where it was decided to present a so-called minibudget in the Assembly which passed this bill the day before it was officially dissolved. The actions of this caretaker government, which lasted more than five months, confirmed that whatever the Constitution might say, the powers of the caretaker government are subject to a very broad interpretation.

Despite its almost fifty years of dictatorship, the Portuguese political system has quickly caught up with the practices of multiparty governments prevalent in most of Western Europe. The authors of the 1976 Constitution and the 1982 amendments may have been aware of the sharp difference between word and deed in the Italian Republic or the French Fourth Republic, but they could not forestall, by a series of measures designed to ensure the supremacy of the executive and in particular the government, the difficulties created by parties divided by factions and tendencies.

With the introduction of true coalition governments in 1980, the PSD has become both the fulcrum and the Achilles' heel of the Portuguese system of government. Since the revolution Portugal has experienced five types of government— PS minority government; an unofficial PS/CDS coalition; governments of presidential initiative; PSD/CDS coalition; and the Central Bloc of the PS and the PSD. Three of these can be considered temporary or transitional solutions. The Socialists themselves have little desire to go it alone, and it is unlikely that the other parties would support such a government. Neither the PS nor the CDS could hope to draw any advantage from what most observers, and especially the members and supporters of both parties, see as an unnatural alliance. As for governments created by the president, at the time they only held on to power through constitutional artifact (parliamentary approval was not even considered), and they never represented a formula for stable government. Nor were they ever intended to. President Eanes confirmed this position when he refused to contemplate a "government of presidential inspiration" to replace Mário Soares's Central Bloc government in the summer of 1985.

Notes

1. Article 110 of the 1933 Constitution also precluded members of the government from sitting in the National Assembly.
2. Jorge Campinos, *O presidencialismo do estado novo* (Lisbon: Perspectivas & Realidades, 1978), p. 232.
3. Marcelo Rebelo de Sousa, *O sistema de governo português antes e depois da revisão constitucional* (Lisbon: Cognitio, 1983), p. 21.
4. CNARPE, "Eanes: A democracia ao serviço de portugal" (Lisbon: CNARPE, 1980).
5. "Discurso proferido pelo presidente da república durante o almoço comemorativo do 3 aniversário da sua reeleição" (Coimbra, 14 January 1984), p. 10. (Mimeographed press release).
6. *Diário de Notícias,* 24 April 1984, p. 8.
7. Luis Salgado de Matos, "Significado e consequências de eleição do presidente por sufrágio universal—o caso português," *Análise Social,* XIX (1983), p. 245.
8. The Estado Novo also gave equal status to parliamentary and government-made legislation. See Marcello Caetano, *Manual de direito administrativo,* vol. 1, 10th ed. (Lisbon: Coimbra Editora, 1973), pp. 90-91.
9. Diogo Freitas do Amaral, *Sá Carneiro, primeiro ministro* (Lisbon: Cognito, 1984), p. 7.
10. Marcello Caetano, *Manual de direito,* 1973, p. 278. See also Lawrence S. Graham, *Portugal: The Decline and Collapse of an Authoritarian Order* (Beverly Hills: Sage Publications, 1975), pp. 29-30.
11. Lawrence S. Graham, "Bureaucratic Politics and the Problems of Reform in State Apparatus," in Lawrence S. Graham and Douglas L. Wheeler (eds.), *In Search of Modern*

Portugal. The Revolution and its Consequences (Madison: University of Wisconsin Press, 1983), p. 232.

12. Decree-law 344-A/83, Article 48.
13. Graham, "Bureaucratic Politics," 1983, p. 236.
14. *O Jornal*, 2 March 1984.
15. Until the 1982 revision he also had to consult the Council of the Revolution.
16. President Eanes had personally chosen Mota Pinto as his prime minister in 1978. However, Mota Pinto had not expected the president to accept his resignation so easily when his government was threatened by two motions of censure in the Assembly; he apparently never forgave Eanes for this show of lack of confidence. In the 1980 presidential elections, Mota Pinto supported General Soares Carneiro against President Eanes.
17. Freitas do Amaral, *Sá Carneiro*, 1984, p. 11.
18. In his unpublished report on Portugal's political class, Vinício da Costa e Sousa has established an "index of technical competence," measured by the number of people with relevant professional skills holding ministerial posts (perfect correlation between the two = 1) and shows that between 1976 and 1984 the index of Portugal's governments only dipped below 0.75 once, with the PS/PSD government formed in June 1983, and even reached a score of 1 with the government led by Maria de Lourdes Pintasilgo in 1979. See Vinício Alves da Costa e Sousa, "Caracterização da classe política portuguesa," mimeo (Lisbon: Instituto Damião de Góis, 1985).
19. Articles 136/g and 190/2 of the 1976 Constitution gave the president the formal power to appoint ministers "at the proposal of the prime minister." The 1982 version maintained this power. According to authoritative sources, this means that the president may refuse to make the suggested appointments, though he has no power to make appointments of his own. See J. J. Gomes Canotilho and Vital Moreira, *Constituição da república portuguesa anotada* (Coimbra: Coimbra Editora, 1980), pp. 282 and 372.
20. Within one month of taking office Rosado Correia had made a detailed report to the Cabinet about a deficit of more than $77 million in the State Secretariat of Public Works, equivalent to a 30 percent spending over the amount allotted to the public works programs, which implied mismanagement by the previous government, or more specifically the previous PSD minister. He also warned that other departments might be in the same plight. Pedro Cid, *O Jornal*, 29 July 1983, p. 7.
21. J. J. Gomes Canotilho and Vital Moreira, *Constituição da república*, 1980, pp. 370-371.

8
The Parliament Without Prestige

Housed in an old monastery which was partly burnt down in the late nineteenth century and only restored in the early 1940s by a regime that had no use for parliamentary democracy, the Assembly of the Republic has emerged as one of Portugal's least understood political institutions. Like all modern parliaments, the Assembly of the Republic, the country's only legislative chamber, has had to adapt to the inexorable expansion of executive power and to the reality of party discipline. However, Portugal's parliamentarians have also had to put up with universally recognized poor working conditions which, despite periodic declarations to the contrary, never feature high on the list of governmental priorities. The 1982 constitutional revision somewhat increased the powers of the Assembly, at least in theory. It strengthened the Assembly's role in the budgetary process, established exclusive legislative powers in certain well-defined areas, and gave Parliament certain powers that formerly belonged to the Council of the Revolution.[1] In the spring of 1984 politicians began the final phase of revising the country's institutions when they rewrote the Assembly's standing orders, or *regimento,* to bring it into line with the Constitution and hopefully to improve the tarnished image of Portugal's parliamentarians. It was expected that the debate would be over by the early summer and the new rules would be adopted by the end of June. But the members raised so much controversy, especially since the main amendments aimed at increasing government control over proceedings and at limiting the powers of the opposition, that the debate dragged on until February 1985.

Organization and Powers of the Assembly of the Republic

Under the 1982 revision legislatures now last four years, unless interrupted by dissolution, ending the curious situation of a legislature which had to complete its official term even if the president had already dissolved it. Sessions are long, lasting from 15 October to 15 June, and the amount of parliamentary business often makes it imperative to extend them for a month or more. Whenever the Assembly is not sitting, many of its duties, except its legislative powers, are exercised by a Permanent Committee chaired by the speaker of the Assembly and made up of its deputy speakers and a number of other members, representing the parliamentary parties according to the principle of proportional representation. The exact number of these is set by the Assembly's standing orders. One of the Permanent Committee's most important powers is that of convening or reconvening Parliament, a power which does not belong to the government constitutionally, though obviously it can use its majority in the Committee to ensure recall of Parliament if necessary. According to Article 177/4 of the Constitution, the president may convene extraordinary sessions of the Assembly but constitutionalists agree that this power is very limited, restricted essentially to matters that need parliamentary authorization.[2]

Normally deputies belong to parliamentary groups (*grupos*), the equivalent of caucuses, which mirror the parties outside Parliament and are firmly under their control. The reality of the parties' hold over their deputies is confirmed by the fact that no deputy may cross the floor to join another group, though he or she may elect to sit as an independent. Often small parties join electoral coalitions headed by larger parties, or even run as independents on a national party slate. Once in the Assembly, the deputies of these small parties may form *agrupamentos*, rather than *grupos*, and enjoy most of the powers of parliamentary groups except the initiating of formal motions to bring down the government. Three such *agrupamentos* existed between 1983 and 1985, the MDP, which ran with the PCP under the APU banner, and the ASDI and the UEDS, both presented on the PS ticket. The Assembly's standing orders even recognized particular rights for a single deputy elected on a party slate; this meant in fact the far-left UDP which regularly got one seat until 1983. Such a deputy has, like his colleagues, the right to join standing committees, to be heard when the parliamentary timetable is set, and to present bills.

The group is the basic unit for parliamentary business. Through the group or the *agrupamento*, deputies join standing committees, have a say on the agenda, ask for debates on government policy (two for each group, one for each *agrupamento* per session), demand the recall of Parliament, request committees of enquiry, exercise the right to initiate legislation, table motions of nonconfidence or of rejection of the government's program, and exercise the right to be informed "regularly and directly by the government on the progress of the main matters of public interest." These powers are not only detailed in the Assembly's standing orders but have also been enshrined in Article 183 of the Constitution. Officially groups elect their own chairman, usually chosen in reality by the party hierarchy, who acts as a parliamentary leader participating in meetings to set the order of business, as party whip, and as the coordinator between the group and the party outside the Assembly.

At the beginning of each session the Assembly elects its speaker and its bureau. The election of the bureau, which oversees the internal administration of the Assembly, normally raises no problems. It is composed of the speaker, the deputy speakers, one member from each of the main parties represented in the Assembly, the secretaries (again one from each party), and until 1985 two deputy secretaries coming from the two main parties. On the other hand, the election of the speaker often involves political considerations, as it affects the relations between the parties forming the governmental coalition. In 1980, the PSD and the CDS agreed that the speaker's office should change annually between the two of them. However, when it came to the CDS's turn to choose the speaker, the PSD refused to support its candidate on the first ballot, claiming that no previous negotiation had been held on who that candidate should be. The following year the CDS returned the compliment by handing in blank votes on the PSD's choice for speaker, complaining that the PSD has violated the agreement. The PSD and the PS came to a similar understanding on a rotating speaker after the elections of April 1983.

Lack of continuity has affected the efficiency of the speaker, not so much in his capacity to chair debates, but as the Assembly's chief administrative officer. Every speaker has his own views on how his duties should be carried out but has little time to act on them before being replaced. There is no room for long-term planning of the Assembly's services, which in turn affects general working conditions. For example, the PSD choice for speaker, Leonardo Ribeiro de Almeida, who presided from 1980 to 1981 and again in 1982, had planned to give deputies more space by extending the parliamentary buildings. These plans were scrapped by his CDS successor. Since the members of the speaker's personal staff are political appointees they leave office when he goes, and new staff members must be trained all over again.

Like most modern parliaments, the Assembly has created a system of standing committees that are becoming increasingly important for carrying out parliamentary business. Committees can have from ten to thirty members; their composition must reflect the representation of parliamentary groups. A deputy may belong to no more than two committees (though provision is made for smaller groups, which have the right to send the same representative to three). The revised *regimento* established thirteen standing committees, organized on a functional basis. They are not all chaired by government supporters, and in 1985 the PCP presided over two: the one on Agriculture and the Sea, and the one on the Condition of Women; and the CDS chaired the committees on Health, Social Security and the Family, Internal Administration and Local Government, and Youth.

The Assembly's standing committees have wide formal powers, since they can be called upon to "give opinions on all problems submitted for their appreciation by the Assembly or by the speaker."[3] In actual fact, they are mainly involved in the legislative process, studying bills at their preliminary stage and then article by article after first reading. Ministers may only attend committee meetings by invitation, but when it commands a majority the government will normally manage to be present to monitor its own legislation. At the various meetings to coordinate the parliamentary groups supporting the government, ministers let it be known that they wish to attend a committee meeting. Thus the committees of the Assembly are unable to show any of the independence displayed by their counterparts under the French Fourth Republic, which often presented revised versions of government bills at variance with the original aims of the government.

Deputies remain divided over the real contribution of committees to parliamentary business. In general, deputies on the government side praise the work of committees, claiming that work is less partisan and proceedings more businesslike in the committees than in the Assembly. Members of the opposition view committees as just another way of imposing the government's will on the Assembly and prefer plenary debates where they have more chance of attracting the attention of the media.

Committees have undoubtedly become more important in Portugal's Parliament; one government supporter suggested to us that their role had become "a question of the survival of the Portuguese parliamentary system." This may be an exaggeration, but it is true that plenary sittings are widely regarded as a futile exercise which has ceased to impress the public, even though many deputies insist that that is where real parliamentary business takes place. The physical conditions in which committee meetings are held leave much to be desired. No specific premises are as yet available, and the members must meet where they can, including in the room where Cabinet meetings are normally held. They do not even have a photocopying machine at their disposal. Under the old *regimento,* committees were not supposed to meet during sittings of the full Assembly; this proved unrealistic as business pressures have forced committees to meet at the same time as plenary sittings. It is still difficult for the public to appreciate what goes on in committees since a record is rarely kept of their meetings in the *Diário da assembleia da república,* the Portuguese equivalent to the Congressional Record. The public must thus rely almost exclusively on the media for information, which is always uncertain as the committees decide for themselves whether meetings are open or in camera.

The PSD speaker elected in October 1984, Fernando Amaral, put some order into committee activity. By the end of the year he announced that committees would provide reports on their activities every two weeks. The new standing orders confirmed the enhanced role of standing committees: their input into the budgetary process was to be institutionalized; they could henceforth meet anywhere in the country; and they could also convene on Saturdays, Sundays, and public holidays.

Until 1985 the Assembly remained absolute master of its own timetable. The chairmen of the various parliamentary groups and *agrupamentos* would meet with the speaker to form the Conference of Chairmen of Parliamentary Groups. On the basis of consensus, the Conference would then adopt the timetable. The government could always insist on priority for what the Constitution calls "matters of national interest requiring urgent settlement,"[4] a phrase open to wide interpretation. During the debate on amendments to the Assembly's standing orders, the government forced through a very important change, hotly contested by the opposition, especially by the PCP. This measure replaced consensus by a weighted vote which now gives each group chairman a number of votes equivalent to his party's numerical strength in Parliament, thereby ensuring complete government control over most business, especially since the government now has the right to participate in the Conference.

All parliamentary groups have a constitutional right to determine the timetable for a certain number of days a year. The old standing orders allowed four days per session for each group supporting the government, six for each opposition group, and two for those parties with only one deputy (or for deputies representing parties which have yet to form a group in Parliament). Above all, this gave the opposition the opportunity to present their own bills. The new *regimento* has tightened the rules for the opposition by restricting the right to set the agenda for six sittings to groups with more than fifty deputies, a position which the PCP and CDS have never achieved, and by completely eliminating the rights of parties with only one representative. Opposition groups or *agrupamentos* with up to twenty-five deputies may organize two sittings per session and those with up to fifty, four. Even the parties supporting the government lose some rights as they set the timetable a maximum of three times a year.

As has been shown, the Assembly's exclusive power to legislate is limited. This power has suffered further erosion with the government's right to request authorization to legislate in matters belonging to the Assembly's "relative right to legislate." Given the strict government control over Assembly business, parliamentary groups have as much chance of seeing their own bills adopted as their counterparts in the majority of other modern parliaments.[5]

Before a bill becomes law it follows a fairly simple, but frequently lengthy, process. After a general debate, and subsequent acceptance, it then goes to committee for detailed scrutiny. The bill can then be returned to the Assembly for final approval without debate. However, once legislation has been approved by the appropriate committee a final vote is often dispensed with. Both the 1976 and 1982 Constitutions are specific regarding labor legislation on which unions and workers commissions must be heard; social security legislation, which must involve consultation with the unions and "other working class organizations"; agrarian reform legislation, on which the Assembly must consult rural workers and small and medium farmer organizations; and legislation affecting autonomous regions, where the latter must also be heard. The form this consultation should take and how much weight should be attached to it is generally not specified.

The 1982 constitutional revision, the 1983 Law on Budget Procedure, and the standing orders adopted in 1985 have increased Parliament's role in budget procedure. Until 1982, the government presented its budget proposals; they were debated and the Assembly then voted a general amount of money for each department. The budget was treated like any other bill, usually after being examined in an ad hoc committee set up for that purpose. The government announced by decree-law exactly how the money would be spent. Under the new rules, the budget (along with a bill laying out the general options of the national plan) first goes to the standing committee on the Economy, Finance, and the Plan and the relevant parliamentary standing committees for their opinions. Each committee must report back within twenty days, to the committee on the Economy, which then has ten days to give a final opinion. The Assembly will then debate the general principles of the budget and the plan for two to five days before voting on them. The Assembly follows this debate with a discussion of the bill, laying out the general options of the national plan and all budgetary proposals involving taxation, borrowing, and other means of raising revenue, article by article. Detailed study of the rest of the budget and the necessary votes for adoption take place in the committee on the Economy. Debate in the Assembly cannot last more than three days, while the committee has a limit of ten days. The committee on the Economy has a further three days to produce a final version of the two bills which are then adopted by the Assembly. The government must now ask for authorization before departments make any changes in their expenditures.

The government has experienced great difficulty in getting its budgets through in time for the beginning of the fiscal year. This has usually meant that the Assembly must vote provisional monthly amounts covering day-to-day expenses. Often the government must also ask for more money than originally provided for, in the form of a supplementary budget. The Central Bloc government claimed an historical first when it got its budget for 1984 adopted by October 1983. Growing tensions within the PSD, differences between the PSD and the PS, and the usual battles between departments prevented that government from repeating the exploit the following year. The Central Bloc government also violated the Law on Budget Procedure, which it had drafted itself, when it announced in August 1984 that with the revisions of Portugal's agreements with the IMF certain budget expenditures could be increased in the area of public works and other public enterprises and made no mention of the need for parliamentary approval.

In a system where the government has so much independent lawmaking power, some provision is necessary for parliamentary control. The Constitution gives the Assembly the right to demand that all decree-laws made in areas which can come under its own jurisdiction be subject to parliamentary ratification. The 1982 revision has simplified this procedure. Now ten members of the Assembly may request that any government decree-law, except one issued under the government's powers of exclusive jurisdiction, be subject to amendment or to a vote refusing ratification during the first ten plenary sittings following its publication. The logic of majority government and party discipline make it highly unlikely that any government will see the Assembly refuse ratification or demand serious amendments, though the situation could occur under a minority government. It is also true that any future Assembly has the right to pass a law effectively cancelling the previously contested decree-law. However, ratification or the request for amendment remains an important instrument of parliamentary control; in effect, it allows the opposition the chance to attack the government and to publicize a decree-law which might otherwise only come to light through close scrutiny of the *Diário da república,* the official bulletin in which all laws and decrees must be published.

The Deputy and the Image of the Assembly of the Republic

In Portugal, as in most Western democracies, members of Parliament have become easy targets for the media and have absorbed much of the blame for the poor functioning of Portugal's political institutions. They have been accused of being underworked and overpaid and acting only as party mouthpieces. Deputies complain that they are, on the contrary, poorly paid, that they lack the necessary conditions to carry out their work effectively and, at least in the case of the opposition, that the government exercises too much control over Parliament. Both sides have a case; much of the problem lies in the structure of the Assembly and in the popular expectations of deputies' proper functions.

Portuguese deputies work under very trying conditions. Very few have individual offices and must therefore either conduct their business, including meeting constituents and members of the press, in one of the big rooms set aside for the parliamentary group or borrow the office of one of the group's official leaders. Often only one telephone exists to receive the messages for all the members of any one parliamentary group and secretarial staff is minimal.

Deputies' salaries have always raised controversy. The basic salary is tied to that of top civil servants, with supplementary fixed amounts for attending sittings of the Assembly and committee meetings. In 1984 a hardworking deputy would earn little more than $500 a month during the parliamentary session. Not surprisingly, Portuguese deputies try to augment their incomes in various ways. The first of these, and the most widely practiced, is a second job. Only civil servants are legally excluded from exercising their profession while in Parliament (though university teachers may continue to teach with no pay). There is nothing to stop lawyers, businessmen, and journalists from carrying on as usual every day in Lisbon or periodically elsewhere. Deputies also go on parliamentary missions, either within Portugal or abroad, for which they receive a statutory per diem.[6]

In the summer of 1981 the Assembly passed a bill awarding deputies a pay increase of 140 percent (at a time when pay increases were officially limited to 16 percent nationally). This raised such an outcry that Prime Minister Pinto Balsemão was forced to postpone (though not cancel) the raises as the country was in a period of austerity. Finally the law was vetoed by the president and shelved.

In October 1984, the government announced its intention to introduce another bill to increase deputies' salaries substantially. Under the new scheme, they would receive a basic monthly salary of $500 with $75 for expenses (still less than 25 percent of the combined income and expense allowance of their British colleagues) and a daily stipend—$20 plus the equivalent of an extra day per week for deputies outside the Lisbon metropolitan area and only $6 with no extra for the others—for each day the Assembly or their committees were in session. They would also get 1/50 of their monthly salary for each committee sitting they attended. The final bill included a generous pension plan, whereby any deputy who had served a total of eight years (not necessarily consecutively), since the election of the Constituent Assembly in April 1975, could expect a life pension equal to 4 percent of his salary for each year served and which would double once he reached sixty. On request, a deputy's surviving spouse, minor or incapacitated offspring, or parents or grandparents in his charge could claim 75 percent of a deceased deputy's pension benefits. Despite an impending presidential veto, the bill was made retroactive to January 1985. As expected, President Eanes cast a political veto against the bill in February 1985 and denounced its provisions for pensions. The PS/PSD majority in the Assembly simply overrode the veto and maintained the bill in its original form.

Since many deputies consider their work in Parliament as a part-time job, it is not unusual to hear complaints of poor attendance in the Assembly. During the debate on the revision of the Assembly's standing orders in 1984, which ironically also attracted few participants, much of the discussion focused on the frequent inability to find a quorum. According to Article 63 of the old standing orders, at least 25 percent of the membership had to be present for plenary sittings before orders of the day, and at least one-third for business taking place after orders of the day. More than half the deputies were supposed to be present for votes, except on questions of procedure. For committees, the quorum was set at half the membership. The new rules relaxed these conditions, so that the Assembly can now function with 20 percent of its members, though the quorum for votes remains the same. Committees need one-third of their members present to hold a meeting, but can only vote if more than half of them are there.

In addition to frequent absences, the practice of "ghost" presences has also been developed. Deputies appear to sign the sheet issued at the beginning of each sitting to indicate attendance and then leave. The sheet can be signed at any time during the sitting. Article 163 of the Consitution stipulates that a member who "exceeds the number of absences provided for in the rules of procedure" should lose his seat. This means missing fifteen consecutive sittings. The sanction is rarely if ever applied.

Deputies can also circumvent these flexible rules on absences. They can take advantage of the right to be temporarily suspended or replaced for a period of up to a year without losing the right to take their seat back again. Originally the right to be replaced depended on having a justifiable reason; the standing orders laid down three of them: prolonged serious illness, urgent professional activity, and the exercise of specific functions within the party. Deputies and parties have interpreted this provision very liberally and replacements have now become a common occurence in the Assembly. Deputies can ask to be replaced for as little as two or three days, and replacements have been increasingly used as a means to avoid the full weight of party discipline in the Assembly.

The parties have become concerned about the deputies' continued absences and are conscious of the unfavorable image that such practices give of the Assembly. In the spring of 1981 the PSD group leader introduced a series of measures in his group to ensure greater participation in parliamentary proceedings. They included persuasion, the signing of additional presence sheets, the need for deputies to justify their absences in writing, preferably with a day's notice, and even fines. These rules had little effect. A year later five PSD deputies were warned that they could not continue to stay away so frequently and another eighteen were told that any future absences would have to follow party rules.[7]

Various factors have contributed to the phenomenon of a badly attended Assembly. Inadequate working conditions and poor pay make the job of deputy increasingly unattractive. The parties must also share much of the blame, for expecting so many of their parliamentarians to remain full-time party activists. The situation is aggravated by the electoral system and by total party control over deputies who have little or no direct links with their constituents. If the electorate in a country with a large rural population does not know which deputy represents it, especially when deputies and parties manipulate party representation in the Assembly at will, then one can hardly be surprised when the voters feel alienated from their representative. Deputies themselves have no incentive to "meet the people." Attempts to correct the situation have failed. For example, the CDS tried to institutionalize monthly meetings between its deputies and their constituents, but quickly had to abandon the experiment when the deputies showed no interest. The deputies themselves feel unappreciated and exist to be disposed of at will by the parties in an Assembly increasingly dominated by the executive.

Despite the negative image of the Portuguese deputy reflected in the media, and the outrage at any suggestions of an increase in his salary, public opinon reacts generally favorably toward the Assembly as an institution. Our survey revealed neither strong antiparliamentary feeling nor an exaggerated view of the Assembly's role as an institution of government. Less than 20 percent saw it as the body that really ruled the country. On the other hand, 64 percent thought the Assembly either extremely necessary or very necessary for the life of the country, against only 14 percent who declared otherwise. Those who considered Parliament necessary gave various reasons for its importance as shown in Table 8.1.

Those who expressed little belief in the Assembly gave answers that suggested a high degree of frustration, rather than an assessment of the effectiveness or noneffectiveness of the functions of Parliament as such, and showed little understanding of its role in the political system (see Table 8.2).

Table 8.1
Why Do You Consider the Assembly Extremely or Very Necessary?
(multiple answer possible)

It approves laws	21%
It solves problems	15
It discusses problems	29
It defends democracy	7
It represents the people	12
It controls government actions	2
It governs the country better	7
Other	2
No response	15

Table 8.2

Why Do You Consider the Assembly Not Very Necessary or Unnecessary? (multiple answer possible)	
Its solves nothing	50%
Unnecessary	8
The deputies do not agree	7
It only wants money	13
The deputies defend their own interests	7
Other	2
No response	20

Relations between the Assembly and the Executive

Both arms of the executive, the presidency and the government, are formally subject to the control of the Assembly, and in turn dispose of constitutional means for influencing Parliament. However, as long as the president remains above the parties, his relationship with the Assembly will be basically that of two rival, separate institutions, whereas the government can always count on party discipline to ensure its political supremacy. This vital difference between the two situations becomes even clearer when the way the two institutions relate to the Assembly is analyzed.

Parliament exercises above all formal powers of control over the president. The Assembly, or its Permanent Committee, grants him permission to travel outside Portugal on official missions or unofficial trips lasting more than five days. He must also seek the Assembly's authorization to declare a state of siege or emergency, as well as for declarations of peace and war. In both of these cases, the government only intervenes to give its nonbinding opinion. Finally, it is up to the Assembly to initiate impeachment proceedings against a president accused of any criminal acts in the exercise of his duties for trial before the Supreme Court of Justice. As for the president, he disposes of essentially negative powers vis-à-vis Parliament. Article 136d of the Constitution gives the president the right to direct messages to the Assembly, but these take place under very restricted circumstances: to announce his resignation and to declare his decision to veto a bill. Only the latter can be considered a means of influencing the Assembly. As noted, the power of the president to reconvene Parliament is also very strictly controlled.

The new Constitution has enlarged the president's power of dissolution. He no longer depends on the favorable opinion of any institution and is under no constitutional obligation to dissolve the Assembly. The only constitutional limits on the power of dissolution are such that an Assembly may not be dissolved during a state of siege or emergency, nor within six months of being elected nor during the last six months of a presidential mandate. The president must also seek the opinion of the Council of State and the parties before proceeding. These opinions do not bind him. When President Eanes consulted the Council of State on whether he should or should not dissolve the Assembly of the Republic in January 1983, the Council voted eight to seven against dissolution. He went ahead with it anyway. Since 1976 the Assembly has been dissolved three times; on all occasions the president claimed that effective government had become impossible. Thus the right of dissolution remains a very powerful weapon in the hands of any president.

The other significant presidential power, the right to veto legislation, has been the subject of much controversy. Under the 1976 Constitution, laws approved by Parliament and decree-laws were sent both to the president and the Council of the Revolution; the Council had five days in which to inform the president about their constitutionality. Then the president had a period of fifteen days to promulgate or veto the bill after hearing the opinion of the Council of the Revolution. A vetoed bill would then go back to the Assembly which would normally have to confirm the decision by an absolute majority of all its members, or, in certain circumstances, confirm their earlier decision by a qualified majority of two-thirds of the deputies present. By taking his time to promulgate a law, the president could exercise a de facto pocket veto since no mechanism existed to force the promulgation of a law. The pocket veto was abolished by the 1982 constitutional revision. The president now has twenty days from the moment he receives a bill (or from the moment when a decision has been rendered by the Consitutional Court on its constitutionality) to promulgate or veto it. This presidential right to veto bills has become a very powerful political weapon. The opposition will put pressure on the president to veto or to submit to the Constitutional Court legislation that it considers either dangerous or highly desirable. The exercise of this right also allows the president to score political points or keep his constituents happy. Such an instance occurred when the president vetoed, unsuccessfully, the Law on National Defense in the winter of 1982 under pressure from the military hierarchy. On the other hand, the decision to send a bill to the Constitutional Court gives the president a chance to avoid taking a stance on controversial issues. The right of referral to the Court allowed the president to sidestep a potential dilemma when confronted with the law on abortion in early 1984. President Eanes sent it to the Constitutional Court, knowing that many of his more conservative followers were against it while his supporters on the left fervently backed it. Since he could not afford to alienate either group by refusing to act, the Constitutional Court provided a convenient solution since the president must abide by its decisions.

Deputies dispose of a whole range of instruments to control the government, both individually and collectively. They can ask questions, as long as they are submitted at least eight days in advance. Instead of a daily question time as in Britain, the Assembly sets aside one sitting every two weeks for members' questions. This has not yet become a regular event and many questions remain unanswered. Since the government is usually flooded with questions it can carefully choose the ones it wishes to take up. Each parliamentary group also has the right to initiate a two-day debate on government policy called an *interpelação*. The *interpelação* is taken seriously by the government, which may treat it as a debate on a motion of censure, even though it does not end with a vote. As this type of debate is still not widely used its infrequent occurence becomes news and helps to breaks the general monotony of reporting on Parliament.

Groups and *agrupamentos,* standing committees, thirty deputies or more, and the prime minister may call for a parliamentary committee of inquiry. Under the new regulations, if one-fifth or more of the members of the Assembly make such a request it must be granted, though each deputy can only do so once every session. According to Article 251/1 of the *regimento,* parliamentary inquiries are undertaken to verify how the Constitution is being respected and to oversee acts of the government and administration. These committees enjoy the same powers as the judicial authorities and present their findings in the form of a report which is first published in the *Diário da assembleia da república* and then debated in Parliament. Committees of inquiry are frequently established and are a favorite instrument of the opposition, especially the PCP. Invariably, the committee either gets bogged down in procedural wrangles and delaying tactics by government supporters or more often meets so infrequently that it is unable to carry out its mandate properly.

Given the relative ineffectiveness of these potentially useful instruments of parliamentary control, attention tends to focus on the big debates, discussion of the new government's program, votes of confidence, and motions of censure. Only one vote of confidence has actually brought about the fall of a government, that of Mário Soares in 1977. As in most multiparty parliamentary systems, the vote of confidence is aimed much more at the parties supporting the government than at the opposition. In early June 1984, Prime Minister Mário Soares surprised observers and all his parliamentary supporters by presenting a vote of confidence in the Assembly, even though he enjoyed an overwhelming majority. The motion was directed at the PSD whose dissidents had been pressuring the party leader and deputy prime minister, Mota Pinto, to push for a Cabinet shuffle. The prime minister's parliamentary maneuver did not achieve its objective of forcing the PSD back into line and of strengthening the cohesion of the coalition. Despite a decision by the PSD's Political Commission to force all its deputies to support the motion at least fifteen members of the party asked for a temporary suspension of their mandate so they could avoid this confrontation.

Any parliamentary group or 25 percent of the members of the Assembly may present a motion of censure against the government. Debate will then take place forty-eight hours later and last for a maximum of three days. If the motion is approved by an absolute majority of the members of the Assembly, the government must resign. The Constitution says nothing about the status of a motion of censure approved by a majority of the members present, but presumably no government unable to muster sufficient support to defeat such a motion could remain politically viable.

Beyond the formal mechanisms that ensure the government's ascendancy over the Assembly lies party discipline. This does not concern merely the parliamentary group but above all the party outside Parliament. Normally, of course, the party leadership in Parliament works hand in hand with the hierarchy outside; frequently the parliamentary leadership simply acts as a relay to ensure that party policy is strictly adhered to.

Parties dispose of varied controls and sanctions in the Assembly. Most widely cited is the practice of asking all deputies to sign a blank letter of resignation which can be brought out at the appropriate time to put pressure on a particularly recalcitrant individual. However, there seems to be little evidence that this measure is actually ever used, even in serious cases of discipline, and most parties deny that this practice even exists. Most controls and sanctions are much less severe but probably just as effective. Through the group chairman, the party may control deputies' participation in debates and not allocate time to one known to oppose the party's position. The deputy can always claim the right to speak as an individual if he feels particularly strongly on any topic, though he may have some difficulty in getting recognized. The most usual sanction is to inform a deputy that he has been replaced for an upcoming debate where he intends to speak against the party position. In extreme cases a deputy who has refused to bow to party pressure and has openly flouted party discipline can be sanctioned by being replaced for an indefinite period. This happened in the case of three deputies who had refused the PSD's strict instructions to vote against the bill on abortion in February 1984. These measures did not satisfy the most zealous supporters of party discipline, and the chairmen of the PSD parliamentary group suggested that a file be prepared on each deputy to be used when preparing future lists of candidates so that the party could veto the "absent, uninterested and undisciplined." This suggestion was considered excessive by the majority of his colleagues. The PS demands that all speeches made by deputies in important debates be cleared first by the group's leadership.

In the absence of any established conscience clause, deputies unhappy with party policy have found other ways to evade party discipline. Occasionally, if they feel obliged to speak out they may just ignore party discipline and insist on their right to address the Assembly, even going so far as to vote against the party line or to abstain. But in most cases, deputies will choose less drastic means of registering their protest. They may miss an important debate and stay away for the vote. They can also emphasize their opposition to the party position by asking to be replaced for that particular debate or even just for the vote. Others may feel the need to make the whole exercise look ridiculous by making declarations in Parliament in obvious opposition to the party position and then proceeding to vote as the party has demanded. And yet others will keep these statements for the press, making it clear where they really stand.

Problems of party discipline become especially acute when the majority of the parliamentary group does not belong to the majority faction that controls the party. This happened in the PS during the second legislature when the parliamentary group opposed Mário Soares and the official party position over the constitutional revision of 1982. Though these deputies finally voted in favor of the constitutional revision, their behavior in Parliament left no doubts about their opposition to it. Tension between the parliamentary group and the party hierarchy reached such heights that the party's Political Commission advised the speaker that the party had decided to change the leader of the parliamentary group. In doing so, the PS showed that irrespective of what the *regimento* might decide about group chairmen being elected by members, the party outside Parliament had the final say. The speaker aquiesced to this violation of the rules in acknowledging the reality of party power over the rights of deputies. During the third legislature, elected in April 1983, a majority of the members of the PSD parliamentary group joined factions hostile to the party's leader, Mota Pinto, and tensions between that majority and the party's leadership were reflected in the vote of confidence imposed by Mário Soares which was discussed earlier.

As most governments since January 1980 have been coalitions, some mechanism has been necessary to ensure coordination between the parties supporting the government. This is achieved in three ways. Occasionally the groups will meet as a whole with members of the government to discuss a particular piece of legislation, and this can operate as a sort of sounding board. Coordination is also carried out on a more regular basis through the weekly meeting between chairmen of the parliamentary groups supporting the coalition and members of the government. Finally, a minister is assigned to watch over relations between the majority parties and the government. Until June 1982, this function was carried out by a minister directly attached to the prime minister's office. Since then a minister of parliamentary affairs has been appointed. This minister combines the duties of a parliamentary leader and chief government whip. He makes sure that the government has a majority and that ministers are available when their presence is called for. He also keeps the government informed about Assembly business and advises the majority parties of the government's position on any particular issue. The Central Bloc government considered this job very important and delegated a senior minister to look after relations with Parliament; it also appointed a secretary of state to assist him and oversee the day-to-day running of government/Assembly relations.

The Rebirth of Parliament?

"Finally Parliament exists," such was the optimistic comment of the director of the *Diário de Notícias* at the end of a long and heated debate on first reading of the government's bill on Internal Security and Civil Protection.[8] Beyond the importance of this particular bill for the future of the country lie the lessons it holds for the Portuguese parliamentary system.

The first hint that the government was preparing a tough law on internal security appeared in the newspapers in late March 1984, but only at the end of May was the public informed that the Cabinet was already discussing the second version of a bill that would be presented in the Assembly in June. It was in the context of terrorist attacks, including a dramatic bank robbery and attempts on the lives of managers of state enterprises, that the police began to put pressure on the government, and particularly on the minister of the interior, for a law giving them a freer hand to fight terrorism and apprehended subversion. The first draft of the bill, based on a report from the attorney general's office, was rejected by several influential ministers (including the second-highest-ranking Socialist in the government, António de Almeida Santos, minister of state and minister for parliamentary affairs), who strongly objected to several unconstitutional articles in the bill. The second version was not much more satisfactory, and Almeida Santos threatened to withhold his signature from the final draft if further improvements were not made. Mário Soares had no choice but to ask his minister of the interior to tighten it up. The bill that went before the Assembly gave sweeping powers to the prime minister, the minister of the interior, and the police forces; it provided for telephone tapping, mail opening, house searches without warrants, preventive detention of suspects, police access to computers and to other information, the possible suspension of public meetings, and special penalities for public servants who refused to cooperate with police inquiries. In a country that had overthrown a dictatorial regime only ten years before, the bill touched on a very sensitive nerve. Understandable opposition came from many quarters, not just from left-wing and liberal intellectuals but also from much of the press, and in particular from influential papers such as *Diário de Notícias, Expresso,* and *O Jornal.* The Press Council also expressed reservations as it worried about the constitutional rights of journalists, and the Union of Prosecuting Counsels' executive denounced the bill's "eminently authoritarian and repressive" character.

To understand the government's determination to push the bill through Parliament, whatever the opposition, it must be remembered that the bill was being debated in the political context of the government's falling popularity and the upcoming presidential elections. Public opinion had also began to doubt the government's effectiveness. The bill on security appeared as an opportunity to create the image of a strong and decisive government, led by a forthright prime minister and likely presidential candidate. By the end of the debate on the first reading a month later, it was by no means certain that the government had made a convincing case.

The government knew it could rely on public apathy, which was confirmed by the total failure of a demonstration against the bill in July 1984 organized by the CGTP, the PCP, and left-wing intellectuals. But the bill met with resistance not only from the opposition parties but also from within the parties of the coalition. It also felt indirect pressure from the president who refused to comment publicly on a bill he had never received, and who let it be known that he could be prepared to veto any such bill if he thought it violated the Constitution. He did not hesitate to grant long interviews to groups created for the purpose of fighting the bill, never denying their revelations about his strong reservations about such a bill.

As soon as the bill was presented in the Assembly, prominent Socialists and Social Democrats announced their opposition to it and remained unmoved even after a four-hour joint meeting of the PSD and PS parliamentary groups addressed by Mota Pinto, Almeida Santos, and Minister of the Interior Eduardo Pereira. Within the PS the opposition was led by Mário Sottomayor Cardia, a former minister of education and a well-known moderate, who attacked the bill for its infringement upon constitutional rights. He announced that he would introduce his own version of the bill, split into four separate parts, with the main emphasis on the fight against terrorism. To forstall a crisis within the PS, a meeting of the Political Commission was called, against the wishes of Mário Soares. After a lengthy debate it gave half-hearted support to the government's bill.[9] A task force, including Sottomayor Cardia, was set up to monitor the bill and propose amendments that would meet most of Cardia's objections. Cardia then agreed to withdraw his four bills. However, dissatisfaction continued to manifest itself within the PS parliamentary group; soon pressure was being put on the dissidents to refrain from showing their opposition in the Assembly. Sottomayor Cardia, obviously unconvinced that any profound changes were going to be made in the bill, insisted on his right to speak as an individual deputy, without using the time alloted to his parliamentary group, despite attempts to silence him. It was then rumored that one particularly fervent Socialist supporter of the government had carefully noted the names of the twenty-four PS deputies who had applauded Sottomayor Cardia's speech in the Assembly and duly handed the list over to Mário Soares. Depite threats from the party leadership, Cardia, supported from the beginning by another prestigious Socialist deputy, Manuel Alegre, and five other members of the PS parliamentary group, finally voted against the bill on first reading. Two others abstained, fourteen declared that they voted for the bill only out of party solidarity, eight stayed away, and one, Manuel Tito de Morais, the speaker, whose opposition to the bill was well known, used his official position as the reason for not participating in the vote. Criticism of the seven rebels in the Political Commission was surprisingly mild and no sanctions were taken against them.

Opposition within the PSD was as great. Members of the parliamentary group showed an equal lack of enthusiasm and several long meetings were held to make them toe the line. Possibly fearing for his authority over the party, Mota Pinto preferred not to involve the party's Political Commission in the debate and gave orders that a former minister of the interior and vice-president of the party, who had already expressed his opposition to the bill on television, should not speak in the debate. On the other hand, pressure to amend the bill from the PSD parliamentary group proved more effective than that from within the PS. The PSD minister of justice, Rui Machete, announced on the last day of the debate that the government would introduce four important changes in the bill at the committee stage, thereby profoundly modifying it. The promise of the amendments was enough to ensure that no PSD deputy disobeyed party discipline, but it did not prevent twenty of them from joining fifteen Socialist deputies in signing a counter-declaration that they only had voted for the bill because of the assurances given by Machete.

In the Assembly itself the battle was fought in a classic parliamentary style. The PCP and the MDP reacted immediately to the bill by presenting a motion calling for its rejection on constitutional grounds. They then introduced a series of delaying tactics which held up the debate for three weeks. The CDS preferred the method of "constructive opposition" and denounced the tactics of the PCP. The

CDS objected to lack of any judicial controls on police actions and the possible infringement upon constitutional rights and introduced a more restrictive bill aimed at combining the need to fight terrorism with constitutional guarantees. It then suggested that if such guarantees were written into the government's bill the CDS could support it; otherwise it would remain adamant in its opposition. As an alternative, it appealed to the government to unite behind the CDS bill, an offer that was turned down. Two days before the end of the debate, the CDS finally declared that it would vote against the government's bill because of the absolute refusal to incorporate the CDS proposals into it.

Because of the PCP's successful stalling tactics and the problems within the PS and PSD groups, the government was forced to request that the parliamentary session be extended until 22 July, more than a month beyond the normal ending of the session. The Assembly's bureau, led by the speaker, suggested that the final vote could be held over until October, but the government refused and advised that it was prepared to hold all-night sittings if necessary to get the debate out of the way before the summer recess. In one final attempt to delay the vote on the bill, the UEDS and ASDI proposed sending the bill back into committee before the end of the first reading. The speaker announced his support for this move but it was rejected by the PS group, with the support of the PSD and the CDS. So, with over sixty of its supporters indicating their dissatisfaction with the proposed legislation, the government got its way; the bill passed on first reading and was then referred to an ad hoc committee of seventeen members, nine of whom came from the government side, to be studied alongside the bills presented by the CDS and the ASDI on the same subject.

In the end, whatever the merits or defects of this bill, the government achieved one overriding objective. It avoided losing face by being forced to withdraw the bill before a vote was taken in the Assembly, or worse, possible defeat. To assert its authority, the government had to resort to a rather curious procedure. It admitted that the bill was faulty and needed amendment, and by a series of leaks and the declaration by Rui Machete let it be known what form these would take. But it insisted that changes to the bill could only be brought in at the committee stage. As opposition grew, the goverment dug in its heels and made retreat even more difficult. In doing so it accomplished the opposite of what had been intended and failed miserably in its aim of projecting the image of a strong government.

The debate over the bill on security showed that the Assembly could manifest the same vitality as any other parliamentary institution. The two main opposition parties played their role by prolonging the debate so that the public could become fully aware of the issues involved. But the most interesting development came within the parliamentary groups supporting the government coalition. Open opposition of a few, who ignored party discipline over a question of principle, and the less public opposition of many more, forced the government to promise changes which profoundly modified the original bill.

The bill on internal security quietly disappeared from the Portuguese political scene. The ad hoc committee which was supposed to report on it in October 1984 rarely met. In the spring of 1985, the media hinted that a totally revised version of the bill would be discussed in committee, but it died with the fall of the Central Bloc government in June 1985.

Formally, the Portuguese Assembly of the Republic has the necessary powers to carry out its functions of legislation, supervision of the executive, and control of the public purse. The increasing role of the executive has followed the general trend experienced in all parliamentary democracies. Even the peculiarly Portuguese distinction between Assembly-made law and governmental legislation resembles the practices of the French Fifth Republic. If the Assembly remains a "Parliament without prestige," it is not because of restrictions contained in the Constitution or in the *regimento*. More attention must be paid to the deputies' material conditions, not just to their salaries, which can attract few full-time politicians of sufficient calibre, but also to secretarial staff, office space, and general support services.

Such changes would not settle the real source of the Assembly's woes: this is, of course, the hold the parties have over their deputies, especially on the government side. No one can expect party discipline to disappear from modern parliaments. It constitutes the very backbone of the organization of parliamentary business. However, one may distinguish between the imperatives of party discipline and the disposal of a deputy's seat at the party's convenience, to the point of rendering the notion of representation in Parliament almost meaningless. Moreover, discipline is applied selectively and not always to the advantage of the reputation of the Assembly. Any deviation from the party line, even on questions of principle, will be strongly sanctioned unless there is a widespread, uncontrollable revolt. Little or nothing happens to the deputy who simply neglects his parliamentary duties.

Notes

1. The powers transferred from the Council of the Revolution to the Assembly include: approval of military treaties, organization and discipline of the armed forces, authorizing the president of the Republic to declare a state of emergency or siege or to declare war and make peace.

2. See J. J. Gomes Canotilho and Vital Moreira, *Constituição da república portuguesa anotada,* pp. 354-55. These instances include requesting permission to declare a state of emergency or siege and the vote on a newly appointed government's program.

3. *Regimento da assembleia da república* (as revised in 1985), Article 38(f).

4. Article 179/2 of the Constitution.

5. In the second legislature, 1980-1983, only twenty-five out of a total of 399 non-government bills were adopted or presented, see *Avante!/Suplemento,* 3 March 1983, p. 3.

6. At the end of 1984, the speaker announced that steps would be taken to end possible abuses. Deputies would no longer be able to go on such trips without permission from the speaker or without informing the Assembly. They would also have to produce a report within five days of their return, which would include details on the initiatives taken, the results of the trip on the country concerned, and the national impact of the trip.

7. Fernando Antunes, "Absentismo preocupa os partidos," *O Jornal,* 23 April 1982.

8. "Afinal o parlamento existe," *Diário de Notícias,* 28 July 1984.

9. The final resolution supporting the government was passed by twenty-six votes to one with ten abstentions. Less than half of the Political Commission's 107 members actually attended the meeting. *Diário de Notícias*, 5 July 1984.

9
The Parties and the Media

Like the masters of the Estado Novo, the politicians of postrevolutionary Portugal view the media as a weapon too potent to escape government control. The Salazar-Caetano era emphasized the need for censorship to protect the people from all potential sources of social and political unrest. The media were not used to mobilize support for the regime, but as a means to silence its critics, however mild. The newspapers, television, and radio of pre-1974 Portugal promoted a bland image of a society where nothing untoward ever happened. Unsettling domestic news items such as suicides, scandals, or even disturbances at soccer matches never reached the papers, let alone the even more strictly controlled electronic media. The Portuguese people could be forgiven for mistrusting their news sources and viewing their journalists with scepticism. Events since the revolution have done little to shake their attitudes.

Freedom of the press became one of the first conquests of the 25 April, but soon a bitter fight for control of information broke out with the Communists as one of the main protagonists. Their opponents accused them of using the media as part of a general strategy to establish a "People's Democracy" in Portugal. After the revolution, the media remained the focus of political controversy as successive governments forgot their leaders' earlier declarations about the sublime value of the freedom of the press and in turn attempted to control radio and television and to neutralize their critics in the widely circulated state-owned newspapers.

The Revolution and the Battle for the Media

In its original program, the MFA declared the abolition of censorship among its "immediate measures." But it also called for the creation of an ad hoc committee to control the press, radio, television, theater, and cinema to "safeguard military secrets and to prevent disturbances which could be provoked in public opinion by ideological aggressions from the most reactionary sections of society." The military respected these principles to the letter when they took power; however, they found them difficult to apply as journalists demanded total freedom of expression.

As the revolution developed, the ideological battle within the media was fought at all levels. News staff, printers, and distributors all believed they had the right to participate in defining the ideological orientation of the newly liberated media, resorting at times to strikes, demonstrations, occupations, and sequestrations to back their positions. Two irreconcilable conceptions of the role of the press in society dominated these struggles. The PCP, the far left, and their supporters in the MFA saw the media above all as an instrument in the service of the revolution. The PS and the parties to their right advocated the pluralist, liberal model prevalent in European democracies. Both sides were convinced that through the media they would succeed in imposing their own vision of the new Portugal.

During this period, the political parties began to organize themselves within the newspapers, and the PCP appeared to be among the best organized to undertake such an operation. Other parties also attempted to control particular papers or to influence the news on radio and television. Despite this apparent confusion and the frantic jockeying for positions, the provisional government drew up a new press law, adopted in February 1975, which has remained in force ever since, with some modifications, despite later government attempts to tighten it up.

Although the new law was drafted during the fight for media control, it firmly reflected a liberal approach close to the Western European model. In some ways it went even further. For example, it gave a newspaper's editorial board the power of veto over the appointment of a newspaper's director. It assured the journalists' right to access to sources of information and the privilege of professional confidentiality. It also created a Press Council along British lines, but with the difference that it also included representatives of the various political parties. The new press law put an end to the MFA's ad hoc committee.

Less than a month after the publication of the press law, an important event for the future of Portugal's media took place. A large part of the press along with the banks were nationalized in the wake of the attempted right-wing coup of 11 March 1975. This happened simply because most of the press was owned by economic groups, through their control of the banking system. This measure intensified the already fierce struggle for control of the media which reached its height during the summer of 1975, especially with the *República* affair.

The daily *A República* had been founded in 1911 and during the 1960s and early 1970s had become the voice of the non-Communist opposition to the Salazar and Caetano regimes. During the late 1960s it was taken over by Socialists and now reflected the views of the PS. Latent tension over editorial policy between the paper's editors, who tended to openly support the PS and Mário Soares, and the workers' commission, controlled by far leftists, came to a head in May 1975. The workers' commission objected to an article hostile to the actions of the Intersindical on 1 May which had prevented Mário Soares from addressing a meeting organized to celebrate that event. The commission called a strike and demanded the dismissal of the newpaper's director. The printers then occupied the paper's premises, appointed another director and began publishing their own version of the paper. The PS organized a demonstration to defend *its* newspaper. The Council of the Revolution finally intervened and ordered the paper closed down. From then on, the issues assumed political overtones that attracted the attention of the international press.

The question seemed so simple: freedom of the press versus totalitarian control. Mário Soares accused the PCP of trying to gag the media by taking over one of the few newspapers left in Lisbon not already under its thumb. The Communist party, which only held a minority position in the workers' commission, had not instigated the affair but was now caught in an impossible position. If it supported Mário Soares it would lose its leadership over the left in favor of its far-left rivals. However, by refusing to condemn the action of the workers' commission, it left itself open to the charges of its accusers. Whatever the truth of the matter, and it is still a subject of controversy in Portugal, this event heralded the decline of the Communist role in the revolution since it effectively mobilized public opinion at home and abroad against it.

There is little doubt that the PCP had succeeded in holding positions in much of the press in Lisbon and exercised some control over television and radio, especially after 11 March 1975. It is equally true that the Communists had little to say in the running of the press outside of Lisbon or of the two radio stations not owned by the state, Rádio Clube Português and the Catholic Rádio Renascença. In the case of these two stations the far left appeared to dominate. Throughout the revolution, the Church fought to regain control of Rádio Renasçenca whose broadcasting antenna finally had to be blown up by the military in November 1975 to put an end to the station's occupation by far leftists. Undoubtedly, the question of Rádio Renascenca played a large part in reinforcing the Church's hostility towards the revolution and in its support for the anti-Communist riots of the summer of 1975.

In assessing the role of the media in the Portuguese revolution, it is revealing to compare the views of two Communists on the whole issue. According to João Paulo Guerra, the "Portuguese revolution is a clear example of the decisive role that the control of the media has in our times for the development of the revolutionary processes, as an integral and inseparable part of the class struggle."[1] This explicit statement of the PCP's view, which certainly reflects its whole attitude towards the media, was not shared by Jacques Frémontier, a member of the French Communist party at the time, who wrote in his very perceptive critique of the revolution that neither "censorship nor installing an absolute monopoly over information has ever convinced anybody of the superiority of socialism: it then only remains to lock up opponents and force them to be silent."[2]

The results of Communist control over much of the media during the revolution hardly supports the view put forward by João Paulo Guerra, which gave the impression of an omnipresent PCP and lent credibility to the rumor of a Communist takeover in Portugal. The Portuguese experience confirms what most research on the impact of the media has concluded, that the media have a much greater effect as instruments of conformism and of reaffirming the status quo than as agents of social or political change.[3] Neither the Communists nor the MFA were capable of breaking through the scepticism and apathy engrained by almost fifty years of dictatorship. Furthermore, they hardly made a dent in the influence held by the Church in the rural areas of northern and central Portugal.

The Media and the Constitution

The role of the media in the new Portugal became a topic of heated debate in the Constituent Assembly which had still to digest the lessons of censorship under the old regime, the battle for control of the media during the revolution, and the inheritance of a large state-owned sector. As could be expected, it settled for a compromise. Through Article 83, which declared in its first paragraph that all "nationalization measures carried out since 25th of April 1974 are irreversible conquests by the working classes," the Constitution ensured that the state sector would remain intact, at least for the foreseeable future. Articles 37, 38, 39, and 40 confirmed the liberal principles already contained in the 1975 press law. Article 37 guaranteed freedom of expression and information, while Article 38 confirmed freedom of the press. To make sure that there would be no return to the ideological conflicts which had opposed the workers' commissions and the journalists, as in the *República* case, paragraph 2 of Article 38 expressly established the right of journalists to participate in the ideological orientation of media belonging neither to the state nor to political parties and forbade any acts of censorship on the part of "other sectors or groups of workers." Article 39 dealt with the peculiar problem of the state-owned sectors in the Portuguese media industry and attempted to solve the dilemma of distinguishing between state ownership and governmental interference. It boldly declared that the state-controlled media should be "used in such a way as to safeguard their independence from the government and public administration" and that "the possibility to express and confront diverse currents of opinion" would be ensured. To strengthen these provisions, the Constitution set up four information councils: one for the press, one for television, one for radio, and one for the national press agency, ANOP. These councils were to be composed of members nominated by the political parties in proportion to their numbers in Parliament. A law passed in 1977 put this number at one per ten deputies, with at least one representative from each party however small its representation in the Assembly. Finally, Article 40 established the right of political parties and union organizations to free air time on radio and television.

The 1982 constitutional revision hardly altered articles 37, 38, or 40, except to make them even more comprehensive. Article 38 was enlarged to give journalists the right of access to sources of information and to give constitutional protection for their professional independence and the right to confidentiality. This article also now allows individual citizens to own periodicals and forbids the concentration of press enterprises. The revised article 40 extends the rights of opposition parties to space for replying to the government in state-owned newspapers.

The various councils set up to monitor the state-owned media in the 1976 Constitution did little or nothing to prevent government intervention. They merely reproduced the partisan composition of the Assembly, thereby giving the government of the day an almost certain majority. In 1982 these councils were abolished to make way for a single Media Council of eleven members. Observers harbored some scepticism about the new council's real ability or will to keep the government in line. In an obvious attempt to eliminate the PCP from the Council, it was decided to jettison the principle of proportional representation in favor of the election of the members of the Media Council by a two-thirds majority of members of the Assembly. Ironically, when these members were chosen in September 1983, the party that had advocated the new two-thirds role, the CDS, was the one to benefit least, since the Assembly appointed four Socialists, four Social Democrats, two Communists, and only one representative of the CDS. At about the same time, the law specifying the Council's powers was adopted by the Assembly, granting, at least on paper, the Council the power of binding decisions and giving it the role of safeguarding the independence of the state-owned media. As we will see, in its first important case the Council proved to be rather more effective than anticipated, despite its overwhelming built-in progovernment majority.

A Newspaper Industry in Crisis

In an age when the press throughout Western Europe and North America has been marked by ever increasing concentration, and the subsequent disappearance of many dailies, Portugal appears at first glance to be the surprising exception. In early 1984, Lisbon and its immediate surroundings could boast nine daily newspapers while the country's second city, Oporto, produced four. These indications of a dynamic press industry mask a much gloomier reality. Circulation figures are low, all but one state-owned newspapers have a deficit, and the privately owned press is also in financial difficulties.

The Portuguese press remains locally oriented. No genuine national newspaper exists, and even the country's best known dailies rarely reach beyond the geographical sphere of influence of the city in which they are published. Thus the four most widely read newspapers in Portugal, the *Diário de Notícias* and the *Correio de Manhã* in Lisbon and the *Jornal de Notícias* and *O Comércio do Porto* in Oporto, find between 75 and 90 percent of their readership in the immediate vicinity. Portugal's newspaper-reading population remains relatively small. According to our survey, only 42 percent of the population claimed to read a daily frequently and only 26 percent a political weekly; just over 20 percent read the newspaper every day, and 15 percent read a weekly at least once a week.

The Portuguese press industry is approximating Western European trends toward, on the one hand, a break with direct links to the political parties and, on the other, a move towards the so-called popular press. However, it has also retained certain national characteristics. The state-owned press remains important and counts for more than 60 percent of the readership of the Portuguese press;[4] the private press is still very often a partisan press with very strong views; and the Portuguese weekly press has developed a character all of its own. The problem for the state-owned press has been to maintain its independence vis-à-vis the government. Its survival depends on government subsidies, which have not prevented at least three state-owned newspapers from going under. Two, *O Século* and *O Jornal do Comércio,* disappeared within two years of the revolution, and the third one, *Notícias da Tarde,* suspended its publication in July 1984 after only two years of existence. The position adopted by these papers toward the government has very much depended on their respective editorial boards. At least two Lisbon state-owned papers, *Diário de Notícias* and *Diário de Lisboa,* have not hesitated to attack government policy, irrespective of the party in power. The *Diário de Lisboa* is considered by many to be a paper close to the PCP and has always assumed positions well to the left, whereas the *Diário de Notícias,* in keeping with its reputation as Portugal's most prestigious daily newspaper, has attempted to maintain a balanced, critical approach both towards the government and the opposition, a quality which one associates with most of the respected Western European newspapers.

Governments have frequently confused state ownership with political control. In September 1983, the Soares government took a decision which has made the life of these state-owned newspapers even more precarious. It decided to reduce the deficits of two Lisbon papers, the *Diário de Notícias* and *A Capital,* by insisting on a series of austerity measures, which included a drastic reduction in staff. It also announced it would no longer indiscriminately subsidize the press. As one weekly pointed out, the government was simply engaging in a fit of pique with the editorial independence shown by the *Diário de Notícias,* directed by a former member of the PS.[5] The government then refused to increase subsidies to state-owned newspapers, forcing them to increase their prices. The same government also attempted to extend its hold over the state-owned press by introducing a new press bill which was intended to prevent the editorial boards of all state newspapers from vetoing the nomination of a director and would have excluded journalists from having any influence on the ideological orientation of those newspapers. The new law would also have affected the press in general, since it put some limits on journalists' access to sources and restricted their right to confidentiality. This bill raised almost unanimous condemnation on the part of the press and the journalists' associations and criticism within the parties forming the government coalition. It was therefore quietly dropped.

The last ten years have seen a growth in the press owned by the private sector. Initially, the privately owned daily press was aggressively partisan. On the left, the PCP established its own newspaper, *O Diário,* and the PS created *Portugal Hoje,* which disappeared in 1982. The right continues to be served by *O Dia* and *O Primeiro de Janeiro,* whose majority shareholder is Freitas do Amaral, former president of the CDS. In 1979 a new paper appeared on the Lisbon scene, the *Correio de Manhã,* modeled on the popular tabloid press which had swept Europe in the 1960s. It became an immediate hit and is now second only to the *Jornal de Notícias* in readership and circulation in the whole country.

The privately owned press has constantly complained of unfair competition from the state-owned sector, which depends on state subsidies. However, they are also helped indirectly by the state, which, through the banking system, gives them easy credit. They also receive government grants to cover their printing costs, based on circulation figures. This aid has not kept them out of financial difficulties, which have hurt most those papers with identifiable political leanings. The Socialist *Portugal Hoje* fell by the wayside, another indication that the PS engenders little ideological commitment even though it was at the time Portugal's strongest party electorally speaking. In 1984, the right also had its problems as *O Dia* and *O Primeiro de Janeiro* struggled to keep afloat, while the rightward-leaning Lisbon evening paper, *O Globo,* tried to stave off the day of decision by switching to the morning, before expiring when sales had fallen to 1,000 copies a day.

The most interesting phenomenon in the private sector has been the growth and popularity of the Portuguese weekly press. The pattern for these weeklies was set by the oldest of them all, *Expresso,* founded during the last year of the Caetano regime. Two other weeklies were created during the revolution, *O Jornal,* sympathetic to the left, and *Tempo,* a paper of the right. Two other important weeklies joined this list in the postrevolutionary period, *O Diabo,* which tends to express very radical right-wing views, and more recently *O Semanário,* which published its first issue in November 1983 and became an immediate success in right-wing circles.

These weeklies are a crossbreed between political weeklies like *The New Statesman* or *L'Express* and the British Sunday newspapers. They publish exhaustive analyses of the stories behind the week's news and articles of a general cultural or political nature and combine this with the latest news, in the style of *The Observer* or the *Sunday Times.* They make little effort to disguise their political bias. The most interesting case amongst them is *Expresso.* Its founder, owner, and longtime director is Francisco Pinto Balsemão, a prominent member of the PSD and former prime minister. Until he gave up the editorship in early 1980, upon becoming a member of the Sá Carneiro government, *Expresso* followed a center-right line, especially critical of the first two governments headed by Mário Soares. This editorial position did not prevent the paper's journalists from writing articles from a different perspective, often sympathetic to positions on the left. Editorially the same orientation was maintained by the paper's next director, Marcelo Rebelo de Sousa, another well-known member of the PSD, associated with its right wing, who gave up the post on becoming a secretary of state in 1981. Although the ownership of the paper remains in the hands of Pinto Balsemão, editorial positions have since shifted towards the center-left and are critical of all governments.

The weekly press has not restricted its activities to reporting the news and presenting analyses and points of view. It has also been accused of trying to make the news, of creating political facts in an attempt to gain readers in a highly competitive market and to influence the course of events. It has not hesitated to stretch the truth, often to back up its own partisan bias. For example, in its 16 July 1981 issue, *Tempo,* which strongly backed the Pinto Balsemão government against the president and his supporters in the Council of the Revolution, published a detailed account of a meeting of the Council of the Revolution on its front page, and a summary of the remarks made by each of the Council's members. The paper itself admitted having invented this sensational "news" by publishing on its back page a stop press paragraph announcing that the alleged meeting had been postponed to the following day! This conduct was rightly censored by the Press Council. The weeklies' predelection for political gossip and floating trial balloons has been developed to a fine art by *Semanário,* which published articles and its own polls throughout 1984 indicating growing support for Maria de Lourdes Pintasilgo's presidential candidacy. It was presumably hoped that this news would influence many people on the left and among the supporters of the outgoing president, General Eanes, to choose a candidate widely thought to have little chance of actually winning the election, because she would repel voters of the center and the right. Although this paper is described on all sides as a rumormonger, it has now become obligatory reading for members of the political class. The highly respected but very competitive *Expresso* and *O Jornal* also indulge in questionable practices to increase their readership. Knowing they cater to the same audience, they periodically fire little salvos in a fight to undermine each other's credibility. In November 1983, *O Jornal* published a scoop, an article written by a journalist who claimed to have firsthand knowledge of conditions in the former Portuguese colony of East Timor, now under Indonesian occupation, and a constant source of guilt for Portugal's political class, which did nothing to prevent the Indonesian invasion of 1975. *Expresso* gleefully denounced the article as "the biggest journalistic fraud in Portugal in recent times," and proved, with convincing evidence, that the journalist in question had never been to East Timor. It also pointed out that an emotional photograph of a crying child which accompanied the article dated from 1969 and had been taken by an American photographer in Vietnam. Such incidents hardly foster faith in the credibility of the Portuguese press.

The attempts by various governments to control the written press were illustrated by the battle over the official state press agency ANOP. This agency, founded in July 1975, had fallen under Communist control for a time and from then on never ceased to be a focal point for controversy involving all political parties. Between 1977 and 1982, the political complexion of the ANOP administration, appointed by the government, changed frequently, and newspapers both left and right accused it of being manipulated by various partisan forces. During the reign of the AD, management and administrative staff close to the PSD was brought in to balance the agency's alleged Communist domination. By 1982 ANOP was rife with rivalry between various political clans. The prime minister, Pinto Balsemão, decided to clarify the situation by announcing that his government would abolish ANOP and create a private press agency Notícias de Portugal, or NP. The new agency began functioning in November 1982, but the government never succeeded in doing away with ANOP and firing its 140 employees, whereas the PS declared it would not necessarily stand by the decision of the Pinto Balsemão government to create NP and to dissolve ANOP. The Central Bloc government announced its own solution to the problem: it would merge ANOP and NP. In the meantime, this policy proved impossible to implement, and Portugal still has two official press agencies receiving equal subsidies from the government; neither enjoys sufficient means to give satisfactory coverage of international events for the Portuguese press.

The Electronic Media: A Story of Government Interference

Governments have backpedalled in their attempts to gain a degree of control over the daily press, but the same is not true of their hold over radio and television. Administrations have changed even more frequently than governments; the height of that instability was reached during the three and a half years of the AD, which made the most blatant move to put radio and television at the service of the government. In the words of the first chairman of the board appointed by the AD, Victor da Cunha Rego, impartiality in state television was unthinkable; on the contrary, "the role television must play is to help the state consolidate itself, defend itself without ceasing to reflect, with balance and rigor, the main questions of public opinion and the main problems of the community."[6] His successor, Daniel Proenca de Carvalho, completed the process and set a pattern from which no government has since deviated.

Unlike the daily and weekly press, radio and television reach out to every region in Portugal. According to our survey, 74 percent of the population listen to the news regularly on the radio and 84 percent watch the news on one of the two television channels. This explains the interest shown by all governments in controlling what is broadcast by the country's only completely national media. Since television is a total state monopoly,[7] and the only nonstate radio station is the Catholic Rádio Renascença, obtaining control has not been a very difficult matter. No government would ever admit that it had exercised any form of censorship, either directly or indirectly. Unfortunately, the recent history of radio—and especially television—in Portugal shows that the electronic media have become the object of both ferocious partisan struggles and direct government intervention. Neither the state television company, RTP, nor the state radio, RDP, and its subsidiary Rádio Comercial, have ever been able to manifest any notable autonomy, such as that shown by the BBC.

Party cells have become so well organized within the RDP and RTP that they have tended, in the words of a former chairman of the RTP, to "assume the role of 'political commissars,' constituting themselves into parallel powers and attempting to enforce decisions."[8] The governing parties themselves are always involved in the appointment of the directors and administrators of the RDP and RTP, to the point where many appointments are seen as nothing more than political party patronage.[9] The nature of these appointments can be seen from the battle over the presidency of the RDP in late 1983. The outgoing president and PSD member, Manuel Magro, had fallen into disgrace among his own party supporters for having failed to promote certain Social Democrats. Magro stayed in his post for three further months waiting for the PS and PSD to come up with a candidate who, in the sarcastic words of one journalist, would fit the profile of "an intellectual chairman, with good relations with the politicians, anti-Eanes and anti-Communist."[10]

Appointments to the governing boards of the RTP and RDP always demand delicate negotiations between the parties of the government coalition; the position of chairman of the board gives rise to the most controversy. Since 1980, government coalitions have been dominated by parties which have customarily appointed two members each to the governing board and have had to negotiate on the chairman. In 1984 the chairman of the RTP board became embroiled even further in internal party politics. The right wing of the PSD, which had opposed the coalition with the Socialists, forced the party to vote in favor of dismissing the governing board of the RTP. The PS reacted to these maneuvers by calling on the prime minister to reject such demands. However, in the end PSD pressure forced the chairman of the RTP, João Palma Ferreira, to tender his resignation in May 1984.

It took four months of tough bargaining between the PS and the PSD to find Palma Ferreira's successor, during a period when the RTP came under heavy criticism for bowing to government pressure. The prime minister put forward his own nominee; as a countermeasure, the PSD deputy prime minister wanted to choose the chairman of the RDP and the majority of the board in exchange. In the end, the parties agreed on a compromise candidate, Manuel João da Palma Carlos, a former Socialist and the RTP's lawyer for disciplinary hearings, a choice which upset the station's journalists, who were never consulted anyway. The deal also included a reduction of the governing board from the five statutory members to three, one from each of the two government parties and the chairman. This would presumably facilitate internal agreement and further reduce any possible resistance to political interference. Since the board appoints and dimisses all program directors at will, the mechanism for government intervention could quickly be put into motion.

The widespread practice of patronage and partisan appointments has produced instability and a top-heavy bureaucracy, as every change of government brings in new staff and the majority of those already employed remain.[11] This unhealthy situation has affected both programming and finances of the RTP and the RDP as their costs—personnel and otherwise—continue to rise while their incomes stagnate. Television suffers most, and at times the RTP has simply had to cancel foreign programs such as "Dallas" for lack of funds. Theoretically the RTP depends on three main sources of funding: government subsidies, advertising, and licenses for television sets. Television already receives more than 50 percent of all advertising revenue in Portugal; trends show that its share of this market has been declining so there is little hope of increases in that sector.[12] As for licenses as a reliable source of income, the RTP can hardly count on a notoriously reluctant public which remains deaf to its pleas and threats to nonpayers. In effect, both television and the state radio must look to government subsidies for their survival, which only increases their vulnerability to political influence.

Accusations of bias, manipulation, and partisanship against state radio and television abound in the Portuguese press and have far too often been substantiated. The former Council for Information on the RTP inquired into such charges. In its report published in July 1981 and supported by its PS, PCP, ASDI, MDP, and UDP members, it concluded that complaints of political manipulation of the RTP and persecution of journalists for political motives were proved beyond all doubt and gave numerous examples to support its contention. A member of the Council for Information on the RTP produced some interesting figures on the bias in favor of the government parties during the AD coalition between 1980 and July 1982. On Channel One (the RTP has two channels) which broadcasts *"Telejornal"*, the most important news bulletin on Portuguese television, between 73 and 85 percent of its news on partisan issues covered the parties of the AD, and only 15 to 27 percent dealt with the opposition parties. Between 1980 and 1983, Channel One divided the time allotted to the various governing institutions in the following proportions:[13]

Government	86%
The President of the Republic	14%
Assembly of the Republic	16%

This period also includes the 1982 debates on the revision of the constitution which focused so much on the work of the Assembly.

The situation did not change with the election of a new government. The press continued to report instances of censorship and manipulation of the news to promote the government and its policies at the expense of objectivity. One account told of a phone call from an adviser to the Ministry of Foreign Affairs which resulted in an extra few minutes being tacked on to the *"Telejornal"* so that a full interview with the visiting German Minister of Foreign Affairs, Dieter Genscher, could be aired. On another occasion, the director of the RTP's daily information service edited part of a speech made by the leader of the PCP, Alvaro Cunhal, at the close of the annual festival held by the party's newspaper, *Avante!*, on the grounds that he was criticizing the government.[14] In some cases, the chairman of the RTP himself intervened directly to ensure that the government received more than its fair share of coverage; he was known to criticize those journalists who failed to adequately acknowledge those in power.[15]

Much of the censorship on radio and television is not even the result of direct intervention but stems from self-censorship, either on the part of the journalists themselves or on the part of their hierarchical superiors. In a gesture reminiscent of the Caetano era, the program director of the RTP and the director of Channel One ordered cuts in an episode of a popular program, *"Viagem através do Homen"* (Journey through Man) because it touched on the seamier, less appealing sides of life such as hunger, drugs, and prostitution. Requests for the cuts were made in the form of advice, with the implicit suggestion that otherwise the program might be withdrawn.

At times, flagrant examples of direct government intervention in television programming hit the national headlines. Two of the most famous cases took place under different prime ministers, Pinto Balsemão and Mário Soares, but concerned the same series, *"Grande Reportagem,"* Portugal's best and most popular program of investigative journalism.[16] One of them also became an important test of the powers and the authority of the country's new Media Council.

The first problem arose with the screening of a program on apartheid which had previously been shown by the BBC "Panorama" in 1982, called "South Africa: To the Last Drop of Blood." Just before the program was to go on the air on 24 May 1983, viewers were told that the film had been suspended because of a recent bomb attack in Pretoria, followed by reprisals against an African National Congress camp in Matola in Mozambique three days later. The RTP claimed it did not want to appear partisan, yet it was later revealed that the South African ambassador to Lisbon had sent the chairman of the RTP a telex expressing his "preoccupation" about showing a film which would be fraudulent and "very partial" and cause distress because of the recent bombings in Pretoria. Though this appeared to be a decision made by the RTP governing board, in actual fact it resulted from government pressure. Through the secretary of state for the media, José Alfaia, the RTP's directors were informed that President Eanes, Prime Minister Pinto Balsemão, and Minister of Foreign Affairs Futscher Pereira had all advised against showing this film on state television.[17] This incident raised totally justified cries of outrage from the press, and the program finally went on two weeks later. However, the significance of this incident lies in the fact that for the first time diplomatic pressure had succeeded in affecting the programs on Portuguese television although other embassies had apparently tried to use similar pressure in the past. To make matters worse, the decision had been taken by a caretaker government which had already lost the elections.

On 15 May 1984, the RTP again cancelled a program on southern Africa. This time it was a film made by the RTP's own journalists on the National Union for the Total Independence of Angola, the main opponent of the government in Angola. The day before the program's scheduled showing, the Portuguese ambassador in Luanda was called in by the Angolan minister of foreign affairs and warned that "the most serious repercussions in Angolan-Portuguese relations would happen if the film were to be shown"; in other words, Angola threatened to cut off diplomatic relations. He added that Angola could not be held responsible for the safety of Portuguese residents in that country should the film be aired. Portuguese exporters with interests in Angola were received by the Angolan Embassy in Lisbon on the same day and told of the possible consequences of showing the film. Later these businessmen saw Mário Soares and informed him of their worry about the impact of the program on Portuguese-Angolan trade relations. In the meantime, the ambassador in Luanda sent a warning telegram to Mário Soares, to his foreign minister, Jaime Gama, and to his minister of state, Almeida Santos, also responsible for the media. The process of withdrawing the program was then set in motion. On the government side, the secretary of state for the media, Anselmo Rodrigues, handled the affair. He began by calling in the members of the governing board of the RTP, minus its chairman, João Palma Ferreira, who was still on holiday and was to resign shortly afterwards. Rodrigues told the members of the board that the decision was theirs but that there could be "consequences" for any disagreement with the government on this subject. The governing board had little choice but to comply with the government's wishes and admitted in a communiqué that it was bowing to political pressure when it claimed that "present legislation compelled the RTP to observe the rules which oblige it to consider the defense of the country's interests."

This incident took place at a very delicate moment in Portuguese-Angolan relations. Only a week previously, in an interview with *O Jornal,* President José Eduardo dos Santos of Angola had accused the Portuguese government of disturbing the entente between Portugal and Angola and criticized Portuguese radio and television and "a certain press" for supporting "terrorists and subversive actions of groups which . . . are dedicated to kidnapping foreign assistants some of whom are Portuguese."[18] In both cases the government was obliged to consider security threats to the numerous Portuguese citizens and emigrants residing in southern Africa, whom the South Africans and the Angolans did not hesitate to suggest as potential hostages.

Most of the press and the journalists' union protested against what was seen as another example of censorship on television. The one exception was the PCP paper, *O Diário,* and the Communist journalists, whose executive issued a communiqué denouncing the program as part of "the very long involvement of the RTP in the anti-Angolan campaign," adding that it "is an act of hypocrisy to consider postponing the broadcast of that program as an act of censorship and to equate this situation with real acts of censorship, and to ignore the partiality of government-controlled information which is sytematically hostile to good relations with the People's Republic of Angola."[19] The year before the party had denounced the suspension of the program on South Africa, but even that incident only deserved a short note on the back page of *Avante!*. Neither the PS nor the PSD, champions of freedom of the press during the revolution, officially stood up and supported the program. The only party that officially denounced the decision was the CDS, which had remained silent during the South Africa affair one year before.

What followed was a nasty battle, involving the authors of the program, the RTP's governing board, the Media Council, and the government, which highlighted the close links between politics and the media. The authors of *"Grande Reportagem"* took their case to the Media Council. Meanwhile, at the end of July 1984, the RTP board decided to dismiss the head of the program, José Barata Feyo, for "just cause" on the grounds that he had published an article in *Expresso* denouncing the original ban. Just over a month later, the RTP announced that it had instituted disciplinary proceedings against Barata Feyo for alleged irregularities over production costs for the program which allegedly had violated currency regulations.

The Media Council brought down its decision in the middle of August, and ordered in a communiqué that the film be shown, declaring: "it is the RTP's inherent duty to organize its programming according to an orientation which respects ideological pluralism and guarantees the rigor and objectivity of information."[20] The RTP's administration did not yet consider itself beaten. It agreed to air the program but in a new series called *"Grande Informação,"* and not *"Grande Reportagem,"* which had been a thorn in the side of various governments since its creation in March 1981. Barata Feyo would not be allowed to introduce it. On the other hand, the coordinating director of information at the RTP, Fialho de Oliveira, obviously unhappy with the way his superiors had handled the whole question, had personally guaranteed to the Media Council that the program would go on the air on 11 September 1984. The board simply ignored this commitment on the pretext that the program's author, Barata Feyo, was still under investigation. When Fialho de Oliveira rescheduled the program for the following week, respecting another (binding) decision issued by the Media Council, the board responded by suspending Fialho de Oliveira for having gone to the Council without notifying it first. Finally, after all this footdragging, and despite high-level pressure to prevent the program from ever going on the air,[21] the film on UNITA was shown at the beginning of October 1984.

Mário Soares had unwittingly thrown oil on the fire when he admitted in a newspaper interview that the government had intervened to pull the program in May because it might be a "pretext for creating difficulties in the relations between Portugal and Angola."[22] This declaration drew a response from the Media Council, which rapped the government over the knuckles for asking for the program to be withheld and chastised the RTP's board for accepting such requests. It also accused the government of dishonesty for denying that it had ever communicated with the RTP. The secretary of state for the media went even further than his prime minister and announced that the government believed that "freedom of information must be subject to the interests of the state."[23]

In spite of its progovernment majority, the Media Council had won its first important case. But the obstructions raised by the RTP's administrative board, which clearly reflected government policy, suggest that television and radio will remain an area of contention.

The media faithfully reproduce the characteristics of Portuguese politics. To begin with, they symbolize the centralization which has increased since 1974. Most of the country's dailies are produced in Lisbon or Oporto, reflect the interests of the readers from those areas, and have no true national distribution. As for the weeklies, they are strongly centered on Lisbon and what goes on there, both in politics and in cultural life. It is therefore not surprising, as our survey has shown, that the readers of the four most important political weeklies in the country come overwhelmingly from Lisbon and to a far lesser extent from Oporto.[24] Radio and television are also very heavily centralized even though the RTP presents a summary of general regional news across Portugal every weekday. In response to this situation, a movement towards private and local radio stations has grown in the last few years, putting pressure on the government to provide frequencies for such stations.

The evolution of the Portuguese media also shows the increasing identification between the state and the parties. The temptation has been too great to resist, and the "colonization" of the all important state-owned media by the government parties and especially by the PSD and the PS has gone on unabated, to the detriment of the quality of the media and their autonomy.

Notes

1. João Paulo Guerra, *"Dossier" communicação social* (Lisbon: Edições Avante!, 1981), p. 12.
2. Jacques Frémontier, *Portugal: les points sur les i* (Paris: Les Editions Sociales, 1976) p. 169.
3. A convincing analysis of the limited impact of the media during the revolutionary process in Portugal is presented by Ben Pimlott and Jean Seaton, "Political Power and the Portuguese Media," in Lawrence S. Graham and Douglas L. Wheeler (eds.), *In Search of Modern Portugal: The Revolution and Its Consequences*, 1983.
4. The state-owned press can be divided into "public" newspapers, wholly owned by the state, and the "state-intervened" papers, which have state and private shareholders. See Warren K. Agee and Nelson Traquina, *A Frustrated Fourth Estate: Portugal's Post-Revolutionary Mass Media* (Columbia, S.C.: Journalism Monographs no. 87, February 1984), pp. 22-23.
5. "O governo e o Diário de Notícias," *Expresso*, 24 September 1983.
6. *Diário de Notícias*, 20 March 1980.
7. "Television shall not be privately owned," Article 38/7 of the 1982 revised Constitution.
8. João Soares Louro, "Instabilidade e sobresaltos na rádio e na televisão," *Diário de Notícias*, 24 April 1984, p. 56.
9. The secretary of state for the media in the Central Bloc government, Anselmo Rodrigues, candidly acknowledged that his government made patronage appointments to these positions and declared that the sharing of the spoils by the governing parties was the "result of the electoral legitimacy which allows for them [i.e. the parties] to appoint the management of these bodies. Do not expect the majority to appoint the minority to positions for which it has competent people" ("Duas agencias? A curto prazo vamos conseguir a fusão," *O Jornal*, 31 August 1984).
10. "Na administração da RDP só Manuel Magro não muda," *O Jornal*, 9 September 1983.
11. Between 1974 and 1983, seventy-eight managers and 130 directors of various services were appointed to the RDP and the RTP (João Soares Louro, "Instabilidade e sobresaltos," p. 56). Between 25 April 1974 and December 1984, the RTP had eighteen different chairmen of the board.
12. Pedro Dionísio, "Publicidade: Radio e imprensa aumentaran vendas à custa da TV," *Expresso*, 2 February 1985. In 1984, Portugal invested only $5.7 per head in advertising, compared to $35.1 in Spain, and $82.3 in France (Nuno Pacheco, "Um império em tempo de crise," *Expresso Revista*, 3 November 1984).

13. António Abreu, "A RTP de Proenca de Carvalho bateu o recorde da manipulação," *O Jornal*, 4 March 1983.

14. "Intervenção de Cunhal censurada pelo director de informação," *O Jornal*, 16 September 1983. The editor of the program who had not even been informed of the cut in advance, sent a letter to the RTP's board of editors to complain about the incident.

15. The interim head of the RTP, João Tito Morais, called in the station's news chiefs to complain about the way television had handled a report on hunger in the Setúbal region and the editing of an interview with the government minister reponsible for the question (Pedro d'Anunciação, "Tito de Morais contra reportagem do Telejornal," *Expresso*, 30 June 1984). In another case, the chairman of the RTP, Manuel João da Palma Carlos, summoned a TV journalist to his office and demanded an explanation for why the *"Telejornal"* had omitted a speech by Mota Pinto, then deputy prime minister, to a meeting of the PSD's National Council. This action brought protests from the editors of the program ("Conflitos entre Palma Carlos e o Telejornal," *Expresso*, 22 December 1984).

16. In a poll taken in March-April 1984 on news programs, *"Grande Reportagem"* came out on top with 68.2 percent of those polled finding the program either good or very good ("Grande Reportagem,noticiários da RRC, Expresso: a melhor imagem" *Expresso*, 12 May 1984).

17. President Eanes later denied making any request to suspend the program.

18. *O Jornal*, 11 May 1984.

19. "Jornalistas comunistas tomam posição," *Avante!/Suplemento*, 26 May 1984.

20. *Expresso*, 18 August 1984.

21. According to an anonymous television source, the RTP board was being subjected to tremendous pressure from "someone important who does not want to see the programme go on the air" ("Gerencia da RTP desmente Soares," *Expresso*, 15 September 1984).

22. Interview with Mário Soares, *Expresso*, 8 September 1984.

23. "Guerência da RTP desmente Soares," *Expresso*, 15 September 1984.

24. Seventy-two percent of the readers of *Expresso*, 55 percent of those of *O Jornal*, 47 percent of those of *Tempo*, and 55 percent of those of *Semanário* came from the greater Lisbon area, compared with 4, 7, 3, and 11 percent from the greater Oporto area.

10
The Politicized Role of the State in the Economy

Although Portugal had initiated a process of industrial development prior to 1974, the country's economic bases were archaic compared with those of other Western European nations. (See Chart 1 in Appendix 2.) The background was one of extreme underdevelopment at the founding of the Estado Novo in 1933: a corporatist structure was then elaborated which intertwined all relevant interests, and a high level of protectionism ensured high profits in commerce and industry. This protectionism included tariffs and regulations to minimize external competition, guaranteed markets and sources of raw materials in the colonies, and active discouragement of internal competition. Through *condicionamento industrial,* for example, the state and existing firms were able to veto the founding of new firms or even the expansion of old firms. The result was a low level of competition, and key areas of the economy were dominated by state-protected monopolies.[1] Eric Baklanoff and other economists have shown how some forty families, of which ten were predominant, owned all the important commercial banks, which in turn controlled a disproportionate share of the national economy. The banks were central to the cartels and economic groups which included basic sectors such as steel, petroleum, cement, and fertilizers. Baklanoff reports that of the 40,051 firms operating in Portugal in 1971, 168 (0.4 percent) held 53 percent of the total corporate wealth.[2] Overall, the economic system can be characterized as private ownership of the means of production combined with extensive state control.

Portugal joined the European Free Trade Association in 1960, which encouraged some outside competition. Protection also decreased somewhat after 1965 when laws that had discouraged foreign investment in the country and the colonies were changed. By the late 1960s many small industries emerged; these were mainly oriented towards export and joint ventures between the Portuguese cartels and foreign corporations. The economy was growing and becoming diversified but was unbalanced. For instance, during the decade 1960-1970, gross domestic product (GDP) growth per year averaged over 6 percent and increased to 7 percent from

1970 to 1973. The secondary sectors, including manufacturing, led the growth rate with a 9 percent increase during 1960-1973. The primary sector including agriculture, fishing, and mining, lagged; agricultural production, which grew by only 1.5 percent per year from 1960 to 1970, dropped to less than half that growth rate during 1970-1973. Between 1960 and 1973 total output (GDP at factor cost) grew by 120 percent in real terms; the secondary sector was over three times greater; the tertiary sector doubled; but the primary sector, mainly agriculture, advanced by only 18 percent. Manufacturing, the major component of the secondary sector, was three times as large at the end of the period.[3] The last ten years of the Estado Novo saw the creation of important projects, including a modern ship-repair and shipbuilding complex, oil refineries, petrochemical plants, vehicle assembly plants, an integrated iron and steel mill, pulp and paper mills, and electronic assembly plants. Meanwhile agriculture stagnated, the domestic market remained weak due to low wages, and more than 1,600,000 Portuguese emigrated (30 percent clandestinely) between 1960 and 1981. The regime was unable to decide whether to become modern and join Europe or remain a colonial power engaged in African wars. The government fully supported the latter option until 1974 with the result that a modern industrial strategy was not consolidated.

With the overthrow of the Estado Novo, which had guaranteed the conditions under which the monopolies had emerged and developed, substantial changes in the economy became necessary. The colonies, which were what the MFA coup was all about in the first place, would be lost with their guaranteed raw materials and markets, wages would have to rise, and competition both internally and externally would have to increase. However, all this changed practically overnight as the revolution altered relations of power and economic structures and injected the state into all parts of the economy. The predominant role of the state in the process of nationalization was facilitated somewhat by its heavy involvement in the pre-1974 monopolies. It must be stressed that the revolution, while involving popular support for a new system after the collapse of the Estado Novo, was not based on a consensus. During late 1974 and 1975, supporters of the old regime disappeared or remained quiet, the PCP took the lead, and the PS and other parties defined their ideology and programs to the left. What took place during these years made some sense at the time, but it was not based on general agreement or a well-defined strategy. Only the PCP and parties and groups to the left had any cohesive program or ideology.

The revolutionary period saw the implementation of a major agrarian reform which changed the structures of tenure relationships in the Alentejo and Ribatejo.[4] Workers' demands and organizations changed; the relationships of power within firms shifted; the percentage of wages in the economy increased (see Table 10.1); and the state, utilizing decree-law 660/74 of 15 November 1974, intervened in private firms. Finally, and probably most importantly, between 14 March 1975 and 29 July 1976, the state directly nationalized 244 firms in key areas of the economy. With each nationalization other firms also came under control of the state, given the economic concentration noted above. The nationalized firms included the

Table 10.1

Portugal: Components of Gross Product, 1973-1983

(percentages)

	1973	1974	1975	1976	1977	1978	1979	1980	1981	1982	1983
Total consumption	81.1	94.0	101.9	94.1	89.6	88.6	88.0	89.2	84.1	83.1	83.8
Private	67.9	79.5	84.6	77.7	74.5	73.9	73.2	73.8	69.2	68.8	69.2
Public	13.2	14.5	17.3	16.4	15.0	14.7	14.8	15.4	14.9	14.4	14.6
Gross investment	26.3	19.3	13.6	19.1	25.2	23.3	22.3	25.1	36.0	37.0	29.0
Fixed	23.8	17.1	17.0	17.7	20.2	20.1	19.1	20.9	31.4	31.6	29.6
Changed in stocks	2.5	2.2	-3.4	1.4	5.0	3.2	3.2	4.2	4.6	5.4	-0.6
Exports of goods and services	25.8	25.9	19.3	16.5	17.4	19.9	25.8	28.1	27.4	26.3	31.5
Imports of goods and services	-33.2	-41.4	-31.4	-29.6	-32.2	-31.8	-36.1	-42.4	-47.5	-46.5	-44.3
Gross product	100.0	100.0	100.0	100.0	100.0	100.0	100.0	100.0	100.0	100.0	100.0
Gross item: Labor's share in national income*	51.6	57.0	68.9	66.6	60.0	56.8	52.9	56.5	56.1	55.3	53.5

Source: Eric Baklanoff, "The State and Economy in Portugal: Perspectives on Corporatism, Revolution, and Reform," Paper presented to Research Conference on State Shrinking, University of Texas at Austin, 1-3 March 1984, p. 8.

*Including employers' contribution to Social Security.

Table 10.2

Participation of the Public Sector in Portugal's Economy Before And After The Revolution, by Industry or Branch

(percentages)

	Traditional public sector (1973)			Public sector after the revolution (1976)		
	Value added	Fixed investment	Employment	Value added	Fixed investment	Employment
Agriculture and fisheries	0.5	–		1.5	24.9	
Mining	1.1	19.9		4.5	15.5	
Manufacturing	–	2.9		13.5	51.0	
Construction	–	–		4.7	21.0	
Electricity gas and water	0.1	–		99.9	99.6	
Commerce	–	2.7		1.9	5.3	
Banking, insurance & real estate	–	–		63.2	23.5	
Transport and communication	0.3	17.4		75.1	85.9	
Administration and defense	100.0	100.0		100.0	100.0	
Education	88.6	96.9		88.6	96.9	
Health	68.4	92.8		69.5	94.2	
Other Services	0.2	–		3.1	45.4	
TOTAL	8.9	10.2	13.4	29.6	47.2	23.7

Source: Baklanoff, "State and Economy," p. 43.

largest and most important in the country: banks and insurance companies; transport, including airline, railroad, and road transportation; oil refining and Portuguese distribution companies; the electric power and petrochemical industries; two of the three principal shipyards; major breweries; cement, fertilizer, and tobacco firms.[5] Nationalization was followed by amalgamation of several private firms in each industry into state monopolies. As Table 10.2 shows, the public sector in 1976 accounted for 47 percent of the country's gross fixed investment (GFCF), 30 percent of total value added (VA), and 24 percent of employment. This substantial expansion of the public sector since the revolution is particularly noteworthy in heavy manufacturing, public services, and in banking and insurance.

The Constitution of 1976 confirmed the large and interventionist role of the state in the economy. Article 1 proclaims that the Portuguese Republic is "involved in a transformation into a society without classes" and in Article 2 the state has as "its objective to ensure the transition to socialism by means of the creation of conditions for the democratic exercise of power by the working classes." Among the fundamental tasks of the state (Article 9) is "the socialization of the means of production." The extensive economic content of the Constitution is located in Title 3 of Part I: Economic, Social, Cultural Rights and Duties; and all of Part II: Economic Organization. Indicative of the extent and specificity of the interventionist, expanding and prosocialist role of the state are the following articles: Part I, Article 50, establishes as a general principle that "the collective appropriation of the principal means of production, the planning of economic development and the democratization of institutions are guarantees and conditions for the implementation of economic, social, and cultural rights and duties." The later listing of rights confers a vast assortment of economic, social, and cultural rights upon workers and attributes to the state the responsibility for their implementation as well as the establishment of relations between the working classes and owners which substantially favor the former. These rights include the right to work (Articles 51 and 52), labor rights (Articles 53 and 54), union organization and workers' commissions (Articles 55, 57 and 58), the principle of collective contracts (Article 58), with the right to strike (Article 59), the prohibition of lockout (Article 60), and the right of cooperative organizations as well as self-management along with private property (Articles 61 and 62). These economic sections are complemented by a vast array of social and cultural rights dealing with such areas as social security, housing, education, the handicapped, etc., all within a perspective of an interventionist and nonliberal role of the state in the country's economic and social life.

The reaffirmation of the socialist character of the Constitution is made at the beginning of the section on General Principles, establishing that "the social-economic organization of the Portuguese Republic is based on the development of socialist relations of production by means of the collective appropriation of the principal means of production and land, as well as natural resources and the democratic exercise of power by the working classes." The most relevant provisions are the following: Article 82 states that "the law will determine the means and the forms of intervention and of nationalization and socialization of the means of production, along with the criteria for determining indemnization." However, that indemnization may not be granted and "all the nationalizations made after 25 April 1974 are irreversible conquests of the working classes" (Article 83). This means that the firms nationalized cannot be denationalized. Article 85 establishes two crucial controls on the free exercise of economic activity: the first affirms that "the law will define the basic sectors in which private economic activity is not permitted," and the second gives to the state the power to monitor and directly intervene in the management of firms "to ensure the general interest and the rights of workers in terms to be defined by the law." It should be noted that the extensive stipulations and regulations on economy and society, which characterize this long (312 articles) and interventionist Constitution, were frequently rhetorical, wishful, and irrelevant. Many simply had little impact and were neglected.[6]

However, several of the articles that relate to the economy in concrete terms were at least formally and legally implemented. Basic legislation passed in 1977 by the Assembly (generally with the votes of the PS and PSD and the opposition—for contradictory reasons—of the PCP and CDS) promulgated and implemented a model of a mixed economy with democratic political power predominating over economic interests. The most important single law was 46/77 of 8 July 1977, which prohibited private enterprises and other similar entities from operating in specified sectors of the economy in line with Article 85 of the Constitution. Three areas were defined as the exclusive jurisdiction of the state: banking and insurance, with the exception of the three relatively small foreign banks, which had not been nationalized, and a variety of funds and investment groups;[7] infrastructure, including electrical energy, gas, communications, transportation and ports and airports; basic industries, including refining of oil, fertilizers, cements, steel, petrochemicals and armaments. This law fulfilled elements of Article 85 and also reaffirmed the irreversibility of the nationalizations made after 25 April 1974.

One of the most polemic issues after the revolution involved indemnization for nationalized properties. Law 80/77 of 28 October 1977 (passed with the votes of the PS, abstention of the PSD, and opposition of the other parties) allowed indemnization under certain conditions. However, only in 1980 did complementary legislation provide for compensation in fact. Other legislation during this period dealt with key aspects of the economy including the following: planning and the formation of a National Council of the Plan to make the economy more rational; a Foreign Investment Code; and the formation of an Institute for Foreign Investment to encourage, regulate, and define areas for foreign investment and agrarian reform.

A review of the Constitution of 1976 and the legislation of 1977 and 1978 confirms that the legal basis was established to regulate the economy in which political power was supposed to control economic power. The old monopolies had been dismantled, and through agrarian reform and the formation of unions structural changes had been implemented. The law concerning indemnizations, reinforced by the law closing sectors to private investment, made it impossible for large economic groups to reconstitute themselves, although the reappearance of smaller groups which had survived the revolution was possible. With a new system of planning that would operate in conjunction with the normal function of the market, and through the creation of a large public sector and structures for discussion among different economic actors, it was hoped that the conditions had been established for a new process of development in contrast to that of the Estado Novo. It seemed as though the new structure of property and the different relationships of power between owners and workers favored the definition of a new and progressive political economy within the perspective of social justice defined in the Constitution of 1976. The new power relationships were illustrated by the outlawing of lockouts, the liberal nature of strike laws, and constitutional restrictions on layoffs. However, the overall approach did not succeed; indeed, both the model defined in the Constitution of 1976 and the ensuing legislation have been part of the political struggle since at least 1978.

Constitutional Revision and the Economy

The revolution, subsequent state intervention and nationalization of firms, and changes in the power relationships between owners and workers were politically feasible in a certain context at a certain time. The political party most responsible for consolidating the new economic model was the PS. It did not favor the nationalizations in 1975, when it was on the defensive against the PCP and Prime Minister Vasco Gonçalves, and in general holds few firm views about either nationalization or denationalization. In the face of great economic and political difficulties, and with the formation of the AD, a new group came to power in early 1980 which was unsympathetic to the changes brought by the revolution and enshrined in the Constitution of 1976. The AD was committed to changing not only the political relationship between president and government but also the economic sections of the Constitution which the incumbent president and Council of the Revolution were guaranteeing. Of particular significance in this regard were the three attempts by the AD governments between 1980 and 1983 to change the law concerning sectors closed to private investment, particularly as it applied to banking and insurance. The solution, as described in Chapter 6, was to be revision of the Constitution of 1976, which was accomplished in August 1982. However, despite the overwhelming public focus on altering the economic section of the Constitution, little of this section was in fact revised.[9] The desire to have a revision, to change the relationship between the presidency (or rather the incumbent president) and government, won out over concern for programmatic changes in the economic section. The AD had to rely on the PS which was unwilling to make any significant changes in the economic section. While a number of minor changes were made in the general principles, with an overall "deideologization" of the Constitution, the overall system of a mixed economy in which the state is predominant continued. For example, Article 85, which provides for the law to define the sectors closed to private firms, remained intact.

What did change, however, was the composition and relationship of the organs of political power. The Constitutional Court took over the Council of the Revolution's role in judging the constitutionality of legislation. The CR had vetoed legislation pertaining to the economic section of the Constitution, particularly the law on sectors; three times it was declared unconstitutional, the last time even against a positive opinion by the Constitutional Commission within the CR. Finally, on 19 November 1983 the Central Bloc government received support in the Assembly for decree-law 406/83 revising two articles of law 46/77 regarding the financial and industrial sections of the economy. It became possible for new private banks and insurance companies to be formed, although certain requirements were specified regarding capital, solvency, etc. In the industrial sector all of the previous areas remained restricted to the state, except cement and fertilizers. The liberalization of banking demonstrates the flexibility of the PS and the PSD which made the original law in 1977, the changing context of power, and probably most of all the serious economic situation which was thought to require changes along these lines. Between 1983 and 1985 four foreign banks and three nationals were established, joining the nine nationalized and three foreign ones already existing. Because of low profitability, the viability of all but three of the nationalized commercial banks is in question. They have excess staff because the *retornados* who worked in these banks in Africa have reserved positions in the banks in Portugal. Further, state firms have expanded to absorb unemployment. Their financial situations are serious, and they will have trouble competing with new banks which do not have this background of excess staff and debts. Indeed, the banks are indicative of the public-enterprise sector as a whole which remains a polemical political question.

Public-Enterprise Controversy

The public-enterprise sector in Portugal consists of approximately eighty firms (see Table A2.2 of Appendix 2). As Table 10.3 indicates, their weight is comparable to this sector in other countries. A further examination of the sectors in which public enterprises are located, in comparison with other countries of the European Community, shows that in terms of the percentage of public firms compared to private Portugal is similar in the energy field (78 percent VA, 69 percent GFCF, and 71 percent employment), slightly less in transports and communications (44 percent, 31 percent, and 36 percent respectively), higher in manufacturing with 12 percent of VA, 51 percent of CGCF, and 9 percent of employment, and overwhelming in banking.[9] The public-enterprise sector thus occupies in Portugal a central and crucial area of the economy.

At least two observations must be made concerning the dynamics of the public-enterprise sector before its role in Portuguese development is examined. First, in Portugal, unlike other countries, this sector expanded almost overnight. Prior to 1974 the role of the state in Portugal was important for control and regulation but

Table 10.3   Weight of Public Enterprises in the Economy
(percentages)

Country	VA 1977	VA 1978	VA 1979	GFCF 1977	GFCF 1978	GFCF 1979	Employment 1977	Employment 1978	Employment 1979
Italy[1]	24.0	24.7	–	49.0[2]	47.1[2]	–	25.0	25.4	–
France	12.8	12.9	13.0	30.7	30.7	30.5	–	–	11.8
United Kingdom	11.6	11.4	11.1	22.7	20.8	20.0	7.7	8.0	8.1
West Germany	10.3	10.4	10.4[3]	12.1	11.9	10.6[2]	9.2	9.1	9.1[3]
Ireland	–	–	9.6[4]	15.0[2]	12.0[2]	12.0[2]	–	–	9.0
Belgium[5]	8.5	8.8	9.0	16.8	16.8	16.2	6.8	6.9	7.0
Greece[6]	–	–	8.1	–	–	11.4[2]	–	–	8.6
Holland	–	–	–	14.4	11.6	10.8	5.6	5.7	5.8
Denmark[7]	–	–	6.0	–	–	10.0	4.5	–	4.1
Luxembourg	–	–	–	5.7	–	–	–	–	–
Portugal[7]	–	19.8	19.0	–	30.0[2]	30.5[2]	–	6.5	6.5

Source: Arminda Manuela de Conceição António José de Sousa Mota, and Adriano Manuel da Rocha Carvalho, O sector empresarial do estado em Portugal e nos países da CEE (Lisbon: Imprensa Nacional and CEEPS, 1983), p. 178.

[1] For 1976, these figures were 23.8%, 46.7%, and 24.6% respectively.

[2] Or investment.

[3] Provisional figure.

[4] For VA in 1970.

[5] The VA in 1973, 1974, and 1975 evolved as follows: 5.4%, 4.9%, and 5.4%.

[6] The figures for VA (1975) and Employment (1976) were 8.1% and 7.9% respectively.

[7] These do not include firms which are controlled, or managed by the state, which in 1977 represented 2.5% of VA, 3.8% of GFCF, and 2.2% of employment.

the level of public ownership (as can be seen in Table 10.2) was slight. The nationalizations were not made gradually, efficiently, or with a preformulated rationale. Rather, they were made by a military-guided but left-oriented government to promote the transformation of Portugal into a socialist economy and society in the shortest possible time. Both the goals of nationalization and the implications in terms of results in the economy and society were greater than in other countries. The shift was radical, abrupt, and politically motivated and has resulted in a politicization of this sector.

Second, the public-enterprise sector is in poor financial shape. Portugal's foreign debt increased from $5.4 billion in 1978 to $13.5 billion at the end of 1982 and finally reached $14.2 billion in 1983, before a second IMF agreement was reached. The share of the foreign debt held by the public-enterprise sector increased from 37 percent of the total in 1978 to 57 percent in 1982.[10] The overall sources of financing can be seen in Table 10.4, which shows the great increase in foreign loans in even one year. Public enterprises have relied heavily on foreign borrowing. Their debts in 1981 represented some 40 percent of the value added of the sector, which is very high. Internally they are in a serious financial situation, as indicated in Table 10.5.

The new agreement with the IMF in 1983, which tightened up considerably such areas as financing and subsidies, aggravated the financial difficulties of the public sector. Three banks (Banco Borges e Irmão, União de Bancos Portugueses, and the Banco Fonseca e Burnay), many industrial firms (Setenave, Companhia Nacional de Petroquimica, etc.), and services (Companhia Nacional de Navegação, Companhia de Transportes Maritimos, TAP-Air Portugal, etc.) are on the edge of financial disaster if not beyond. In early 1985, for instance, just to establish financial stability for eighteen firms under the control of the Ministry of Industry and Energy would have required almost U.S. $3 billion.[11] Before dealing with the causes of the many problems in the public-enterprise sector, it would be useful to highlight the potential importance of this sector for Portuguese development.

Table 10.4

Sources of Financing for the Public-Enterprise Sector

	1980	1981
Self-financed	17%	7%
Provision of Capital	15	9
Obligations	–	3
Internal Credit	24	17
External Credit	40	61
Other	5	4

Source: Portugal Central Department of Planning.

Table 10.5

Financial Predicament of Public-Enterprise Sector

(in Millions of U.S. Dollars.)

	1977	1978	1979	1980	1981
Industry	-29,1	-15,1	29,5	19,6	-272,8
Electrical energy	1,2	1,6	-16,5	1,0	1,0
Transports	-45,6	-96,2	-123,8	-257,3	-240,0
Communications	4,9	5,2	9,2	13,6	15,3
Other	-38,7	-26,2	2,5	-18,9	-17,6
Total	-107,8	-128,8	-99,0	-243,0	-514,0

Source: Portugal Central Department of Planning.

Portugal remains the most underdeveloped country of Western Europe with general indices far below the other less-developed countries, including Greece and Spain. (See Table A2.1 in Appendix 2.) In the context of Portuguese underdevelopment any strategy for growth, and finally development, will require a coherent plan. Unfortunately, planning has been less successful since 1976 than it was under the Estado Novo, although it was given prominence in the 1976 Constitution and the program of the first constitutional government. Considering the size, linkages, centrality, and generally modern characteristics of the public-enterprise sector, it must be involved in a strategy for development in Portugal. The economist João Cravinho notes that prior to nationalization this sector was the fulcrum of the whole modern sector.[12] The value added of the public-enterprise sector, excluding banks and other financial institutions, indicates the capital-intensive and generally strategic character of this sector (See Table 10.6).

The most comprehensive study available on the public sector also highlights its importance for Portuguese development by emphasizing its size, role in basic services, amount of investment, and utilization of relatively modern technology.[13] The role of public-sector enterprises is particularly obvious if we recall that as *public* enterprises they should, in principle, be under the control of the state and thus an instruments in a planning strategy.

Portugal's membership in the European Community in 1986 increases the potential positive role of the public-enterprise sector. Application for accession was made in 1977 and, after several delays, complications, and ongoing negotiations caused by disagreements within the Community, and the requirement of joining Portugal's application to that of Spain, was finally agreed to in early 1985. Much has been written about the Community and its implications for Portugal. Portugal is at present very underdeveloped; its new industries were founded behind high tariffs and other nontariff barriers in a context which changed with the oil shocks and the revolution. Most of the industrialization is weak, and agriculture is particularly inefficient with 28 percent of the economically active population producing but 12 percent of GDP. The motivation for the application in 1977 and its acceptance by the Community in 1978 was based mainly on political grounds.[14] In principle Portugal should also benefit economically. This requires adaptation and modernization of policies in at least agriculture and industry. So far this adaptation has not been forthcoming, and Portugal remains generally unprepared for the likely impact of accession even considering its ten-year transition period.[15] This lack of preparation is nowhere more obvious than in the public-enterprise sector, potentially important for development in the face of accession to the European Community.

Table 10.6

Value Added of Public-Enterprise Sector

(in millions of U.S. dollars, 1978 prices)

	1978	1979	1980	1981	1982*
Industry	620	882	933	926	913
Electrical energy	346	382	366	346	511
Transport	564	548	504	553	551
Communications	328	344	344	413	400
Social communications	31	40	53	55	
Agriculture	4	4	6	6	440
Commerce	75	113	46	151	
Fishing	26	28	20	15	
Misc.	22	22	26	310	
Total	2016	2363	2298	2775	

*estimate

Source: Portugal Central Department of Planning

The Economic Crisis

Probably the single most important reason for the disarray in the public-enterprise sector is the macroeconomic situation of the country in which this sector plays an important role. Portugal, lacking a wide and diversified resource base, having gone through a revolutionary process after a longer period of protection, and stripped of the colonies, has a weak economy. Following the revolution, the country encountered severe balance-of-payments problems and had to turn to the International Monetary Fund in 1978 for a standby agreement whereby foreign states agreed to loan the country $750 million. The overall results of the measures were positive, and between 1978 and 1981 the economic situation improved substantially.[16] As noted in Table 10.1, labor's share of GDP decreased. The considerable reduction in real wages after 1976 helped improve Portugal's competitive position in foreign markets exports, including tourism and services, which increased from 16.5 percent of domestic expenditure in 1976 to an average of 27 percent in 1979-80. Further, total consumption, which had exceeded domestic expenditure by two percentage points in 1975, averaged just under 89 percent in 1979-80. With renewed private saving and a much improved climate for investment, capital formation (gross investment) rose sharply from a low of 13.5 percent in 1975 to an average of over 24 percent in 1979-80.[17]

However, with the second oil shock of 1979 and the simultaneous electoral policies of the AD government, the economic situation deteriorated sharply. The AD won in the interim elections of late 1979 and faced regular legislative elections in late 1980 as well as presidential elections shortly thereafter. The AD government pursued an electoral strategy in economic policy by forcing inflation down from 24 percent to 16 percent, expanding internal demand by 6.2 percent, increasing disposable income by 3 percent, increasing private consumption by 4.5 percent, and promoting a real increase in salaries of 4 percent. To do so required maintenance and even revaluation of the overvalued escudo, maintaining or increasing subsidies and borrowing.[18] This resulted in incredible leaps in the current account deficit from $1,251,000,000 in 1980, to $2,852,000,000 in 1981, and $3,245,000,000 in 1982. By 1982 the deficit amounted to 13 percent of the GDP, and the total foreign debt in 1983 of $14,200,000,000 required $2,500,000,000 just for service. Even with gold and foreign-exchange reserves in 1982 of $6,473,000,000 these deficits and accumulated debts were completely impossible to carry. Thus when the Central Bloc government came to power in mid-1983 it had to turn quickly to the IMF for another standby agreement. Negotiations were finalized in October 1983 for $480 million of loans, which opened the way to further international credit.

The terms of agreement with the IMF were standard and included a reduction of balance-of-payments current account deficit from $3.2 billion in 1983 to $1.25 billion in 1984, and a reduction in the budget deficit from 13 percent of GDP in 1982 to 7 percent in 1984. The following major programs were included as well: adoption of public-sector policies to tighten expenditures, principally through wage restraint, and to increase public revenues, principally through higher taxes and by raising administered prices; limited growth in total domestic bank credit; pushing up the prices of subsidized import commodities to reflect real costs; restraining nominal increases in wages to levels significantly below the rate of inflation; and, after a devaluation in mid-1983, maintaining crawling peg exchange rate adjustments for the escudo to ensure competitiveness of Portuguese exports. This amounted to an emergency economic program which resulted in extremely constrained economic policies; essentially, just managing the debt. In 1983 there was no real growth, and in 1984 growth actually declined by approximately 2 percent. In 1983 inflation was 30 percent and unemployment increased to 10 percent of the work force, or approximately half a million. Real wages dropped by 9 percent in 1983 and subsidies on foods, transport, and other necessities were abolished. The economy was unquestionably in recession.

The significance of the overall economic situation for the public-enterprise sector is complex. As noted above, the public-enterprise sector bears more than 50 percent of Portugal's foreign debt. It cannot be assumed, however, that this is due to irresponsibility on the part of the directors, as the government uses this sector for a number of purposes. One of these is to help finance the overall state debt by using the larger enterprises, such as Petrogal, to extend their loans abroad.[19] The government has also used them to maintain prices, even through subsidies which are incredibly complicated, and to keep unemployment down by retaining excess staff.[20] The public-enterprise sector has been used less as an instrument for overall development than as one element in a larger economic policy, or group of policies, to avoid or at least delay some of the serious implications of the economic crisis. With the second IMF agreement, however, less flexibility was available and the enterprises can no longer be maintained as they have in the past. Layoffs occurred, some firms were on the verge of bankruptcy, and the Ministry of Industry and Energy demanded $1,650,000,000 from the state for what was owed by public sectors to the eighteen public firms under its control.[21]

Disarray and Politicization of the Public-Enterprise Sector

There are two other main reasons for the disarray in the public-enterprise sector. First, the debate over this sector raises fundamental philosophical and economic disagreements within the political and economic elite. The debate concerns not only the way the public sector was created, but also the issue of privatization and the responsibility of the state sector for the country's economic ills. Constitutional revision did not offer a solution to this issue.

The other major reason deals with the technical and political problems of the enterprises themselves. Their supervision, or control (*tutela*), is divided among a number of ministries, depending on the nature of the firm. Technical control is exercised by the ministry involved in the area; economic-financial control is with the Ministry of Finance; social control involves the Ministry of Labor; and, depending on the particular issue, other ministries may be involved, such as the Ministry of Commerce regarding prices.[22] Controls suffer from poor coordination, and the managers feel very tightly constrained.

In addition, the appointments of managers and boards of directors of the firms are highly politicized. The three major political parties which have been in government since 1976 have all placed their members in top positions in these firms.[23] Not unreasonably, these individuals may have political rather than technical expertise. This practice may help build up the party system but does little for the firms. Further, the firms cannot easily take steps to promote increased efficiency; their top-heavy nature, an almost built-in instability due to changes in the government, and an all too frequent struggle between the parties for positions militate against efficient business procedures. The instability has been increased since 1982 with decree-law 464/82 of 9 December which altered the 1976 Statute of Public Managers. The position of public manager was redefined to encompass "individuals nominated by the government for the organs of management for public firms and for organs of firms in which the state has a role." The conditions of pay, prerequisites, and mandate were changed with the result that "the public manager can be freely dismissed by the entities that nominate him, and the dismissal can be based on the mere convenience of needs." (Article 6-1). This has, if anything, increased the instability and politicization of public firms. The public-enterprise sector serves the overall economic and political purposes of particular governments and parties.

What may be concluded from this discussion on the role of the state in the economy? Due to the particular context, timing, and process of the revolutionary period the state's role in the Portuguese economy is predominant. However, there is little agreement on this role or its instruments which are a constant source of political conflict. Despite the constitutional revision and subsequent opening of the banks and other areas to private investment, the role of the state remains large and is an integral part of the economic crisis and the governments' manner of dealing with it. The role of the state is more important in the context of access to the European Community in 1986. However, there are no simple solutions to the problems raised by the role of the state in the economy because of its centrality in such areas as subsidies and employment; its administrative problems with divided control; and most of all because of the high level of politicization with political appointees occupying key positions in the firms. In this area, as in others, the parties have played a preeminent role in defining the general character of the political and economic system in postrevolutionary Portugal.

Notes

1. See Elizabeth Leeds, "Salazar's 'Modelo Económico': The Consequences of Planned Constraint," in Thomas Bruneau, Victor M.P. da Rosa, and Alex Macleod (eds.), *Por-

tugal in Development: Emigration, Industrialization, the European Community (Ottawa: University of Ottawa Press, 1984), for an analysis of the development strategy and its results in industrialization and emigration, pp. 13-51.

2. Eric Baklanoff, "Reforming the Portuguese Revolution: Perspectives on the Nationalization-Redistribution Syndrome," *Annals of SECOLAS*, Vol. 15 (March 1984), p. 38. Baklanoff draws these data from Maria Belmira Martins, *Sociedades e grupos em Portugal* (Lisbon: Editorial Estampa, 1973), p. 16. See, also, his *The Economic Transformation of Spain and Portugal* (New York: Praeger Publishers, 1978).

3. Eric Baklanoff, "The State and Economy in Portugal: Perspectives on Corporatism, Revolution, and Reform," paper presented to Research Conference on State Shrinking, University of Texas at Austin, 1-3 March 1984, p. 8. On this general topic see also the now-classic Francisco Pereira de Moura, *Por onde vai a economia portuguesa?* 4th ed., (Lisbon: Seara Nova, 1974). Tremendous details on all aspects of the economy, investment, agriculture, the European Community, etc., can be found in the four volumes resulting from the First and Second International Conferences on the Portuguese Economy, 10-13 October 1976 and 26-28 September 1979, sponsored by the German Marshall Fund of the United States and the Fundação Calouste Gulbenkian (Lisbon: Fundaçào Calouste Gulbenkian, 1977 and 1980).

4. We have not dealt specifically with the topic of agrarian reform in this book for two reasons. First, with very few exceptions the topic is not as relevant in economic terms as it was during the revolutionary period. Second, there is abundant literature on this topic, including a World Bank study and a series edited by António Barreto, minister of agriculture during the first constitutional government after 1976. For the former, see World Bank, *Portugal: Agricultural Sector Survey* (Washington: The World Bank, 1978), and for the latter, see António Barreto, *Memória da reforma agrária* (Lisbon: Publicações Europa-America, n.d.). By mid-1985 five of these volumes had been published.

5. A complete listing and description of the 244 firms is found in Maria Belmira Martins and J. Chaves Rosa, *O grupo estado: Análise e listagem completa das sociedades do sector público empresarial* (Lisbon: Edições Jornal Expresso, 1979).

6. For this argument see Marcelo Rebelo de Sousa, *Direito Constitucional* (Braga: Livraria Cruz, 1979), pp. 340-45.

7. Baklanoff, "State and Economy," p. 11, notes that the nationalized banks at the end of 1977 held 98 percent of all commercial bank capital and equal shares of commercial loans and deposits.

8. These minor changes are analyzed in great detail by A.L. de Sousa Franco, "A revisão da constituição económica," *Revista da Ordem dos Advogados,* September-December 1982, pp. 601-88. He states that "the fundamental principles of the economic constitution were not radically modified," p. 686.

9. For extensive details, see ibid., p. 178-84.

10. Baklanoff, "State and Economy," p. 20. For the whole issue of debt, see in particular Abel Moreira Mateus, *Crescimento económico e dívida externa: O caso de Portugal* (Lisbon: Instituto de Estudos para o Desenvolvimento, 1982), and IED, *Seminário sobre crescimento económico e dívida externa: O caso de Portugal* (Lisbon: Instituto de Estudos Para o Desenvolvimento, 1983).

11. For the eighteen public enterprises under the Ministry of Industry and Energy (MIE), see MIE, *O sector empresarial do estado na indústria e energia: Análise e propostas de atuacão* (Lisbon: MIE, 1984).

12. João Cravinho, "Portugal: Um pais em crise entre o 'desplaneamento' e as políticas de estabilização," in Manuela Silva et al., *O planeamento económico em Portugal* (Lisbon: Livraria Sá da Costa Editora, 1984), p. 63. Also of importance for understanding development, and particularly industrialization, is the monograph by Klaus Esser, Guido Ashoff, Ansgar Eussner, and Wilhelm Hummen, "Portugal's Industrial Policy in Terms of

Accession to the European Community" (Berlin: GDI, 1980); and Maria José Constâncio, Adriano Pimpão and Rui Carvalho, *Uma estrategia para a industrialização portuguesa* (Lisbon: Instituto de Estudos Para o Desenvolvimento), 1984.

13. Arminda Manuela da Conceição António et al. *O sector empresarial,* 1983, p. 239.

14. The political justification by the Commission is made very clearly in the "Opinion on Portuguese Application for Membership," *Bulletin of the European Communities,* Supplement 5/78 (transmitted to the Council by the Commission on 19 May 1978), p. 7.

15. On the impact of entry for Portugal see, for example, the GDI publication cited in note 16, as well as the following: João Cravinho, "Structural Adjustment in Portugal in the Face of Entry to the EEC," and Jorge Braga de Macedo, "Portugal and Europe: The Dilemmas of Integration," in Thomas Bruneau, Victor M.P. da Rosa, and Alex Macleod (eds.), *Portugal in Development,* 1984; Rainer Eisfeld, "Political and Economic Problems of Portugal's Accession to the EC," *Assuntos Europeus,* no. 3 (1982), pp. 345-81; IED, *Problemas relacionados com a adesão de Portugal à CEE* (Lisbon: Instituto de Estudos Para o Desenvolvimento, 1981); and the very useful interview with the ex-minister of finance and vice-director of the Bank of Portugal, Victor Constâncio, in *O Jornal,* 10 February 1984.

16. For the 1978 IMF agreement, see in particular the following: Barbara Stallings, "Portugal and the IMF: The Political Economy of Stabilization," in Jorge Braga de Macedo and Simon Serfaty (eds.), *Portugal Since the Revolution: Economic and Political Perspectives* (Boulder, Colorado: Westview Press, 1981); J. Silva Lopes, "IMF Conditionality in the Stand-By Arrangement with Portugal of 1978," in John Williamson (ed.), *The Lending Policies of the International Monetary Fund* (Washington, D.C.: Institute for Internatioanl Economics, 1982); and Hans Schmitt, *Economic Stabilization and Growth in Portugal,* Occasional Papers of the IMF, no. 2 (Washington, D.C.: IMF, April 1981).

17. Baklanoff, "The State and Economy," p. 26.

18. João Cravinho, "Portugal: Um País em Crise," in Silva et al. *O planeamento económico,* 1984, pp. 63-64. For a discussion of the economic policies of the AD government of Sá Carneiro by his minister of finance and the plan, see Aníbal A. Cavaco Silva, *A política económica do governo de Sá Carneiro* (Lisbon: Publicações Dom Quixote, 1982). See also his "Finances públicas e contas externas: A 'história' dos desequilíbrios," *Diário de Notícias,* 24 April 1984, pp. 50-51.

19. This is briefly noted in the MIE, *O sector empresarial,* p. 166, and was pointed out frequently in our interviews in 1982 and 1983.

20. Some of these points are noted in Baklanoff, "State and Economy," p. 19, and are normally emphasized in our interviews with managers of the firms.

21. *Diário de Notícias,* 24 January 1985.

22. MIE, *O sector empresarial,* 1984, pp. 134 and 162.

23. This was a key theme which emerged in our interviews with managers of firms as well as political figures. It has been noted frequently in the press. See, for instance, *Expresso* of 15 December 1984 in the interview with Pedro Ferraz da Costa, President of CIP, on this point. "The strength of the parties fundamentally is based in or resides in the public firms, in the distribution of positions, in the creation of clienteles. . . ." The same theme was emphasized in *Expresso,* 2 February 1985, in indicating the political affiliation of the directors of the nationalized banks.

Conclusion

The most obvious feature of Portugal's new constitutional regime is the increasing dichotomy between the logic of partisan politics and the aims of the Constitution. Neither the document drafted in 1976 nor the revision of 1982 have produced a long-term solution to the most pressing political problem, government stability. Between 1976 and 1986, no legislature went its full term and no government survived more than two years. However, one institution stands out as a model of stability and continuity, the presidency, a situation which may well be jeopardized by the 1982 revision and the demands of party politics.

The government crisis of the summer of 1985, which led to the dissolution of the Assembly and subsequent elections in October, highlighted the inherent weaknesses in the constitutional changes of 1982. If the crisis had occurred one month later, President Eanes could not have used dissolution to break the deadlock, since the president may no longer dissolve the Assembly during the last six months of his mandate. In fact, the country could have been saddled with a hung parliament for almost a year, because the revised Constitution forbids parliamentary elections within ninety days of presidential elections. This last condition effectively reduces the possibility for a Portuguese president to follow the example of his French counterpart, who can use dissolution to create a parliamentary majority in the image of his own presidential majority in the wake of a successful election or reelection.

President Eanes managed to symbolize stability because he stood above the party fray. This extraordinary situation, akin in some ways to the myth of de Gaulle in France, could not outlast the dictates of political reality. As in the French Fifth Republic, the presidency has become a party affair. This could hardly be avoided. Even in 1976 and 1980, President Eanes depended on explicit partisan support for his election while insisting on his total autonomy from the parties. His main rival in 1980, General Soares Carneiro, was clearly a creature of the AD, a wholly partisan candidate. In 1985, two of the most prominent presidential candidates, Mário Soares and Diogo Freitas do Amaral, identified themselves with parties, despite their attempts to broaden their appeal. Since no one party can hope to attract the support of an absolute majority of the electorate (even the AD, the closest the post-1976 governments have come to a coherent parliamentary majority, could not achieve that) any victory in future presidential elections will depend on a circumstantial majority which will give no guarantee of future stability. Party behavior has shown that no possible coalition is immutable. Furthermore, any deal involving the promise of the prime ministership for one party in exchange for its support for the presidential candidate of another would immediately weaken not only the future president's room to maneuver but also the prestige, and hence the legitimacy, of the presidential office as a source of stability.

The presidency has become a focal point for all parties. The Communists, who nurture few illusions about joining the "government of national salvation" which they demand, know that they can decisively influence the choice of president, as they did in 1980. They can support a candidate and hope for some consideration in return; equally, they can withhold their votes to help defeat a candidate. The importance of the presidency for the other parties made itself felt in 1984-85 when it overshadowed all other political issues. The life of the Central Bloc government seemed to hinge on the presidential aspirations of Mário Soares; this ultimately became a stumbling block as many elements in the PSD rejected the implicit subordination of their party to the PS, and the Social Democrats could not come up with a credible candidate of their own. As for the newly formed PRD, from the beginning tensions appeared between supporters and opponents of the candidacy of Maria de Lourdes Pintasilgo, who was unacceptable to the outgoing president, Ramalho Eanes, for whom the party was supposed to have been founded in the first place. The president has become the leader of a partisan coalition. This is a new feature of Portuguese politics.

Most academic observers in Portugal have concluded that the political system can best be characterized as a "semipresidential regime." The proponents of this concept, borrowed from Maurice Duverger,[1] base their argument on the fact that the president is elected by universal suffrage; the government is responsible before the president and the Assembly; the president has the power to dissolve Parliament; and, additionally, he can exercise real powers and can control the government's activities.[2] But as Jean-Claude Colliard has pointed out, a president can only use the constitutional powers at his disposal if the party system is highly fragmented, as in Finland, or if the parties constituting the majority in Parliament acknowledge the president's authority as being over that of the prime minister, as in France.[3] Undoubtedly, President Eanes exercised his constitutional powers to the full and used his political skills to set important precedents, such as refusing to automatically accept government shuffles or implausible nominees for prime minister. But in the first case the president never had to carry out his threat, and in the second, he quite rightly surmised that the proposed candidate could never succeed in reconstituting a moribund coalition. The Italian president may also influence the choice of premier to a large extent, but by no stretch of the imagination would one call Italy a "semipresidential regime."

The fundamental question is this: has the president been able to act independently of other institutions? The answer must be a qualified no. With one crucial exception, the president must either act on the advice of the prime minister or be constrained by the political complexion of the Assembly. He cannot dismiss the prime minister at will, he cannot choose his ministers (powers which successive presidents of the French Fifth Republic have established), and his legislative veto can be overridden by a determined Assembly. He can dissolve Parliament on his own, but, as we have seen, his power is constitutionally restricted. During the two terms of President Eanes, neither of Colliard's conditions prevailed. Things would certainly have been different had Eanes commanded a coherent majority in the Assembly. One can also imagine that, in the unlikely event of a partisan president supported by a stable parliamentary majority, the president could wield very real executive political powers. We must therefore conclude with Colliard that everything depends, not on the letter of the constitution, but on "the form of political game brought about by the president's position vis-á-vis the party system."[4]

Portuguese politics has been marked by a visible trend toward concentration of power. Within the parties, the leader, supported by a relatively small executive, has become the main source of decision making. In the PCP and the PS, no one can doubt the ascendency of the secretary-general over his party. In the PSD and the CDS the phenomenon is somewhat less obvious. Freitas do Amaral and Sá Carneiro enjoyed almost complete control over their respective parties. Their successors have had much less success. However, both parties favor centralization and the concentration of power, and the militants seem to be forever seeking a leader capable of wielding undisputed authority. Within the state apparatus, the government has increasingly become the center of power, calling on the parties to exert pressure on their deputies when necessary, so that the Assembly, more often than not, acts simply to give the government its stamp of approval. Finally, in keeping with a strong Portuguese tradition, political and cultural power continues to reside in Lisbon, even though economic power has tended to shift back to the industrial region of Oporto-Braga in the north.

This concentration of power has not gone unnoticed; obvious reactions against it are evident within the parties. Many of the problems in the PSD can be traced back to provincial resentment of a perceived Lisbon-oriented domination over a party with deep roots in rural Portugal. From the very beginning, the debates that centered around the creation of the pro-Eanes PRD reflected rivalries between groups based in the capital and the members from the provinces. On a more general level, the reaction to the domination by Lisbon, the source of many antigovernment rebellions in the past, was expressed in the great popularity of President Eanes, himself a product of rural Portugal. For many, he represented the antithesis of intraparty and interparty squabbles, of the search for personal advantage through politics,[5] and symbolized down-to-earth traditional Portuguese values.

The consolidation of the party system has reinforced the trend toward concentration of power. Party splits have had little or no effect on voter support for the main parties. No breakaway party has been able to sustain itself for any length of time, and postrevolutionary politics tells many stories of splinter parties which have simply disappeared from the political scene. Each political party seemed to occupy fully its own ideological space. The far left has all but evaporated to the advantage of the PCP. The PS has virtually swallowed the UEDS and the ASDI. On the center right and the right, there was apparently little room outside the PSD and CDS. Voters seemed to follow the elites.

However, our 1984 survey revealed that 65 percent of the respondents thought that a large number of Portuguese were discontented with the existing parties. The basis of a new political force came from the undeniable popularity of President Eanes. Again in our survey, we asked the respondents to rank the degree of sympathy they had for ten political personalities. President Eanes with a average rank of seven (one was low and ten high) ranked a full point higher than the next personality and the degree of disagreement with this rank was less than all other personalities. Eanes himself remained equivocal about the whole idea of this party as it began to take form in 1984-85 and could not give it his official blessing without losing his image as an independent president, above party politics. Further, it was not clear where the PRD would find its constituency. In our survey, of those responding that they thought there were a large number of Portuguese who were discontented with the present parties, 36 percent indicated that the appearance of a new party was necessary. The calling of early parliamentary elections in June 1985 did not prevent the PRD from winning an unanticipated 19 percent of the vote.

Conflicts between institutions, between parties, and within parties have been aggravated by the personal dimension which has always played an important part in Portuguese political culture. The personalization of politics occurs in all countries, but in a nation like Portugal, with a relatively small political class, personal relations can greatly influence politics. It would be a gross oversimplification to reduce politics to the infighting of partisan coteries or cliques, but the personal factor affects the ease with which political negotiations are conducted. The relations between President Eanes and Mário Soares, the personal antipathy between certain "barons" of the PSD and Pinto Balsemão, the personal settling of scores between the ex-Secretariat and the Soaristas within the PS have all had adverse repercussions for the Portuguese political system. In our interviews with politicians, this theme was constantly invoked and we were struck by the intensity of sentiment frequently expressed. It also helped us to understand the ferocity of certain polemics and the difficulties involved in resolving them.

Despite the problems facing the Portuguese political system, one is tempted to echo Galileo and declare *eppur si muove*. It could be argued that Portugal has fared no worse than Italy, which has long since learned to live with ephemeral governments and endless crises. But one must seriously ask whether this, the most underdeveloped country in Western Europe, can afford the luxury of unstable governments when faced with the economic legacy of the Estado Novo, the trauma and costs of decolonization, and the upheaval of the revolution, all of which have left it unprepared to bear the hardships of the general economic crises of the 1970s and 1980s. As Portugal joins the European Community, there will be even greater economic challenges which will demand more decisive and responsible leadership than the poliical parties have offered, with few exceptions, since the revolution.

Notes

1. See Maurice Duverger, *Echec au roi* (Paris: Albin Michel, 1978) and "A New Political System Model: Semi-Presidential Government," *European Journal of Political Research,* 8 (1980), pp. 165-187.
2. See for example, António Nadais et al., "Constituição da república portuguesa," 1983, pp. 231-233.
3. Jean-Claude Colliard, *Les régimes parlementaires contemporains,* 1978, p. 280.
4. Ibid., p. 281. See also Colliard's preface to Emídio da Veiga Domingos, *Portugal político,* 1980, p. 18.
5. For the first year of the revolution, Eanes directed the RTP but took only his Lt. Colonel's pay and not the higher salary that normally went with this post. He also strongly resisted all increases in politicians' salaries, including his own. The salary of the president of the Republic remained the same from 1973 to 1985, despite inflation between these years.

Epilogue
The Paradoxes of Portuguese Politics

As the results of the parliamentary elections began coming in on the night of 6 October 1985, a feeling of disbelief spread through the Portuguese political system. The six-month-old Democratic Renewal party, with a long list of neophyte candidates, running on a program based on little more than support for President Ramalho Eanes and the need to bring morality into parliamentary politics, had taken 18 percent of the vote. Not only had it outdistanced the Communist-dominated APU and the conservative CDS, it had also reduced the PS share of the vote to just over 20 percent. At the same time, the clear winner was the PSD, whose new leader, Aníbal Cavaco Silva, had brought down the government coalition to which it belonged and had forced the election. Despite its full share in the government's austerity policy and its being the main cause of government instability, the PSD had managed to shift all the blame on to its partner, the Socialist party, and to score the best election result in its eleven-year history.

Observers quickly claimed that nothing would be quite the same as before in Portuguese politics. The poor showing by the PS had dashed Mário Soares's presidential aspirations. The country's stable four-party system had been irremediably shaken. Anything could now happen in the coming presidential elections. As the events unfolded between 6 October and the first ballot of the elections for the presidency on 26 January 1986, it became clear that it was not so easy to break the established pattern of Portuguese politics, and in particular the solidity of the party system. These events also revealed the many paradoxes that made up the reality of political life in Portugal.

Undoubtedly, the PRD had been able to capitalize on growing discontent with the existing parties, particularly amongst voters on the left and the center left. Some 73 percent of its support came from disaffected Socialist supporters and another 6 percent from the PSD. Surprisingly, the PRD also attracted almost 18 percent of its vote from those who had previously supported APU,[1] which had the effect of giving that coalition its worst result since its creation. However, as one analyst pointed out, the PRD received much of its vote from the urban lower middle classes in commerce, industry, and the services and from small business people, an electorate particularly unstable and easy to mobilize.[2] The PRD also owed much of its success to the support it received from President Eanes, whose wife participated actively in the party's campaign. The President's first involvement in partisan politics belied the political neutrality that had contributed so much to his prestige and set off a decline in his political reputation which subsequent events accelerated.

The PSD more than made up for these losses to the PRD with support from Socialist voters, from new voters, and above all from the CDS, which lost some 14 percent of its 1983 vote to the PSD.[3] With these gains from the CDS and the orientation imposed on the party by its new conservative leader, who had established his authority in a way no leader had done since the death of Sá Carneiro, the PSD had undeniably shifted to the right.

As the clear winner of the election, even with only 30 percent of the vote, the PSD was called on to form a government, the second minority government in the regime's short history. Constrained by the realities of its position in the Assembly of the Republic, the Cavaco Silva government could only go through with its conservative program if it could consolidate its position. The country's built-in left-wing majority excluded any possibility of gaining support for such a program in the Assembly in the near future, especially given the poor relations between the PSD and CDS. Cavaco Silva needed a victory for the presidential candidate whom he had supported before winning the leadership of the PSD in May 1985, Diogo Freitas do Amaral. Only thus could he hope to complete the strategy dreamed up by the late Sá Carneiro of a conservative coalition backed by a conservative president. The results of 6 October had paved the way for one of the possible scenarios of the coming presidential elections.

The Presidential Candidates and Their Base of Support

Outgoing President Ramalho Eanes was constitutionally barred from running for a third term; so he hoped to find a suitable candidate who could build a similar coalition to the one that had reelected him in 1980 and who would allow him to come back in 1991. The first serious "Eanista" candidate for the presidency appeared within two weeks after the legislative elections. He was Colonel Manuel da Costa Brás, a participant in the revolution of 1974–1975 and head of the High Authority against Corruption. After announcing publicly his availability as a candidate, he received open backing from President Eanes. He seemed in many ways an ideal choice, despite a lackluster public personality. He had an unblemished track record and his moderate image could attract votes from the center left and the center right and could certainly count on the type of discreet but effective support the PCP had given President Eanes in 1980. Unfortunately, Colonel Costa Brás could only obtain the first of the four conditions that he laid down for declaring his candidacy: that he should be supported by the President, that he should get the backing of the PRD, that Maria de Lourdes Pintasilgo should withdraw in his favor, and that he could rely on absence of opposition from the 25 April Association, to which he belonged.

President Eanes's support did not suffice to swing the PRD behind his candidacy. Not only did many members of the PRD lean toward Maria de Lourdes, but the PRD leadership resented the way they had been left out of the preliminary negotiations and put in a "take it or leave it" situation. As for Maria de Lourdes Pintasilgo, she had no intention of stepping down for anybody. Finally, though the 25 April Association could not officially support any candidate, many of its more influential members stood openly behind the Pintasilgo candidacy and therefore did not look on her potential rival with any enthusiasm. Under these conditions, Costa Brás could do little but drop out of the race less than two months after announcing his readiness to run. This whole affair dealt a serious blow to President Eanes's authority, and hence his prestige, and left him with under three months to prepare his succession.

As Costa Brás left the political stage, another possible "Eanista" candidate stepped forward, Francisco Salgado Zenha. He had served as second in command in the PS until his break with Mário Soares over the latter's withdrawal of support for President Eanes's bid for reelection in 1980. Known to be close to Eanes, Zenha publicly declared his candidacy in mid-November, without laying down conditions. This time most of the PRD leadership rallied behind the new candidate. President Eanes himself left little doubt about his own support and finally appeared on television on Zenha's behalf in the closing stages of the campaign.

In the meantime the PCP put forward a candidate of its own, a longtime member of the party hierarchy, Angelo Veloso. The party never hid the fact that it was repeating its 1980 tactic of running a candidate to take full advantage of free television and radio time without any intention of remaining in the race till the end. Zenha did not particularly appeal to the Communists. He had fought against them in 1975 over the issue of forming a single labor-union federation and had been a faithful member of the Socialist party and Socialist-led governments until 1982. Moreover, his reputation as a renegade, or at best a maverick, within the PS, could hurt his chances of winning over Socialist voters. He was not an effective public speaker and lacked the capacity to mobilize the electorate on his own. On the other hand, he enjoyed the unqualified support of President Eanes, the one man who could possibly rally enough votes behind a candidate to beat Mário Soares on the first ballot, and thus avoid the choice the PCP most feared, that between Soares and Freitas do Amaral. With obvious reluctance, the party announced its support for Zenha at a National Conference held only three weeks before the first round of voting. But it did not officially withdraw its own candidate until four days before the vote.

For the PCP, two vital issues were involved. First, it wanted to ensure that it would play a determining role in the election of the new president, so that it would not be excluded from the one institution of the executive branch where it could still hope to exert some influence. Of greater long-term importance, because it concerned the party's very existence, was the need to reassert its authority over its electorate. The party had lost the votes of almost 20 percent of its constituency in the October elections, and opinion polls and press reports indicated that many Communist supporters were preparing to vote for Maria de Lourdes Pintasilgo, a candidate that both the party and President Eanes had already rejected. The PCP was about to show that it still controlled its vote and that it would never again suffer the setback of the 1976 presidential elections, when many of its voters backed Otelo Saraiva de Carvalho over its own candidate and gave the party its worst electoral defeat since 1974.

Although President Eanes had found his candidate, he could not recapture the ground lost with the Costa Brás fiasco. The PRD, victim of its own rapid rise to fame, could not sustain the hopes it had carried. Against the advice of Eanes, it plunged into the local elections of 15 December 1985, without realizing that it could only meet with defeat. The PRD's campaign began very badly when it had to withdraw from the municipal race in Lisbon because of alleged irregularities in the signatures on its official nomination papers, not a happy event for a party that had called for a new political morality. Participation in the local elections proved to be a strategic error. As in most countries, local elections usually involve local issues, even though these are often mixed with questions of national party politics, and largely favor incumbents. By definition, the PRD could not count on the latter, except for those who had defected from other parties. It was therefore no surprise, except perhaps for the PRD leadership, that the party's share of the vote dropped from over 18 percent in October to less than five percent in December. Party leaders were particularly upset with President Eanes's wise refusal to lend his name to this PRD campaign.

The party was also experiencing problems with the presidential elections. The bulk of the leadership followed Eanes's second choice, realizing that another rebuff to the outgoing president would irremediably destroy his authority and his public image. However, the PRD membership and its electorate were deeply divided. Many felt committed to Maria de Lourdes Pintasilgo, while others could not bring themselves to rally behind a candidate too dependent on the PCP.

While President Eanes and the Communist party were searching for the ideal candidate, two other contenders identified with the left were grappling with their own problems. The first, Mário Soares, had to rid himself of the very negative image attached to his two years as head of an unpopular government that he had been unable to control, and to the election disaster of October 1985. Surveys consistently placed him well behind the other serious hopefuls. Everything seemed to indicate that if President Eanes could come up with a viable and attractive candidate, Mário Soares could forget his presidential dreams. On the other hand, he could count on the solid support of his own party machine, including the members of the ex-Secretariat, and a growing number of influential members of the moderate left, who had earlier set up a special election committee, the MASP (Movement for the Support of Soares for the Presidency, which his most enthusiastic supporters had translated into English as Make Amiable Soares President!). The Soares strategy was aimed at creating a candidacy of the center, which would build on Socialist support—obviously estimated originally at much higher than the 20 percent received in October—to forge a coalition stretching from the fringes of APU to the PSD. The objective was to get to the second ballot and then beat the candidate most clearly identified with the right, Freitas do Amaral, who, all polls confirmed, would be his most likely opponent. This strategy, it seemed, could only fail if President Eanes found a candidate acceptable to the PRD, the PSD, and the PCP. The Soares strategy received a boost with the early withdrawal of General Mário Firmino Miguel, the candidate backed by former PSD president—the late Carlos Mota Pinto, and the subsequent takeover of the PSD leadership by Cavaco Silva.

To Soares's left appeared Maria de Lourdes Pintasilgo who had been preparing her entry in the race for over two years and who seemed to be gathering strength in all the polls. She did not enjoy the support of any of the big parties and had to rely on her many enthusiastic supporters who came from outside the ranks of the PCP, the PS, and the small Marxist-Leninist parties, and on part of the former military left. As a prominent left-wing Catholic and an ex–prime minister who had made her mark as a social reformer during her short stay in office in 1979, she hoped to gain support from an electorate more and more disenchanted with the existing parties. Although she had been President Eanes's personal choice for prime minister in 1979, he rejected her candidacy for the presidency. Pintasilgo did not meet the profile of the ideal "Eanista" candidate. She was too far to the left, which paradoxically made her unacceptable to the PCP, and above all had announced her ambitions without consulting the President, which would have made her appear to force his hand. She could certainly not have agreed simply to act as Eanes's stand-in for the next five years.

More than other candidates, it can be said that Maria de Lourdes Pintasilgo fell victim to public opinion polls. In the early days, they showed her well ahead of all the other contenders, but she forgot that they were putting her against an unpopular prime minister and a host of undeclared possible candidates. Bolstered by the enthusiasm of her supporters, she overestimated the real appeal of her candidacy. When Zenha threw his hat into the ring, the situation began to change. Polls showed that a lot of PRD support was going to the new candidate, after Eanes made it clear that he backed him. Zenha's popularity grew even further when the PCP came out in his favor and decided to actively campaign for him. As Zenha's standings in the polls improved, some of Pintasilgo's supporters, fearing that a Communist-backed candidate could win the three-way race on the left, shifted their support to Mário Soares in the last two weeks of the campaign. Unlike the other candidates, she had no hard partisan support or party machine to fall back on.

The only candidate on the right, Freitas do Amaral, had already turned down an offer from Sá Carneiro to run as the Democratic Alliance's candidate in 1980 and had publicly announced in the summer of 1984 his decision to withdraw from the presidential race. He changed his mind in April 1985 when General Firmino Miguel officially dropped out of the running, partly for family reasons and partly because the PSD leadership at the time appeared incapable of mustering solid support behind his candidacy. Freitas do Amaral could count on the support of his old party, the CDS, but had to wait until after the October elections to win that of the PSD. Cavaco Silva, a strong supporter of the former leader of the CDS, had had to beat a tactical retreat at the PSD congress at Figueira da Foz in May, in which he won the presidency of the party, and had endorsed a motion which left the PSD's options open. After the October elections, Cavaco Silva, in the name of the party, negotiated a deal with Freitas do Amaral in which the candidate agreed not to attempt to increase the powers of the president as laid down in the 1982 revised constitution and not to use the presidency to favor his own party or to create a new one.[4] This position caused some friction within the PSD hierarchy, with the more progressive elements, like former prime minister Francisco Pinto Balsemão, expressing a preference for Mário Soares, but surveys indicated that the mass of the party's electorate supported Cavaco Silva's choice.

The First Round

The results of the first ballot confirmed the strength of the traditional parties. The three candidates supported by the old parties received the overwhelming vote of their "natural" electorate. Freitas do Amaral polled 91 percent of those who voted PSD in October 1985 and more than 90 percent of the CDS vote, while Mário Soares took 91 percent of the Socialist vote and Salgado Zenha received the support of 90 percent of those voting APU. The PRD split its vote five ways, giving approximately one third to Freitas do Amaral, while the remainder preferred to join the 25 percent of the electorate that abstained, a relatively high number for Portuguese elections.[5] Maria de Lourdes Pintasilgo was obviously hurt by the lack of a firm party base and her disappointing result showed there was little room for so-called independent candidates in presidential elections.

Freitas do Amaral had done extremely well and had taken 320,000 votes more

Table E1

Results of the First Ballot of the Presidential Elections,
26 January 1986 (as a percentage of the votes cast)

Candidate	Percentage of Votes
Diogo Freitas do Amaral	46.3
Mário Soares	25.4
Francisco Salgado Zenha	20.9
Maria de Lourdes Pintasilgo	7.4

than the CDS and the PSD combined vote in October. Most of this new support came from the PRD and former abstentionists. Mário Soares had only made a modest recovery after the shock of the legislative elections but still remained far behind the PS's potential maximum of 37–38 percent. However, it was enough to put him on the ballot for the second round on 16 February.

If President Eanes could find little solace in the results, having thrown his full support behind a candidate who drew some 70 percent of his vote from the traditional Communist electorate, the PCP could feel satisfied that it had reasserted its authority over its voters, with less than 9 percent going to Maria de Lourdes Pintasilgo. On the other hand, it now had to face the dreaded dilemma of choosing between those it called the "two candidates of the right."

The Left Against the Right

As its Tenth Party Congress in December 1983, the Portuguese Communist party had flatly stated that under no circumstance could it vote for Mário Soares in the coming presidential elections. The moment of truth had now arrived. Communist abstention would mean certain victory for Freitas do Amaral. Worse, the party might not be followed by its electorate, even though most Communist voters shared their party's antipathy toward Mário Soares. But could it endorse the man who had fought so hard against it during the revolution and who had staked so much of his reputation on his anticommunism? Two days after the first ballot, the PCP's Central Committee announced that a special Party Congress would be held one week later to confirm its decision to vote for Mário Soares, without supporting him. It justified its position by declaring that Communists "cannot remain with their arms folded before the grave and imminent threat to democracy which comes with the possible election of Freitas do Amaral."[6]

At the Congress, the unprecedented happened. Two delegates voted against a resolution to vote for Soares, breaking with the hallowed tradition of unanimity. In fact during the week preceding the Congress, almost 800 meetings took place among party members, and only a majority supported the party's new position.[7] Before the second ballot, the party held over 200 public meetings to convince its voters to fall into line.[8]

The PCP's historic decision accentuated the atmosphere of bipolarization that built up between the two ballots. The two defeated candidates of the left called on their supporters to rally behind Mário Soares. As the campaign continued, left-wing intellectuals and artists, most far left parties (except the Maoist MRPP) came out in favor of the "candidate of the left." In the unions, the situation was a little more complex. The CGTP adopted the same position as the PCP, but the UGT remained divided and took no official position. However, it was no secret where the sympathies of the majority of the leadership lay. Freitas do Amaral had claimed in his television debate with Mário Soares that tens of union leaders supported him. This was strongly denied by the UGT, and according to its secretary-general, Torres

Couto, a PS member of the Assembly of the Republic, only 44 of the 220 members of the federation's national leadership supported Freitas do Amaral, compared with 149 who openly backed Soares.[9] The UGT's president, a member of the PSD, was among those 44 supporters. Most of the employers' associations, with the exception of the AIP, made an appeal for Freitas do Amaral. Both candidates contributed to this growing polarization as they increasingly radicalized their discourse and caricatured each other. Freitas do Amaral tried to play on anticommunism by emphasizing that Soares had PCP support and hinting he had made a deal with the PCP, an insinuation that both the Communist party and Soares forcefully rejected. Mário Soares dropped his centrist stance and assumed the language of the left, with reference to the conquests of the revolution and the suggestion that the victory of his opponent would open the way for the forces of an (unidentified) antidemocratic right.

The flux of new supporters to the Soares campaign created a feeling of momentum that Freitas do Amaral found difficult to counter. Having already reached the normal limit of the electorate of the right and thwarted by the PCP's decision to vote against him rather than abstain, he could not call on much extra ammunition. Prime Minister Cavaco Silva had originally declared that he could only participate in the campaign for the second ballot, but he finally appeared on TV to support Freitas on the eve of the first round, thus leaving his candidate no fresh strength in reserve to draw on in his final battle against Mário Soares.

Soares's Narrow Victory

As in most tight races, the number of abstentions in the second round dropped, falling to under 22 percent. Despite his greater capacity to mobilize the first ballot undecided vote, Freitas do Amaral was unable to defeat the temporary union of the left. A close examination of the results show that Soares actually lost votes, compared to the combined vote of the left, in those areas where APU consistently takes more than 15 percent of the vote, namely Beja, Evora, Faro, Setúbal, and Lisbon, an indication that some Communist voters found it difficult to support a longtime opponent. But the loss was relatively small and a transfer of almost 800,000 APU votes (more than 90 percent of its October vote) from Zenha and Pintasilgo to

Table E2

Results of the Second Ballot of the Presidential Elections,
16 February 1986 (as a percentage of the votes cast)

Candidate	Percentage of Votes
Diogo Freitas do Amaral	48.7
Mário Soares	51.3

Table E3

Percentage of Total Number of Registered Voters Received by the Presidential Candidates on Both Ballots, January–February 1986

Candidate	% of Vote First Ballot	% of Vote Second Ballot	Difference
Freitas do Amaral	34.6	37.7	+3.1
Mário Soares (plus Zenha plus Pintasilgo)	40.1	39.7	−0.4

Soares more than compensated for it. He also picked up more than 550,000 PRD votes, which had either gone to one of the other two candidates of the left or had abstained on the first ballot.[10] In terms of the percentage of the vote in both ballots, Mário Soares failed to regain the total vote of the left in any district in the country.

Freitas do Amaral, on the other hand, improved his position both in absolute figures and in the percentage of votes taken everywhere in Portugal. He lost some 5,000 former Socialist votes to Soares and made no inroads into the APU electorate, but he more than made up for the weaknesses with an extra 70,000 votes from the PRD and 47,000 from PSD voters who had previously abstained.[11] The difference in the movement of votes between the two candidates can be appreciated more clearly if we compare their percentage of the votes on both ballots in terms of the number of registered voters.

The Presidential Election and Portuguese Politics

With the victory of Mário Soares, Portugal had its first civilian president ever to be elected by universal suffrage and its first civilian president since 1926. This election emphasized the degree to which Portuguese politics had become civilianized. The two main military contenders for the presidency, General Firmino Miguel and Colonel Costa Brás, had been forced to withdraw for lack of solid support, and other military hopefuls preferred not to push ahead with their candidacies. Some military officers played a prominent role in the election organization of Salgado Zenha and Maria de Lourdes Pintasilgo, but many of them were already on the retired list and none occupied important positions in the military hierarchy. As for the 25 April Association, it was split between Zenha and Pintasilgo and could not adopt an official, unequivocal position. The last blow to public military involvement in politics came with the forced withdrawal of Lietuenant Colonel Vítor Alves, a leading member of the 25 April Association, as head of the PRD list for Lisbon in the December local elections, for the reasons we have already given.[12]

The presidential elections revealed the fragile nature of the PRD. Not only did its electorate divide its vote between all the candidates, but this same electorate refused to recognize the authority of the party's acknowledged leader, President Ramalho Eanes. At the same time, over 70 percent of those who voted for this party in October backed Mário Soares on the second ballot, a strong sign that sociologically the PRD belonged to the Portuguese left.

Finally, the disarray of the PRD electorate, which had so emphatically expressed its dissatisfaction with the existing party system in October 1985, and the surprisingly poor showing of Maria de Lourdes Pintasilgo, the only candidate totally independent of any party machine, suggest that the four traditional parties still largely control Portuguese politics.

The battle for the presidency, the dominant political issue from 1982 to 1986, highlights some fundamental paradoxes of politics in Portugal. The two candidates in the second ballot had both worked actively to reduce the powers of the president during the debate over constitutional revision, and yet both sought this position rather than the more powerful office of prime minister. Both claimed they would make full use of presidential power and would not assume a low profile. The reasons for this apparent contradiction reside in the fact that both men probably thought they could use their links with their former parties and their political experience to influence politics and could hope at some time to find a parliamentary majority which coincided with their own natural support. The presidency also provides a more stable position than that of prime minister, which gives its holder an advantage within the political system.

A second paradox is the artificial bipolarization that the present electoral system has imposed. Freitas do Amaral, who had constantly proclaimed the traditional left/right cleavage to be obsolete and who knew that sole support of the right would not bring him victory, could not escape the realities of Portuguese politics. He became the prisoner of a right-wing rhetoric that he could have preferred to avoid. On the second ballot he had to pin his hopes on a Communist call for abstention or widespread disobedience on the part of the Communist electorate. Mário Soares also sought to avoid bipolarization that would make him dependent on Communist votes. He had long aimed at a centrist coalition, around the PS and the PDS, but like his rival he had to come to terms with a situation that pitted right against left. Soares fully assumed the role of leader of the left between the two ballots, but as soon as his election was assured, he distanced himself from that position by proclaiming that he considered himself the "president of all the Portuguese."

The Communist party defied the forecasts of its imminent demise by becoming a vital part of the Soares victory. It did so reluctantly and for negative reasons but it proved once again that it could not be counted out of the political system. Yet, as its support for Zenha and then for Soares shows, the PCP can only positively influence the outcome of an election if it does not become an overwhelming source of support for a candidate. Unlike former President Eanes, President Mário Soares cannot presume an attitude of benevolent neutrality on the part of a PCP that has always considered him one of its main targets. So, much of the Soares presidency will be taken up with the search for a viable alternative coalition for the 1991 elections.

The coalition that made Soares president was purely circumstantial and could not hide the deep divisions that continue to mark the Portuguese left. In that sense, the first ballot provided a more accurate measure of political reality than the induced bipolarization of the second round. Both ballots confirmed the persistence of a fundamentally united right. It may never mobilize enough votes to win the presidency, as long as the PCP falls behind a candidate recognized by all segments of the left, but it disposes of a potential springboard to launch a parliamentary majority in the image of the Democratic Alliance, since 43 percent of the vote will suffice, to give a decisive victory to a united electoral coalition. With the election of a civil president dependent on the parties, the conditions now exist not for a vaguely defined semi-presidential political system but for a balance between a government of the center right and a president from the center left, which could well become a prevalent feature of Portuguese politics.

Notes

1. Calculations based on the figures given in José António Lima and Luís Fraga, "A revolução de 6 de Outubro", *Expresso-Revista,* 12 October 1985.
2. Jorge Gaspar, "Permanecem as linhas da força da geografia eleitoral," *O Jornal,* 11 October 1985.
3. José António Lima and Luís Fraga, "A revolução."
4. For the main points of the PSD's conditions, see *Expresso,* 19 October 1985.
5. Calculations based on the model of vote transfers drawn up by José António Lima and Luís Fraga, "AD regressa e renasce o PS," *Expresso-Revista,* 1 Feburary 1986. In the 1980 presidential elections the abstention rate was just under 16 percent.
6. *Avante!,* 31 January 1986.
7. Santos Pereira, "XI Congresso: nâo ver, nâo ver, mas pôr a cruz," *Expresso-Revista,* 8 Feburary 1986.
8. Figures based on information in *Avante!,* 6 and 13 February 1986.
9. Nuno Pacheco, "UGT: Soares 149, Freitas 44," *Expresso,* 14 February 1986.
10. Figures based on the estimates of José António Lima and Luís Fraga, "A vitória impossível," *Expresso-Revista,* 22 February 1986.
11. Ibid.
12. For the first time since 1982, the new Cavaco Silva government did not appoint its Minister of Defense to the office of deputy prime minister. This had much more to do with the structure of a one party minority government than a deliberate decision to downgrade the prestige of the ministry closest to the armed forces.

Appendix 1
The Sample Survey:
Questionnaire and Sample

The survey was supported by the SSHRCC grant and administered for the authors by NORMA (Sociedade de Estudos para o Desenvolvimento de Empresas) under the supervision of Dr. Mário Bacalhau. The questionnaire contains sixty-four main items, forty-four subitems of which sixteen are open-ended, and a series of questions to control for age, sex, class, and region of the respondent. The authors and Dr. Bacalhau elaborated the questionnaire utilizing items from a survey carried out by Thomas Bruneau and Mário Bacalhau in 1978 (published as *Os portugueses e a política quatro anos depois de 25 de abril*) as well as items from surveys conducted in Spain by Juan J. Linz, Richard Gunther, G. Shabad, and Giacomo Sani. Following a pretest, the questionnaire was applied to a sample of 2,386 respondents, who were interviewed in person, between 8 March and 13 April 1984. There was a 12 percent return interview to verify the quality of the interviews.

The universe of the survey was the Portuguese population, resident on the Continent (excluding the Azores and Madeira), eighteen years of age or more and living in localities of ten or more persons. According to the census of 1981, this universe consisted of 6,481,000 persons. The respondents were selected according to a sampling strategy utilized by NORMA which takes into consideration the electoral districts (regions), socio-cultural regions, and localities which may be considered sociological units. For example, the two listings that follow show the number of respondents per electoral district, and the size of population per locality.

The selection of the sample was drawn by chance throughout in order to guarantee all elements in the universe equal probability of appearing in the sample. Chance was ensured by means of different methodologies at the following stages: selection of the localities, selection of the sampling points, selection of the families, and selection of the individual to be interviewed.

After the interviews were conducted, the open questions were coded and all questions arranged according to a number of variables, such as region, locality, sex, age, class, religion, etc., and cross tabs with other preselected variables were prepared. These resulted in seven volumes of tables which have been utilized in the preparation of this book. In addition, the computer tape is available with the full data set for future analysis.

Appendix 2
General Data on Industry and Economy

Table A2.1

Comparative Indicators (1980)

	Portugal	Spain	EEC/10	Greece
Population (millions)	9.9	37.4	270.9	9.6
GDP at market prices (billion ECU)	17.3	152.0	2,017.3	28.8
GDP per capita (ECU)	1,750.0	4,061.0	7,448.0	3,000.0
GDP per capita (purchasing power parities)	3,464.0	5,479.0	7,703.0	4,333.0

1 ECU = 1.39 US $ (exchange rate mid-1980)

Data source: Eurostat (1982)

Table A2.2

Portugal Public Enterprises

---

1. Agriculture and Fisheries

    Agriculture

    - Companhias das Lezírias

    Fisheries

    - SNAPA - Soc. Nac. dos Armadores da Pesca do Arrasto
    - CPP - Companhia Portuguesa de Pesca
    - PESCRUL - Sociedade de Pesca de Crustáos
    - SNAB - Sociedade Nacional dos Armadores do Bacalhau

2. Exctractive Industries

    - ENU - Empresa Nacional de Uranio
    - Ferrominas
    - EMMA - Empresa Mineira e Metalúrgica do Alentejo

3. Manufacturing Industries

    Food, Drink, and Tobacco

    - FRIANTARTICUS - Frigoríficos de Cascais
    - FRIGARVE - Empresa Frigorífica do Algarve
    - CENTRALCER - Central de Cerveja
    - UNICER - Uniao Cerverjeira
    - Fábrica de Tabacos Micaelense
    - TABAQUEIRA - Empresa Industrial de Tabacos

    Paper, Printing, and Publishing

    - PORTUCEL - Emp. de Celulose e Papel de Portugal
    - EPDP - Empresa Pública do Jornal "Diário Popular"
    - EPNC - Emp. Pública dos Jornais Notícias e Capital
    - INCM - Imprensa Nacional Casa da Moeda

    Chemicals and Related Activities

    - CNP - Compnhia Nacional de Petroquímica
    - Petroquímica e Gás de Portugal
    - QUIMIGAL - Química de Portugal
    - Indústrias Nacionais de Defesa (INDEP)
    - Petróleos de Portugal (PETROGAL)

    Nonmetallic Minerals

    - Fábrica-Escola Irmãos Stephens
    - CIMPOR - Cimentos de Portugal

    Basic Metals

    - Sideurgia Nacional

    Shipbuilding

    - Estaleiros Navais de Viana do Castelo
    - SETENAVE - Estaleiros Navais de Setúbal

(Table A.2 cont'd)

4. Electricity, Gas, and Water

   • Electricidade de Portugal (EDP)
   • Empresa de Electricidade do Acores (EDA)
   • Empresa de Electricidade da Madeira
   • EPAL - Empresa Pública das Aguas Livres

5. Construction and Public Works

   • Dragagens de Portugal (DRAGAPOR)
   • FPUL - Empresa Pública de Urbanização de Lisboa

6. Commerce

   • Administracao-Geral do Acúcar e do Alcool (AGA)
   • Emp. Pública de Abastecimento de Cereais (EPAC)
   • GELMAR - Emp. Distribuidora de Produtos Alimentares

7. Transports and Communications

   Land Transports

   • Caminhos de Ferro Portugueses (CP)
   • Companhia Carris de Ferro de Lisboa, SARL
   • Metropolitano de Lisboa (METRO)
   • Rodoviária Nacional (RN)
   • Servicos de Transportes Colectivos do Porto

   Sea Transports

   • Companhia Nacional de Navegação (CNN)
   • Comp.^{a} Portuguesa de Transportes Marítimos (CTM)
   • DOCAPESCA - Soc. Concessionária da Doca de Pesca
   • SOCARMAR - Soc. de Cargas e Descargas Marítimas
   • TRANSTEJO - Transportes Tejo

   Air Transports

   • Aeroportos e Navegação Aérea (ANA)
   • Servico Acoreano de Transportes Aéreos (SATA)
   • Transportes Aéreos Portugueses (TAP)

   Communications

   • Correios e Communicações de Portugal (CTI)
   • Telefones de Lisboa e Porto (TLP)

8. Banks, Other Financial Institutions, Insurance, and Financial Services

   Banks and Other Monetary and Financial Institutions

   • Banco Borges & Irmao
   • Banco Comercial dos Acores
   • Banco Espírito Santo & Comercial de Lisboa
   • Banco de Fomento Nacional
   • Banco Fonecas & Burnay
   • Banco Nacional Ultramarino
   • Banco Pinto & Sotto Mayor
   • Banco de Portugal
   • Banco Portugues de Atlantico
   • Banco Totta & Acores
   • Caixa Geral de Depósitos
   • Crédito Predial Portugues

- FINAGESTE - Empresa Financieira de Gestao
- Instituto de Participaçoes do Estado
- Sociedade Financeira Portuguesa
- Uniao de Bancos Portugueses

Insurance

- Alianca Seguradora
- Companhia de Seguros Acoreana
- Companhia de Seguros Bonanca
- Companhia de Seguros Império
- Companhia de Seguros Mundial Confianca
- COSEC - Companhia de Seguros de Crédito
- FIDELIDADE - Grupo Segurador
- PORTUGAL RE - Comp.ª Portuguesa de Resseguros
- TRANQUILDADE - Seguros

Building and other Services

- EPPI - Empresa Pública de Parques Industriais
- Empresa Regional de Parques Industriais
- ANOP - Agencia Noticiosa Portuguesa
- ENATUR - Empres Nacional de Turismo

9. Public Services

Radio, Television, and Cinema

- Teatro Nacional de S. Carlos
- Radiodifusão Portuguesa
- Radiotelevisão Portuguesa

Source: This listing is drawn from Arminda Manuel da Conceição Antonio, Antonio José de Sousa Mota, and Adriano Manuel da Rocha Carvalho, O sector empresarial do estado em Portugal e nos paises da CEE. Lisbon: Imprensa Nacional and CEEPS, 1983, pp. 463-466.

Chart A2.1

Structural Development of Portuguese Industry

Pre-World War II	Traditional domestic market-oriented industries	Textiles, clothing, hats, leather, footwear, clay, glass, paper, dye industries works, foundries, matches, soaps, tobacco, beverages
	Traditional exporting industries (natural advantages)	Cork, olives, sardines, quality wines
1945/48 to 1960/61	Infant industries of the 1950s	Basic metallurgy, metal processing, mineral oil, chemicals, paper and printing
	Labor-intensive exporting industries	Textiles, clothing, foodstuffs, beverages, tobacco, wood products (furniture), cork
1961 to 1970/73	Infant industries of the 1960s	Finished chemical products, steel, mechanical engineering, transport equipment, metals and metal goods, nonmetal products, electrical equipment, raw materials for papermaking, tomato concentrates
	Labor-intensive exporting industries (labor-cost advantage)	Textiles, clothing, footwear, leather articles (new labor-intensive (labor-cost products),[a] electrical, electronic advantage) and optical products, toys ("offshore industries of the new type"), ship repairs[a]
1970/73 to 1980	Infant industries of the 1970s	Intermediate and finished chemical products, chemical fibres, plastics, heavy electrical and heavy metal products, mineral oil industry, shipbuilding, steel, household appliances, electrical appliances, switches, etc., plant construction

1980/81 to 1990	Infant industries of the 1980s	Basic and intermediate petrochemical products, chemical fibres, plastics, fertilizers, steel products, shipbuilding, automotive industry of the "new" type, electrical household appliances, agricultural machinery and equipment, office machines, electronic household appliances, textile machines, motorcycles
	New capital-intensive exporting industries	Petrochemicals, chemical products, steel, heavy metal products,[b] plant construction[c]
	Traditional exporting industries	Textiles, clothing, footwear, leather articles
	Labor-intensive exporting industries	Antique-styled furniture, other furniture, ceramics, metal goods, glassware, other handicraft products[d]

[a] from the second half of the 1960s.

[b] as far as economies of scale play only a limited role.

[c] particularly suppliers to the major industrial products in Sines and near Porto, who are already beginning to use their experience for exports.

[d] also for tourists.

Source: Klaus Esser, et. al., "Portugal's Industrial Policy in Terms of Accession to the European Community," Occasional Paper no. 60. (Berlin: German Development Institute, 1980, p. 81).

Bibliography

Books and Articles

Agee, Warren K., and Nelson Traquima. 1984. *A Frustrated Fourth Estate: Portugal's Post-Revolutionary Mass Media*. Columbia, South Carolina, Journalism Monographs, no. 87, February 1984.

Aguiar, Joaquim. 1983. *A ilusão do poder: Análise do sistema partidário português, 1976-1982*. Lisbon: Publicações Dom Quixote.

Aguiar, Joaquim. 1985. *O pos-salazarismo*. Lisbon: Publicaçòes Dom Quixote.

Almada, Teresa. n.d. *Diário da reforma agrária*. Lisbon: Publicações Europa-América.

Bacalhau, Mário. n.d. *Inquérito à situação política: Eanes A Solução?* Lisbon: Heptágono, Estudos e Publicações, SARL.

Baklanoff, Eric. 1978. *The Economic Transformation of Spain and Portugal*. New York: Praeger Publishers.

Barreto, António. n.d. *Memória da reforma agrária*. Lisbon: Publicações Europa-America.

Belmira Martins, Maria. 1973. *Sociedades e grupos em Portugal*. Lisbon: Editorial Estampa.

Belmira Martins, Maria, and J. Chaves Rosa. 1979. *O grupo estado: Análise e listagem completa das sociedades do sector público empresarial*. Lisbon: Edições Jornal Expresso.

Braga de Macedo, Jorge, and Simon Serfaty, eds. 1981. *Portugal Since the Revolution: Economic and Political Perspectives*. Boulder: Westview Press.

Bruneau, Thomas. 1976. "Church and State in Portugal: Crises of Cross and Sword." *Journal of Church and State,* vol. 18, no. 3 (Autumn), pp. 463-490.

Bruneau, Thomas C. 1984. *Politics and Nationhood: Post-Revolutionary Portugal*. New York: Praeger Publishers.

Bruneau, Thomas, and Mário Bacalhau. 1978. *Os portugueses e a política quatro anos depois do 25 de abril*. Lisbon: Editorial Meseta.

Bruneau, Thomas, Victor M.P. da Rosa, and Alex Macleod, eds. 1984. *Portugal in Development: Emigration, Industrialization, the European Community*. Ottawa: University of Ottawa Press.

Caetano, Marcello. 1973. *Manual de direito administrativo*. vol. 1, 10th ed., Lisbon: Coimbra Editora Limitada.

Caetano, Marcello. 1974. *Depoimento*. Rio de Janeiro: Distribuidora Record.
Caetano, Marcello. 1978. *Constituições portuguesas*. Lisbon: Editorial Verbo.
Campinos, Jorge. 1978. *O presidencialismo do estado novo*. Lisbon: Perspectivas & Realidades.
Campinos, Jorge. n.d. *Ideologia política do estado salazarista*. Lisbon: Portugalis Editora.
Canotilho, J.J. Gomes, and Vital Moreira. 1980. *Constituição da república portuguesa anotada*. Coimbra: Coimbra Editora.
Cavaco Silva, Aníbal A. 1982. *A política económica do governo de Sá Carneiro*. Lisbon: Publicações Dom Quixote.
Colliard, Jean-Claude. 1978. *Les régimes parlementaires contemporains*. Paris: Fondation Nationale de Science Politique.
Conceição António, Arminda Manuela da, António José de Sousa Mota, and Adriano Manuel da Rocha Carvalho. 1983. *O sector empresarial do estado em Portugal e nos países da CEE*. Lisbon: Imprensa Nacional and CEEPS.
Condomines, Jonas, and José Durão Barroso. 1984. "La dimension gauche-droite et la competition entre les partis politiques en Europe du Sud (Portugal, Espagne, Grece)," *Il Politico*, no. 3, pp. 405-438.
Costa e Sousa, Vinício Alves da. 1985. "Caracterizacao da classe política portuguesa." Lisbon, Instituo Damião de Góis, mimeographed.
Cunhal, Alvaro. 1976. *A revolução portuguesa: O passado e o futuro*. Lisbon: Edições Avante!
Cutileiro, José. 1971. *A Portuguese Rural Society*. Oxford: The Clarendon Press.
Deubner, Christian, Guy Clausse, and Michael Noelke. 1984. "Economic Relations between Spain and Portugal in a Twelve-Nation European Community." Brussels: European Research Associates.
Di Palma, Giuseppe. 1977. *Surviving Without Governing: The Italian Parties in Parliament*. Berkeley: University of California Press.
Di Palma, Giuseppe. 1980. "Founding Coalitions in Southern Europe: Legitimacy and Hegemony" *Government and Opposition*, vol. 15, no. 2 (Spring), pp. 162-89.
Domingos, Emídio da Veiga. 1980. *Portugal político: Análise das instituicões*. Lisbon: Edições Rolim.
Donges, Juergen B., et al. 1982. *The Second Enlargement of the European Community: Adjustment Requirements and Challenges for Policy Reform*. Tubingen: JCB Mohr.
Durão Barroso, José. 1983. *Le système politique portugais face a l'integration Europeenne*. Lisbon: Associação Portuguesa para o Estudo das Relações Internacionais.
Durão Barroso, José. 1983. "Capacidade de adaptação e incapacidade de decisão: O estado português face à articulação política desde 1974." Paper presented at colloquium on formation and modes of action of social groups in Portugal after 1950, Bad Homburg, 12-15 December.
Duverger, Maurice. 1978. *Echec au roi*. Paris: Albin Michel.
Editorial Progresso Social e Democracia. 1984. *Atlas eleitoral*. Lisbon: EPSD.
Eisfeld, Rainer. 1982. "Political and Economic Problems of Portugal's Accession to the EC" *Assuntos Europeus*, no. 3, pp. 345-81.
Esser, Klaus, Guido Ashoff, Ansgar Eussner, and Wilhelm Hummen. 1960. "Portugal's Industrial Policy in Terms of Accession to the European Community." Occasional Paper Number 60, German Development Institute. Berlin.
Figueiredo, Antonio de. 1975. *Portugal: Fifty Years of Dictatorship*. Middlesex: Penguin Books.
Freitas do Amaral, Diogo. 1983. *A lei de defesa nacional e das forças armadas*. Coimbra: Coimbra Editora.
Freitas do Amaral, Diogo. 1984 *Sá Carneiro, primeiro ministro*. Lisbon: Cognitio.

Freire Antunes, José. 1980. *O segredo do 25 do novembro*. Lisbon: Publicações Europa-America.
Frémontier, Jacques. 1976. *Portugal: les points sur les i*. Paris: Editions Sociales.
Gallagher, Thomas. 1983. *Portugal: A Twentieth Century Interpretation*. Manchester: Manchester University Press.
Gaspar, Jorge, et al. 1984. *As eleições para a assembleia da república 1979-1983: Estudos de geografia eleitoral*. Lisbon: Instituto Damião de Góis.
Gaspar, Jorge. 1983. "L'abstention electorale au Portugal, 1975-1980." *Finisterra* XVIII, 35, pp. 65-97.
Gaspar, Jorge, et al. 1982. *As eleições para as camaras municipais*. Lisbon: Instituto Damião de Góis.
Gaspar, Jorge, and Nuno Vitorino. 1976. *As eleições de 25 de abril: Geografia e imagem dos partidos*. Lisbon: Livros Horizonte.
Goldey, David. 1983. "Elections and the Consolidation of Portuguese Democracy: 1974-1983." *Electoral Studies* vol. 2, no. 3, pp. 229-240.
Graham, Lawrence S. 1975. *Portugal: The Decline and Collapse of an Authoritarian Order*. Beverly Hills: Sage Publications.
Graham, Lawrence S., and Douglas Wheeler, eds. 1983. *In Search of Modern Portugal: The Revolution and Its Consequences*. Madison: University of Wisconsin Press.
Graham, Lawrence S., and Harry M. Makler, eds. 1979. *Contemporary Portugal: The Revolution and its Antecedents*. Austin: University of Texas Press.
Guerra, João Paulo. 1981. *'Dossier' comunicação social*. Lisbon: Edições Avante!.
Harvey, Robert. 1978. *Portugal: Birth of a Democracy*. London: The Macmillan Press, Ltd.
Herz, John H., ed. 1983. *From Dictatorship to Democracy: Coping with the Legacies of Authoritarianism and Totalitarianism*. Westport: Greenwood Press.
Huntington, Samuel P. 1957. *The Soldier and the State*. Cambridge: Harvard University Press.
Huntington, Samuel P. 1984. "Will More Countries Become Democratic?" *Political Science Quarterly*, 99 (Summer), pp. 193-218.
Instituto de Estudos para o Desenvolvimento. 1981. *Problemas relacionados com a adesão de Portugal à CEE*. Lisbon: IED.
Instituto de Estudos para o Desenvolvimento. 1984. *Uma estratégia para a industrialização portuguesa*. Lisbon: IED.
Instituto de Estudos para o Desenvolvimento. 1985. *Portugal e a Europa: O fim de um ciclo migratória*. Lisbon: IED.
Instituto Português de Opinião Pública e Estudos de Mercado. 1973. *Os portugueses e a política: 1973*. Lisbon: Moraes Editores.
Lavau, Georges. 1969. "Le parti communiste dans le système politique français, in Frédéric Bon (ed), *Le communisme en France*. Paris: Armand Colin.
Lijphart, Arend. 1984. *Democracies: Patterns of Majoritarian and Consensus Government in Twenty-One Countries*. New Haven: Yale University Press.
Linz, Juan J. 1978. *The Breakdown of Democratic Regimes: Crisis, Breakdown, and Reequilibration*. Baltimore: Johns Hopkins University Press.
Linz, Juan J. 1979. "Europe's Southern Frontier: Evolving Trends Towards What?" *Daedalus*, Winter, pp.175-209.
Linz, Juan J. 1980. "The New Spanish Party System," in Richard Rose, ed., *Electoral Participation: A Comparative Analysis*. Beverly Hills: Sage.
Loureiro dos Santos, José Alberto. 1980. *Forças armadas, defesa nacional e poder político*. Lisbon: Imprensa Nacional—Casa de Moeda.
Macleod, Alex. 1984. "Portrait of a Model Ally: The Portuguese Communist Party and the International Communist Movement, 1968-1983." *Studies in Comparative Com-

munism, XVII, 16 *(Spring), pp. 31-52*.
Macleod, Alex. 1984. *Le révolution inopportune: Les partis communistes français et italien face à la révolution portugaise*. Montréal: Nouvelle Optique.
Marvall, José. 1982. *The Transition to Democracy in Spain*. London: Croom Helm.
Maxwell, Kenneth. 1976. "The Thorns of the Portuguese Revolution." *Foreign Affairs*, January, pp. 250-270.
Maxwell, Kenneth. 1980. "The Communists and the Portuguese Revolution." *Dissent*, Spring, pp. 194-206.
Maxwell, Kenneth. 1982. "The Emergence of Portuguese Democracy," in John H. Herz, ed., *From Dictatorship to Democracy: Coping with the Legacies of Authoritarianism and Totalitarianism*. Westport: Greenwood Press.
Maxwell, Kenneth, ed. 1984. "Portugal Ten Years after the Revolution." Reports of three Columbia-Gulbenkian Workshops. New York: Research Institute on International Change.
MDP Parliamentary Group. 1984. "Breve história do MDP/CDE em 1984." Lisbon, mimeographed.
Medeiros Ferreira, José. 1983. *Ensaio histórico sobre a revolução do 25 de abril*. Lisbon: Imprensa Nacional-Case de Moeda.
Middlemas, Keith. 1980. *Power and the Party. Changing Faces of Communism in Western Europe*. London: André Deutsch.
Miranda, Jorge. 1982. *Manual de direito constitucional*. vol. 1, 2nd ed. Coimbra: Coimbra Editora, Ltd.
Miranda, Jorge, and M. Vilhena de Carvalho. 1982. *Constituição da república portuguesa depois da primeira revisão constitucional*. Lisbon: Rei do Livros.
Mujal-Leon, Eusébio. 1976. "The PCP and the Portuguese Revolution." *Problems of Communism*, 26, January-February, pp. 21-41.
Mujal-Leon, Eusébio. n.d. "The Portuguese Elections of April 1983: The Portuguese Party System in Flux," in Howard Penniman, ed., *The World Votes: 1983*. Durham: Duke University Press. (Forthcoming).
Nadais, António, António Vitorio, and Vitalino Canes. 1983. "Constituição da república portuguesa. Texto e comentarios à Lei no. 1/82." *Supplement to Revista Jurídica*, Associação Académica da Faculdade de Direito de Lisboa, January.
Nogueira Pinto, Maria José. n.d. *O direito da terra*. Lisbon: Publicações Europa-America.
Opello, Walter C. Jr. 1978. "The New Parliament in Portugal." *Legislative Studies Quarterly*, III, 2 (May), pp. 309-334.
Opello, Walter C. Jr. 1978. "The Second Portuguese Republic: Politico-Administrative Decentralization Since April 25, 1974." *Iberian Studies VII*, no. 2 (Autumn), pp. 43-48.
Opello, Walter C. Jr. 1981. "Local Government and Political Culture in a Portuguese Rural County." *Comparative Politics* 13, no. 3 (April), pp. 271-289.
Opello, Walter C. Jr. 1985. *Portugal's Political Development: A Comparative Approach*. Boulder: Westview Press.
Parkin, Frank. 1975. *Class Inequality and Political Order*. London: Paladin.
Partido Comunista Português. 1977. *VIII Congresso do PCP*. Lisbon: Edições Avante!.
Pereira, José Pacheco. n.d. *Conflitos sociais nos campos do sul de Portugal*. Lisbon: Publicações Europa-America.
Pridham, Geoffrey, ed. 1984. *The New Mediterranean Democracies: Regime Transition in Spain, Greece and Portugal*. London: Frank Cass.
Rebelo de Sousa, Marcelo. 1979. *Direito constitucional*. Braga: Livraria Cruz.
Rebelo de Sousa, Marcelo. 1983. *Os partidos políticos no direito constitucional português*. Braga: Livraria Cruz.
Rebelo de Sousa, Marcelo. 1984. *O sistema de governo português antes e depois da revisão*

constitucional. Lisbon: Cognitio.
Robinson, Richard. 1979. *Contemporary Portugal*. London: George Allen & Unwin.
Rodrigues, Avelino, Cesário Borga, and Mário Cardoso. 1974. *O movimento dos capitães e o 25 de abril: 229 Diaspara derrubar o fascismo*. Lisbon: Moraes Editores.
Rodrigues, Avelino, Cesário Borga, and Mário Cardoso. 1976. *Portugal depois de abril*. Lisbon: António dos Reis.
Rodrigues, Avelino, Cesário Borga, and Mário Cardoso. 1979. *Abril nos quartéis de novembro*. Lisbon: Livraria Bertrand.
Rose, Richard, and Ezra Suleiman, eds. 1980. *Presidents and Prime Ministers*. Washington: American Enterprise Institute.
Salgado de Matos, Luis. 1983. "Significado e consequências da eleição do presidente por sufrágio universal-o caso português" *Análise Social* XIX, pp. 235-259.
Santamaria, Julian, ed. 1982. *Transición a la democracia en el sur de Europa y America Latina*. Madrid: Centro de Investigaciones Sociologicas.
Santana Lopes, Pedro, and José Durão Barroso. 1980. *Sistema de governo e sistema partidário*. Lisbon: Livraria Bertrand.
Sartori, Giovanni. 1976. *Parties and Party Systems: A Framework of Analysis*. vol. 1. Cambridge: Cambridge University Press.
Santos, Alberto. 1980. "La peninsule ibérique: enjeu stratégique," *Les cahiers de la fondation pour les etudes de la défense*, no. 18.
Schmitter, Philippe. 1975. *Corporatism and Public Policy in Authoritarian Portugal*. Contemporary Political Sociology Series. Beverly Hills: Sage Publications.
Silva, Manuela, et al. 1984. *O planeamento económico em Portugal: Lições da experiencia*. Lisbon: Livraria Sá da Costa Editora.
Soares, Mário. 1976. *Portugal: quelle révolution? Conversation avec Dominique Pouchin*. Paris: Calmam-Lévy.
Stock, Maria José, et al. 1985. *Os partidos em congresso, 1981*. Evora: Gabinete de Investigação e Acção Social.
Tiersky, Ronald. 1974. *French Communism: 1920-72*. New York: Columbia University Press.
Tsoukalis, Loukas. 1981. *The European Community and its Mediterranean Enlargement*. London: George Allen & Unwin.
Tucker, Robert C. 1969. "The Deradicalization of Marxist Movements" *American Political Science Review*, 61 (June).
Vitorino, António. 1984. "O sistema de governo na constituição portuguesa de 1976 e na constituição espanhola de 1978." *Revista Jurídica*, 3 (January-February), pp. 33-79.
Wiarda, Howard. 1977. *Corporatism and Development: The Portuguese Experience*. Amherst: University of Massachusetts Press.
Wiarda, Howard. 1980. "Spain and Portugal," in Peter Merkl ed., *Western European Party Systems*. New York: The Free Press.
Williams, Alan. 1984. *Southern Europe Transformed. Political and Economic Change in Greece, Italy, Portugal and Spain*. London: Harper and Row.

Newspapers and Journals

Newspapers

Diário de Notícias
Expresso

O Jornal
Semanário

Party Newspapers

Acção Socialista (PS)
Avante! (PCP)
O Militante (PCP)
Portugal Socialista (PS)
Povo Livre (PSD)

Journals

Análise Social
Estudos de Economia
Estudos sobre o Comunismo
Prospectivas

Reports and Statistics

OECD, Economic Surveys: Portugal
Banco de Portugal. Report of the Board of Directors
Ministério da Administração Interna, Secretariado Técnico dos Assuntos para o Processo Eleitoral. Election Results from 1976-1983.

People Interviewed

Joaquim Aguiar
Leonardo Ribeiro de Almeida
Vitor Alves
Diogo Freitas do Amaral
Teresa Ambrósio
António Arnault
Francisco Pinto Balsemão
Augusto Pinto Baptista
Alfredo Barroso
Xavier de Basto

Carlos Brito
José Luis Nogueira Brito
Francisco Sarsfield Cabral
Miguel Caetano
António Campos
António Capucho
Mário Sottomayor Cardia
António Lopes Cardoso
Alberto Arons Carvalho

Sousa e Castro
Vítor Constâncio
Eugénio Anacoreta Correia
João Cravinho
Fernando Diogo
Emanuel Jardim Fernandes
Carlos Correia Gago
Jaime Gama
Bernadino Gomes
Oehen Goncalves
António Guterres
João António de Morais Leitão
Pedro Santana Lopes
José da Silva Lopes
Rui Machete
Luis Filipe Madeira
Guilherme d'Oliveira Martins

Jorge Miranda
Vital Moreira
Helena Cidade Moura
José Luis Nunes
Maria de Lourdes Pintasilgo
Joaquim Dias da Silva Pinto
Francisco Lucas Pires
João Salgueiro
Jorge Sampaio
Diana Smith
Marcelo Rebelo de Sousa
Maria José Stock
Vasco Rocha Vieira
José Luis Cruz Vilaca
António Vitorino
José Vitorino
Francisco Salgado Zenha

Index

Abortion, 114
Acção Socialista (newspaper), 68-69
AD. *See* Democratic Alliance
Agrarian reform, 3, 54-55, 111, 182, 196(n4)
Agrupamentos. *See* Assembly of the Republic
AIP. *See* Portuguese Industrial Association
Alegre, Manuel, 161
Alfaia, José, 176
Almeida, Leonardo Riberio de, 148
Alves, Vítor, 16, 21, 211
Amaral, Diogo Freitas do, 16, 17, 93, 133, 138, 170, 208, 211
   CDS, 78, 80, 89
   elections, 212-213
Amaral, Fernando, 149
Amaral, João Mota, 93
Angola, 2, 3, 176-177
ANOP, 168, 172-173
ANP. *See* National Popular Action
Armed Forces Movement (MFA), 2, 3, 8, 12, 46, 102, 119
   media and, 165-166, 168
Armed Forces, General Staff of, 12, 14–15, 17, 19, 20
APU. *See* United People's Alliance
ASDI. *See* Independent Social Democrat Action
ASP. *See* Portuguese Socialist Action
Assembly of the Republic, 4, 5, 18
   agrupamentos, 147, 150, 157
   committees, 148-149
   deputies, 152–154
   executive branch, 155-159
   grupos, 147, 157
   organization, 146-147, 148
   party control, 148, 158-159
   power, 147, 150, 157-158, 163
   salaries, 152-153
Associations, 98-101
Avante! (journal), 60, 63
Azevedo Gomes, António de, 139

Balsemão, Francisco Pinto, 77, 79-80, 124, 137, 176
   AD leadership, 94, 121
   Expresso, 171, 172
   press, 172-173
   PSD, 82, 83, 90
   rule, 133, 136
Balsemão government, 16, 94
Banking, 188, 190. *See also* Economic crisis; Economy; International Monetary Fund
Brás, Manuel de Costa, 205-206, 211
Budgets, 134, 150-151. *See also* Assembly of the Republic; Economy; International Monetary Fund

Cabinet, 135, 136. *See also* Governments
Caetano, Marcello, 2, 26, 27, 77
Caetano government, 94
CAP. *See* Confederation of Portuguese Farmers
Capital, A (newspaper), 170

229

Captains' Movement, 21
Cardia, Mário Sottomayor, 160-161
Caretaker governments, 142-143. *See also* Governments, resignations
Carlos, Manuel João de Palma, 174
Carneiro, Antonio Soares, 4, 15, 22-23, 24, 79, 105, 121
Carta Aberta, 103. *See also* General Union of Workers
Cartels, 99, 108. *See Also* Economy
Carvalho, Daniel Proença de, 173
Carvalho, Otelo Saraiva de, 12, 47, 48, 53
Casqueiro, Manuel, 111
Catholic Church, 99, 113-115, 167, 168
CCP. *See* Portuguese Confederation of Commerce
CDE. *See* Democratic Electoral Committee
CDS. *See* Social Democratic Center party
CEM. *See* Monarchy Electoral Committee
Central Bloc government, 29, 48, 66, 92, 108, 151, 173, 193, 199
  and CPCS, 111-113
  formation, 80, 90, 91, 124
CEUD. *See* Electoral Committee for Democratic Unity
CGTP. *See* General Confederation of Portuguese Workers
CGTP-IN. *See* National Confederation of Portuguese Workers-National Intersindical
Christian Democratic party (PDC), 78
Christian Democrats, 75(n6), 87
CIP. *See* Confederation of Portuguese Industry
Civil control
  Law on National Defense, 16-17
  military, 17, 18, 22, 24
Civil service, 134-135. *See also* Deputies
CNAE. *See* National Council of Entrepreneurial Associations
CNARPE. *See* National Committee for the Reelection of President Eanes
Coalitions, 28, 29, 30, 31, 55, 64, 66, 80, 211
Coalition governments, 49, 77, 91, 213
  See also Central Bloc government; Democratic Alliance; PS/PSD government
Collective Production Units, 55
Colonial empire. *See Ultramar*
Colonies, 1-2, 3, 182
Comércio do Porto, O (newspaper), 169
Commercial Association of Lisbon, 111
Commercial Association of Oporto, 111
Committee for Economic Affairs, 133
Communism, 3, 27, 54. *See also* Portuguese Communist Party
Communist party. *See* Portuguese Communist Party
Communists, 27, 45, 47, 103, 199. *See also* Portuguese Communist Party
Confederation of Portuguese Farmers (CAP), 110-111, 112
Confederation of Portuguese Industsry (CIP), 109-110, 111, 112
Constituent Assembly, 4, 27, 78, 118, 168
Constitution (1933), 120
Constitution (1976), 4, 5, 11(n1), 12, 13, 14, 29-30, 51, 78, 118, 185
  adoption of, 118-119
  economy, 185-188
  governmental structure, 133, 140
  labor movement, 102-103, 116(n22), 185
  legislative powers, 132, 156
  1982 revisions, 16-17, 29, 61, 120, 121-125, 129, 143, 187-188
  parliament, 147, 155
  political parties, 29-30, 51, 61, 78, 119-120
  presidential parties, 120-121, 136
  public opinion, 123-124
Constitutional Court, 122, 123, 156, 188
Corporative Chamber, 1, 26
Correia, João Rosada, 142
Correio de Manhã (newspaper), 169, 170-171
Costa, Adelino Amaro da, 15, 78, 80, 133
Costa, Alfredo Nobre da, 137
Costa, Manuel Soares, 139
Council of State, 130
  activity, 122-123
  role, 140-141, 155-156
Council of the Revolution (CR), 12, 13-14, 56, 167
  dissolution, 16, 17, 22
  purpose, 118-119, 120
Coups, 3, 4, 10, 12, 78
CPCS. *See* Permanent Council for Social Coordination
CR. *See* Council of the Revolution
Crespo, Vítor, 91, 137
Cultural organizations, 101
Cunha, Correia, 77
Cunhal, Alvaro, 60, 63

Decolonization, 3
Decree-law 3/74 (1974), 14
Demilitarization, 8. *See also* Military
Democracy, 3, 4, 30, 78. *See also*
    Constitution (1976); Revolution
    (1974-1975)
Democratic Alliance (AD), 4-5, 19, 94, 173
    coalitions, 28-29, 31, 77, 79, 80, 87, 90-91, 138
    collapse, 80, 91
    constitutional revision, 121, 122
    control of military, 15, 16, 18
    economy, 187, 193
    labor unions, 106-107, 111
Democratic Electoral Committee (CDE), 27
Democratic Renewal party (PRD), 28, 48, 201
    elections, 207-208, 209, 211, 212
Deputies, 154
    power, 156-157, 158, 163(n6)
    salaries, 152-153
Development, 3, 4, 5, 181, 191-192
Dez anos para mudar Portugal, 67, 71
Dia, O (newspaper), 170, 171
Diabo, O (newspaper), 171
Diário, O (newspaper), 170, 177
Diário da assembleia da república, 149, 151, 157
Diário de Lisboa (newspaper), 170
Diário de Notícias (newspaper), 169, 170
Document of the Nine, 29
"Document of the 199," 47

Eanes, António Ramalho, 4, 5, 12, 15, 20, 56, 91, 112, 128-129, 176
    constitution, 120, 121, 122
    military control, 18, 19, 20
    politics, 16, 198, 201
    presidential power, 131-132, 137, 143, 145(n16), 155-156
EC. *See* European Community
Economic Crisis, 104, 107, 112, 193-194
Economy, 1, 2, 5, 10, 181
    cartels, 108-109
    constitution, 185-186
    control, 98-99
    legislation, 186-187
Egidio, Melo (general), 20, 24
Elections, 11, 32, 34, 40, 79, 105, 129, 201
    Estado Novo, 26, 27
    1975, 4, 27-28, 61, 75(n5), 78
    1976, 4, 47, 53, 56, 61

1979, 4, 15, 28, 29, 31, 79
1980, 4-5, 15, 24, 28, 29, 31, 71
1982, 28
1983, 19, 28, 76(n36), 80, 124
1985-1986, 22, 92, 93, 206, 207-208
Electoral Committee for Democratic Unity (CEUD), 27
Electoral law (1979), 30, 31
Electoral system, 30-31, 61, 216
Emigrant votes, 31
Estado Novo, 1, 2, 3, 98, 113, 128, 144(n8)
    economy, 98-99, 109, 181-182
    elections, 26, 27
European Community (EC), 4, 5, 191-192, 195
European Free Trade Association, 181
European Union for Christian Democracy, 87
Expresso (newspaper), 171, 172

Faria, Leite de, 78
Farmers' unions, 111
Farm owners' associations, 111
FEPU. *See* United People's Electoral Front
Ferreira, João Palma, 174, 177
Ferreira, Lemos (general), 13, 20, 23
Feyo, José Barata, 177
First Republic, 1
Foreign investment, 5. *See also*
    International Monetary Fund
Foreign Investment Code, 186
FP-25. *See* Popular Forces of the 25 April
Freedom of the press, 165, 167, 177
Freemasons, 77
FRS. *See* Socialist Republican Front
Fund for Unemployment, 134

Gama, Jaime, 138, 177
GDP. *See* Gross Domestic Product
General Confederation of Portuguese
    Workers (CGTP), 53, 54, 55, 101, 112, 209
    activities, 103-104
    as pressure group, 106-108
General Union of Workers (UGT), 53, 55, 68, 101, 102, 103, 106, 112
    elections, 209-210
    political parties, 105-106
    pressure group, 107-108
German Social Democratic Party (SPD), 4
GFCF. *See* Gross fixed investment
GIS. *See* Socialist Intervention Group
Globo, O (newspaper), 171

Index

Governments, 4, 14, 127, 132, 145(n18)
   coalitions, 138, 139, 144
   formation, 136-137, 138, 139-140
   media, 172-173, 175-176, 179
   resignations, 140-141, 142-143, 157
   shuffles, 141-142
   structure, 133-136
   See also Central Bloc government; Democratic Alliance; PS/PSD government
"Grande Informação," 178
"Grande Reportagem," 176, 177, 188
Gross Domestic Product (GDP), 181-182, 192, 193
Gross fixed investment (GFCF), 185, 188
Grupos, See Assembly of the Republic
Grupos econômicos. See cartels
Guterres, António, 32, 71

High Council of the Army, 19
Higher Council for National Defense, 17-18, 19, 122, 123
d'Hondt electoral system, 30, 31, 61
Humanitarian organizations, 104

IMF. See International Monetary Fund
Independent Social Democrat Action (ASDI), 28, 29, 31, 47, 122, 147, 162, 175
   founding, 75, 90
Information councils, 168
International Confederation of Free Trade Unions, 4
International Monetary Fund (IMF), 4, 5, 112, 151, 190, 193-194
International Security and Civil Protection, 159-163
Intersindical, 101-102, 103. See also General Confederation of Portuguese Workers

Jornal, O (newspaper), 171, 172
Jornal de Notícias (newspaper), 169, 171
Jornal do Comércio, O (newspaper), 170
JUC. See University Catholic Action

Labor laws, 108
Labor unions, 53, 54, 101
   Constitution and, 102-103
   politics, 98, 101, 103-104
Law on Budget Procedure (1983), 150, 151
Law on National Defense (1982), 14, 15, 16-17, 18, 19, 20, 122, 156

Law on National Security, 48
League for Union and Revolutionary Action, 45
Left. See Political left
Legislation, 14, 150, 156, 159-163, 166, 186-187. See also Assembly of the Republic; Constitution; individual laws
Legislative process, 135-136
Liberal democracy, 4, 100. See also Democracy
Liberal marcelista, ala, 77
Lisbon Trade Fair, 110
Lopes, Ernâni, 138-139
Lourenço, Vasco, 20, 21

Machete, Rui, 22, 84, 136, 161, 162
MAD. See Movement for a Democratic Debate
Magro, Manuel, 174
Maoist People's Democratic Union (UDP), 31, 103, 175
MASP. See Movement for the Support of Soares for the Presidency
MDP. See Portuguese Democratic Movement, 31
Media, 178-179
   censorship, 177-178
   constitution, 168-169
   electronic, 173-179
   government manipulation, 175, 179(n9)
   revolution, 165-168
   See also Newspaper; Radio; Television
Media Council, 169, 176, 177-178
Melo, Eurico de, 90
MES. See Movement of the Socialist Left
MFA. See Armed Forces Movement
Miguel, Mário Firmino, 14, 22, 89, 93, 211
Militante, O (publication), 60
Military, 18, 21, 23, 211
   civilian control, 15-16, 17, 18, 22, 24
   political involvement, 12-15, 16, 22, 25(n4), 56
   See also Armed Forces Movement
Ministry of Agriculture, 111, 139
Ministry of Corporations and Social Welfare, 98
Ministry of Defense, 14, 17, 19
Ministry of Finance, 111, 134, 195
Ministry of Industry and Energy, 190, 194
Ministry of Labor, 195
Ministry of the Interior, 14, 15
Monarchy Electoral Committee (CEM), 27

Index

Morais, Manuel Tito de, 161
Moreira, Adriano, 89
Mota, Joaquim Magalhães 77, 79, 90
Movement for a Democratic Debate (MAD), 47-48
Movement for the Support of Soares for the Presidency (MASP), 207
Movement of the Socialist Left (MES), 70

National Assembly, 1, 26, 27
National Committee for the Reelection of President Eanes (CNARPE), 48, 128
National Confederation of Farmers, 111
National Confederation of Portuguese Workers-National Intersindical (CGTP-IN), 103
National Council, 93
National Council of Entrepreneurial Associations (CNAE), 111, 112
National Council of Portuguese Entrepreneurs (CNEP), 111
National Council of the Plan, 186
Nationalization, 3, 55, 182, 185, 186, 190, 191
National Political Commission (PSD), 82-83
National Popular Action (ANP), 26, 27, 77
National Union (UN), 26. *See also* National Popular Action
NATO. *See* North Atlantic Treaty Organization
Newspapers, 169-172, 178
Nobre, Eugénio, 142
North Atlantic Treaty Organization (NATO), 13, 17
Notícias da Tarde (newspaper), 170
Notícias de Portugal (NP), 170
NP. *See Notícias de Portugal*

Oliveira, Fialho de, 178
Oporto Industrial Association, 111, 112

Pacheco, Miguel, 105, 106
Parliament. *See* Assembly of the Republic
Parliamentary groups. *See Assembly of the Republic*
Pato, Octávio, 47, 53
PCP. *See* Portuguese Communist Party
PDC. *See* Christian Democratic party
Pereira, Eduardo, 160
Pereira, Futscher, 176
Permanent Council for Social Coordination (CPCS), 104, 107, 108, 111-113

Permanent Secretariat for Public Enterprises, 134
Pintado, Xavier, 78
Pintasilgo, Maria de Lourdes, 4, 47, 211, 212
   government, 140, 143
   support, 76(n27), 209, 210, 212
Pinto, Carlos Mota, 22, 79, 145(n16), 153, 207
   Central Bloc rule, 90, 92, 93
   Internal security, 160, 161
   and PSD, 82-83, 84, 90
   resignation, 140, 142
Pires, Lucas, 87, 89
Pluralism, 4, 6-7, 78, 99, 102
Political Commission of the PCP, 58
Political left, 54
   post-revolutionary, 47-48
   pre-revolutionary, 45-47
   society, 48-50
   See also individual political parties
Political parties, 102
   activities, 198-199
   electoral system, 30-31
   Estado Novo, 26, 27
   importance, 5-7
   local participation, 32, 76(n30)
   media, 172, 173-174
   membership, 57-58
   parliament, 147, 148
   post-revolution, 27, 28, 100
   small, 28, 29
   stability, 40-41
   system, 29-30, 199-200
   See also individual political parties
Political right, 78
   affiliations, 48-49, 87-88
   society and, 48, 75(n6)
Politicians, 8, 11(n6), 15, 16, 21, 23
Popular Democratic party (PPD), 3, 4, 28, 61, 77
   funding, 27, 77-78
   See also Social Democratic party
Popular forces of the 25 April (FP-25), 48
Popular Monarchist Party (PPM), 29, 31, 79
Portugal Hoje (newspaper), 68, 170, 171
Portugal Socialista (journal), 68
Portuguese Communist Party (PCP), 7, 16, 27, 40, 47, 114, 147, 160
   affiliation, 48, 49
   control of MDP, 61, 62-63, 64
   deradicalization, 51-52

elections, 12, 28, 31, 53, 129, 209-210, 212, 213
internal security bill, 161, 162
labor unions, 102, 103
media, 166, 167, 168, 169, 170, 175
membership, 57-58, 60, 75(nn4,11,18)
organization, 57-58
political survival, 52-57
post-revolution, 47, 51, 53
revolution, 3, 46, 51
Portuguese Confederation of Commerce (CCP), 110, 111, 112
Portuguese Democratic Movement (MDP), 31, 47, 147, 161, 175
autonomy, 62-64
coalition, 55, 61
Constitution and, 118, 122
elections, 61, 76(n27)
identity, 64-65
Portuguese Industrial Association (AIP), 109, 110, 111, 112
Portuguese Socialist Action (ASP), 45
Povo Libre (publication), 82
PPD. *See* Popular Democratic Party
PPM. *See* Popular Monarchist Party
PRD. *See* Democratic Renewal party
Presidential power, 17, 18, 120-121, 123, 128, 138, 156, 199
constitutional revisions, 130-131
government formation, 136-137, 140-141, 143
parliament, 155-159
political parties and, 208-212
Press law, 166
Primeiro do Janeiro, O (newspaper), 170, 171
Prime minister, 17, 133-134, 135, 136, 137, 140
Private investment, 124. *See also* Economic crisis; Economy
PS. *See* Socialist party
PSD. *See* Social Democratic party
PS/PSD government, 19, 20, 21, 107, 134
Public-enterprise sector, 188-192, 194-195
Public funding, 30
Public opinion surveys, 9, 32-34, 35-39, 49, 88, 203-204
abortion, 114-115
church attitudes, 113, 114
constitutional revision, 123-124
labor unions, 108, 116-117(n27)
presidential power, 129-130
PSD and CDS governments, 88, 94, 96

Public Security Police, 23

Radio, 178-179
censorship, 175-176
government control, 173, 174-175
Rádio Clube Português, 167
Rádio Comercial, 173
Rádio Renascença, 167, 173
RDP, 173, 174, 175
Rebelo de Sousa, Marcelo, 91, 93, 171
Reform, 2, 52, 92
Rego, Victor da Cunha, 173
República, A (newspaper), 166-167, 168
Republican National Guard, 23
Retornados, 3
Revolution (1974-1975), 3, 45, 46, 165-168, 182, 185
Right. *See* Political right
Rodrigues, Anselmo, 177
Roman Catholic Church. *See* Catholic Church
RTP, 173, 174, 175, 179
censorship, 176-178, 180(nn15,21)
Council for Information on the RTP, 175
Sá Carneiro, Francisco, 5, 15, 23, 24, 121
AD, 90-91
PPD, 77, 78, 79
PSD, 66, 82, 89-90
rule, 15, 83, 94, 133, 138, 140
Sá Carneiro government, 137, 140
Salazar, António de Oliveira, 1, 2, 113, 120, 128
Salazar government, 94
Santos, Amadeu Garcia dos, 14, 19, 20, 22, 24
Santos, Antonio de Almeida, 74, 138, 160, 177
Santos, José Alberto Loureiro dos, 13, 14
Seabra, José Augusto, 142
Secretariat of Collective Units of Production, 111
Século, O (newspaper), 170
SEDES, 77
Semanário, O (newspaper), 171, 172
SI. *See* Socialist International
Silva, Anibal Cavaco, 1, 90, 93, 207, 208, 210
Soares, Mário, 13, 14, 19, 76(n42), 80, 122
elections, 92, 93, 138, 206-211, 212, 213
government, 137, 139, 141, 157, 170
internal security bill, 160, 161
MDP, 62, 63

media, 166, 167, 176-177, 178
opposition, 72, 73-74
PS, 66, 67, 68, 70-71, 72-73, 91
Social Democratic Center (CDS) party, 3, 4, 7, 15, 40, 77, 79, 81, 87, 89, 114, 148, 169
  affiliation, 48, 49
  coalitions, 31, 79, 80
  Constitution and, 119, 121, 124
  elections, 28, 31, 208-209
  founding, 27, 78
  ideology, 87, 88
  membership, 84, 86-87
  support, 76(n37), 78, 96
Social Democratic party (PSD), 3, 7, 15, 16, 22, 27, 48, 66, 77, 92, 114, 151
  activism, 62-63
  coalitions, 31, 79, 90-91
  Central Bloc government, 29, 91-93
  Constitution and, 119, 121
  deputies, 153-154
  elections, 28, 31, 93-94, 137, 207-208, 209, 210
  ideology, 87-88
  influence, 141-142
  internal dissidence, 79-80, 81
  internal security bill, 161, 162
  labor unions, 54, 105
  leadership, 89-90
  media, 171, 173, 179
  membership, 84, 86-87
  organization, 81-82, 83-84
  parliament, 148, 157, 158, 159
  support, 82, 83-84, 96
Social Democratic Reformist Union Tendency (TESIRESD), 105-106
Social Democrat Union Tendency (TSD), 106
Social Democrats, 27, 48, 77-78, 88, 96, 105-106, 160
Socialist International (SI), 4, 67-68, 88
Socialist Intervention Group (GIS), 70
Socialist party (PS), 3, 4, 7, 16, 18, 22, 25(n14), 32, 41, 46, 47, 54, 71, 76(n45), 114, 147, 151, 158, 187
  affiliations, 49, 66
  coalition politics, 66, 90
  Communists and, 53, 65-66
  electoral system, 31, 129
  factions, 28, 29
  founding, 27, 47
  internal security bill, 160-161, 162
  MDP, 61, 64

media, 166, 171, 173, 175, 179
  programs, 66-68
  PSD, 66, 92
  support, 68-69, 76(nn36, 37, 43, 44)
Socialist Republican Front (FRS), 28, 31, 66-67, 71
Socialists, 45, 47, 53, 68, 160
  labor unions, 102, 103, 105
  political parties, 27, 49
  See also Social Democratic Center party; Social Democratic party; Socialist party
Social organizations, 101
South Africa, 31, 176, 177
SPD. *See* German Social Democratic Party
Spínola, Antonio, 78
Statute of Opposition Rights, 63
Statute of Public Managers (1976), 195
Strikes, 107, 116(n22)

"*Telejornal,*" 175
Television, 179
  censorship, 175-176, 177-178
  government control, 173, 174-175
Tempo (newspaper), 171, 172
Tengarrinha, José Manuel, 63, 64
Ten Years to Change Portugal. *See Dez anos para mudar Portugal*
TESIRESD. *See* Social Democratic Reformist Union Tendency
Trinidade, Aurélio, 19
TSD. *See* Social Democrat Union Tendency
25th April Association, 20-21, 22, 23

UDP. *See* Maoist People's Democratic Union
UEDS. *See* Union of the Democratic and Socialist Left
UGT. *See* General Union of Workers
Ultramar, 1-2
UN. *See* National Union
Union Movement, 101-103
Union of the Democratic and Socialist Left (UEDS), 28, 29, 31, 47, 122, 147, 162
Unions. *See* Labor unions
United People's Alliance (APU), 28, 62, 211
  activity, 62, 63
  affiliation, 48, 49
  coalition, 31, 55
  stability, 40, 41
  support, 76(n37), 207
United People's Electoral Front (FEPU),

61. *See also* United People's Alliance
University Catholic Action (JUC), 7

Veloso, Angelo, 205

Vieira, Vasco Rocha, 13
Voting, 35, 37, 40-41. *See also* Elections

Zenha, Francisco Salgado, 69, 208, 211, 212